Final Time

A Husband's Reflections on His Wife's Terminal Illness

by Robert G. Esbjornson

Robert Esbjornson

To Shirley,
I remember you, after
all these years!

Gah 12/8/94

1

ISBN 0-943535-10-7

Produced in the United States of America
Primarius Publishing
Minneapolis, Minnesota

TABLE OF CONTENTS

PREFACE
An Invitation

I invite you into an intimate time of my life as revealed in the pages of a personal journal I kept during and after my wife Ruth's terminal illness and death. It was a time of loss of someone dear to me, a time in which I had to face our mortal **and** moral limits and to work my way beyond the experience itself to the meaning of the experience.

This account includes excerpts from the journal I wrote as the story was taking place and ethical reflections written during the second year after Ruth's death. The journal is a combination of narrative and meditation which I wrote day by day as I experienced the events. Beginning when my wife Ruth discovered she had breast cancer, the journal covers her final illness until her death in April 1990 and continues with excerpts written after her death, when I was dealing with loss. It describes not only the external story of my wife's final days but also the inner story of my thoughts, feelings and prayers.

The journal was written as the story was taking place, not after the events. I knew Ruth was going to die but not exactly when. I knew I would be involved in her care but not precisely how. The account is as direct and disorderly as the days' events. Because I wanted to preserve as much of the immediate and original flow of what happened and of my reactions, I have included, verbatim, selections from the journal. However, it was necessary to edit the raw material to make some corrections, clarifications and explanations to render the account more readable.

I wrote from the standpoint of "the person by the bedside" as I, next of kin, experienced the loss of my wife who was my best friend for fifty years, nearly 45 of them in marriage. Therefore, it is not the story as Ruth or someone dying would tell it, nor is it written from the standpoint of a professional medical practitioner who is also dealing with ethical questions.

The experience of Ruth's illness and death confronted me with not only our mortal limits but with moral challenges as well. Since her death I have been composing my reflections about the experience, not as a participant

4

but as an ethicist trying to make some sense of the moral meaning of what happened. Facing terminal illness and death is not just an encounter with mortality but with moral experience, because it is a time when we cannot escape making decisions about matters of significance to ourselves and others under conditions of uncertainty about motives and consequences.

I have written the reflections as an ethical analysis of significant factors that influenced the decisions and actions that took place in Ruth's and my story. During my years of teaching ethics I saw that the heart of the story is not the recent development of medical technologies that have stirred so much interest in bioethics. Rather, it is the relationship between those who give medical care and those who receive it, a relationship that is a moral affair, not just a medical matter.

The reflections have become an effort toward formulating an ethics for patients, for those of us who enter the world of medical professionals when we need their expert knowledge and skills. When we enter that world, we do not cease being moral persons with rights or responsibilities, but we do become engaged in a collaborative effort with the professionals to attain results of importance both to ourselves and them.

You may hesitate to enter such a personal story, fearing you will intrude on my privacy, or feeling reluctant to think about your own mortal and moral limits. I cannot guarantee that reading this will be easy or meaningful. I have taken the risk of making my thoughts public, and I ask you to take the risk of reading what I have written. In other words, this book presents you with a moral choice you can't escape, simply because the book has come into your life. Even the decision not to read it is morally significant. You can't be entirely certain of either your motives for reading it, or refraining from doing so. And you can't be entirely certain of the consequences that might develop in either case.

We humans move inexorably toward death and we experience little deaths along the way; in other words our life stories are made up of a series of deaths and rebirths as we age. In his journal about his final days of living, **In The Face of Death** (New York: Viking Penguin, 1989), Peter Noll, dying of bladder cancer, said he wrote "to present my situation as average and, at the same time as exemplary, in order to convince the reader that it makes sense to examine the issues of dying, death and the notions of the beyond while we are still alive."

I hope reading this account and analysis of my experience helps to convince you to act on Noll's advice.

I have been thinking about who might take this book in hand. Many persons sooner or later stand in the place where I have been, watching while a person they cherish suffers and dies. We are those who stand by and with the dying while the professional care-givers walk in and out. We who are close to the dying can only watch, and wait and try to care in appropriate ways. My journal shows that ordinary people can cope with loss, not only in action but in the inner life of the mind and spirit—clumsily, perhaps, but with the compassion and help of the community of friends and its web of relationships, we are kept from falling into the sucking quicksand of despair and loneliness.

You may be one who has not yet had this experience, but you know that you may well have one like it in the future, and you may be better prepared for it by entering into my experience and thoughts. I encourage you to do so, to break away from our culture's resistance to anticipating and preparing for the future. Of course, you can't control the future, but you could be better prepared for it, the way training prepares athletes, surgeons or musicians for future performances.

You may be, as I was, the husband watching by the bedside of a woman you love. Although wives survive husbands more often, husbands are also the survivors. A man's experience is not quite the same as a woman's. Men are, or seem to be, less willing to talk about their inner experience, their feelings, and how they are coping with loss. That does not mean they do not need to do so. Perhaps my description will give others warrant to express their feelings too. I gained so much from Martin Marty's book, **A Cry of Absence** (San Francisco: Harper & Row, 1983), and from C. S. Lewis's **A Grief Observed** (New York: Bantam, 1976)—books written after the deaths of their wives. Maybe other husbands could receive some help from mine.

Perhaps you are one of the professional medics, a physician, or a nurse, or some other skilled care-giver. I invite you to cross over into my experience of receiving your ministrations and return to your roles of care-giving with new understandings of yourself and me and those like me. Cross over, be with

6

me at 2 a.m. when a crisis develops and there is no one available to help, and feel what it is like for an inexperienced care-giver to be there.

You may be a professional ethicist. An ethicist myself, I know the occupational hazard of my profession—we traffic in generalities, theories, abstractions. We incline toward writing papers and books for other ethicists, our peers. My experiences as a teacher and as a person dealing with illness and death have moved me to see ethics as a **practical** discipline. You may be interested as a professional in such a story for academic discussion by ethicists. However, you may someday have to live in the face of the approaching death of someone you love and make decisions about what you ought to do. Perhaps this account will be of value to you as preparation for such a time in your life.

Whoever you are, I invite you to join me in this venture. I don't assume that my personal experience is the model for others, but there are common, if not universal, features in our personal stories that make it possible to communicate with and learn from each other.

All I can do is to be a hospitable host, inviting you to enter my life and share it for a short time. In **The Way of All the Earth: Experiments in Truth and Religion** (New York: MacMillan, 1972), John S. Dunne calls crossing over into another person's life, another culture and another religion the "spiritual adventure of our time."

You could read my story as you would a mystery story, as one curious about the outcome. I suggest a different way: Plunge into the journal as if you were entering into another person's life experience at some point in the middle of that life. Imagine yourself as being in my place, writing over a period of time, and then read it over a period of time. As you read, think of yourself in conversation with me. When something you read strikes you, stop and think about it and what you would say to me. If you are inclined, write down your response. This is what I do in my journals. Such reading could be called meditative reading, not reading for adventure or information.

I hope you will not read as rapidly as possible, never stopping to ask yourself, "What should I think or say?" These are readings of the heart, by the heart and for the heart. The heart is the core of the self, and the heart is the center from which flows the creative energies of a person's life. I write for your heart from my heart.

8

Part I
The Beginning of the End
July 1987 - November 1989

Discovery of Cancer

Ruth and I were on a vacation trip to the Rocky Mountain National Park in Colorado when she discovered a lump on her right breast the night of July 24, 1987, in a motel in Billings, Montana. She did not tell me until we were in Rapid City, South Dakota, on our way home because she said she wanted me to have a time free from stresses of family life. She was afraid she might have the same cancer that killed her mother. My thoughts moved from hope that it was a benign tumor to fear that she would have a painful terminal illness and die.

Decision in Vermillion, South Dakota

During a stopover with our son Carl and his family, I called Dr. Randy Beahrs, a physician in St. Paul, Minnesota. A friend of mine who had been a student in my biomedical ethics class, he had offered his help if ever I had any medical problems. He advised going right away to Mayo Clinic in Rochester and offered to make arrangements for Ruth's immediate admittance.

Diagnosis and Treatment

I called Mayo Clinic in Rochester, Minnesota, when we got home. An appointment with a surgeon had been made for the following Tuesday, August 4, 1987.

We arrived on the fourth floor at 8 a.m. and waited for about an hour. The surgeon and his resident talked to Ruth first and then the resident examined her. She was very competent and caring, and Ruth liked her. The surgeon then came in and also examined her. Their opinion was that a biopsy was necessary because of the size and location of the tumor. If the tumor was malignant, they would perform a radical mastectomy to remove the breast and lymph glands that might be malignant.

Ruth was concerned about the effect of diabetes at a time of surgery. They assured her that diabetes would afford no major problem, because they often operated on diabetic patients and knew how to take care of them. They were right—as we saw later.

A mammogram, a sonic scan, blood tests, an X ray and an exam by a general physician occupied Ruth the rest of the day. The physician said that her general condition was very good, and she should come through the operation very well (which she did).

In the evening, our daughter Louise, our son Carl and wife Rilla, and their daughters Rachel and Rebekka joined Ruth and me in a Best Western motel. There was much talk about hospitals, cancer patients, postoperative developments and the like.

At one point Louise initiated prayer. Carl, Ruth and I added our prayers. Four-year-old Rachel prayed in her own way, obviously caught up in the spirit of the occasion. Settling down from the raucous play with Louise that preceded the prayers, she listened and watched very attentively and quietly. She stood on the bed, swaying and talking in words we did not understand but very obviously praying to God, not addressing us, with a most joyful expression. Then she sang a little song she made up in response to a chorus Louise sang and did a little dance. Louise said that God understood her prayer even if we didn't. It was a very devout moment, an unforgettable event in our family.

August 5 was a day of waiting. Louise and I went with Ruth to the hospital at 7 a.m. Preparations for surgery took about an hour. She left for the OR by 8:15 and came back around 11. Carl and Rilla came later with the children. We waited all day for the report. Ruth was groggy, nauseous and had a dry mouth, but she felt no pain. We didn't see the resident surgeon until 8 p.m. Because the tumor in the breast and those in the lymph glands were malignant, they had performed a radical mastectomy to remove them. The children were allowed to be with us all day as we stood by Ruth. Ruth was in and out of sleep most of the day, but she looked very good.

Louise and Rilla talked about the situation over and over. Both had worked in hospitals, Rilla as an aide and Louise as a chaplain. As a woman, Rilla felt deeply for Ruth and said that she felt Ruth would be very upset. I didn't think so. I knew Ruth would be fine during the crisis, though she might collapse later. I was insensitive to Rilla's need to talk and I apologized to her. Ruth and I had talked already about this being cancer and the grief of losing each other. I am not sure Louise and Rilla realized how close we were, how often we had to deal with the immediate possibility of her death in a diabetic coma.

August 8, 1987

I am observing the intricacies of medical technology and specialized services. The hospital teems with staff, each person with a specific role. For example, a nurse who had been a student of mine came only to give a blood sugar level test; that is all. One medic from the clinic and another from the hospital took Ruth's diabetic history. The charge nurse sees to monitoring her care, urination, IV, blood pressure and the like. Beyond them are record keepers, technicians, cleaners, dieticians, and others—a huge, costly operation. And finally the whole system is defeated by death. Even so, it may give us extra years.

Mayo is an international medical center, with top-of-the-line application of medical knowledge and technology. The clinic is formidable and intimidating, yet lifesaving. The MDs are cautious and reserved, not easily lured into personal relations or irrelevant chatter. They are pleasant, polite, yet superior and well-confident they know more than their patients. It must be difficult not to develop what we ethicists call "strong paternalist" attitudes. We who receive their services must seem ignorant savages in our imprecise ways of expressing concern and asking questions. We may even appear ridiculous when we try to impress them with what we know or want to know. I know a little about medical practice and technology. If I find the experience intimidating, I can imagine it is even more so for the many persons who know far less. Medical technology makes us passive and subdued.

11

If and when doctors have too many patients to review on rounds, they don't have enough time for personal relations. They obtain their knowledge from the patients' charts, from X rays, ultrasonic scans, chemical analyses of blood, computerized kits for measuring blood sugar, blood pressure and temperature. They compare the specific with general profiles stored in data banks, huge masses of information gained from exams and tests of thousands of patients.

Even the physical layout of the medical center subdues me. The waiting rooms teem with ailing people and their families; the corridors and stations are alive with medical care-givers, all performing esoteric tasks. There are closed doors and areas not accessible to patients. Computer screens everywhere remind one of the collective mind and memory created by people with vastly more complex intellects. More and more Mayo strikes me as a Large Mind. Even the doctors seem like front men or women interfacing between this Mind and the little folk who don't understand what is going on.

I sense a wariness in the doctors in their contacts with us. Maybe it is the way all surgeons and oncologists become, because they deal with apprehensive patients who are scared and don't hear or want to hear what they say. Or maybe it is the gap between their level of expert knowledge and the common folk's level. Or perhaps it is a fear of malpractice suits.

One does not come to Mayo to engage in gregarious conversation but to take advantage of what one hopes is the latest state of the art. The process is efficient. Ruth was examined and tested on her first day here and in the operating room the first thing the next morning. She is routed and shunted from one place to another, according to a communication system that normally works very well here.

The ward in Methodist Hospital is a circular arrangement with the nurses' station in the center and rooms radiating from a corridor surrounding it. Ruth's requests are respected. She gets

prompt and courteous attention from pleasant and competent
persons. A nurse whose name was Smith impressed us, in
particular, by her compassion and competence.

I can imagine a symbiotic relationship between technology
and ethics that could go bad if relationships get out of balance.
Technology is enabling; ethics is guiding. Some kind of need fuels
the efforts leading to technological innovations. Humans value
something not yet attained, even if it is only the value of satisfying
curiosity and the desire for new knowledge. And so we humans
think, dream and compute.

On Thursday, August 6, Ruth felt good when she awoke. She was
cheerful and hungry. Her recovery began well and continued so until she was
dismissed from the hospital on Sunday morning, August 9. Her oncologist
said that no postoperative chemotherapy or radiation therapy would be
necessary. They prescribed an antihormone drug called tamoxifen [Nolvadex],
which might prevent recurrence of the cancer by blocking the effects of
estrogen, which stimulates breast tissue to grow and thus could lead to cancer.
The Federal Drug Administration had just approved the drug for use by post-
menopausal women after breast cancer surgery. The only side effect might be
an effect on the bones and result in osteoporosis.

She was euphoric for about a week after the surgery. She said, "When I
woke up after the operation and realized I was still alive, it was like the
beginning of new life. Everything seemed fresh and new. I had survived. I was
not in for a painful end, not for the present at least."

Crisis with Diabetes

Our neighbors Ross and Lavinia Bloomquist gave us the use of their
condominium in Palm Bay, Florida, for a week in February 1989. Our pattern
for the week was getting up early, eating breakfast, doing our prayers and
readings, going for beach walks, lunch, nap, more reading, watching TV in the
evening or going for another beach walk.

On Wednesday, February 15, I described a severe insulin reaction in
my journal.

13

Ruth's sugar was so high it was off the register, so she took more insulin and went to the bedroom for a nap. Later I heard her snorting. I rushed into the bedroom to find her in deep shock, glassy eyes staring without seeing, unresponsive, and convulsing. I tried to give her a jelly form of glucose, which she could not swallow. So I called 911 and within minutes the emergency squad and ambulance crew came, took over, monitored her heart, gave her an injection, and got her back to consciousness within minutes. All of it was done gently and competently. The ambulance took her to the Holmes Regional Medical Center in Melbourne. Her blood sugar count was 6—lower than the doctor had ever seen. The medical care stabilized her enough so she could be released by 2 p.m. It was a sobering episode, making us aware of our mortality and grateful [again] for competent and compassionate volunteers and medics.

We returned to our pattern the next day. The beach walks were most refreshing and interesting. The air was mild and there was a breeze off the Atlantic, with the surf strong with sizable breakers. The gulls, sandpipers, pelicans and an occasional crane were interesting characters. A few sunbathers, fishermen and women, and hikers populated the beaches in the morning. Surfers waited for the right waves. Poetry should be written about such times.

On the way home we read Madeleine L'Engle's **Two-Part Invention: The Story of a Marriage** (New York: Farrar, Straus, Giroux, 1988), about her interesting and happy marriage that lasted for forty years. She told of the relationship with her actor husband in the context of the theater world and the poignant experience of losing him through a painful death by cancer. Reading it turned out to be, for me at least, a preparation for what I would experience—sooner than I realized at the time.

Ruth's insulin reactions were occasionally so severe that she was not conscious enough to take care of herself. Her care was sometimes beyond my ability as well. They were near-death experiences and in a way prepared me for losing Ruth.

In August Carl and his family surprised us with a visit, and we had a happy time together for several days.

After her operation in August 1987, Ruth had regular three-month checkups at Mayo Clinic, which revealed no signs of cancer. She was feeling fairly well until the autumn of 1989, when she began to suffer headaches and weakness affecting her legs.

Recurrence of Cancer

In early November 1989, Ruth had what was to have been the last of the regular three-month checkups at Mayo Clinic. The tests were negative, but her oncologist, James Ingle, discovered a lump in her right armpit and advised surgery.

November 15, 1989

Yesterday Louise led us in prayer before she left. We were interrupted twice by phone calls, so some of the serious intensity of Louise's prayers was diminished. Reflecting on the experience, I realized that it is not the eloquence of prayers that matters but rather basic trust. God's good will is not dependent on our zeal. So I pray, not as a psychological gimmick but to give God attention and put Ruth in God's care. From that core comes energy for appropriate action.

November 16, 1989

Today, in my deep well, I sense a girding of gladness, a joy of life, even now after Ruth's surgery and a long, tedious day of waiting. In St. Mary's outpatient surgical ward, patients are lined up on gurneys like cars waiting at a ferry crossing. There are inevitable delays with so many to care for. We came in at 9 a.m. and left after 6 p.m., nine hours. Ruth had Novocaine, felt pain, heard everything but saw nothing; her eyes were covered with towels.

15

November 18, 1989

"Be strong, take courage, all you who hope in the Lord"
(Psalm 31:24).

*A word for Ruth and me today. The power and glory of God moves me to look at all that happens as a challenge to do God's will, and that takes some figuring out. Ruth and I have to cope with illness. If she or I should develop a terminal condition, should we forgo treatment that is costly and painful but which results in extending our lives a few months? Who benefits by such heroic effort? Who suffers? It is very difficult to accept mortality. I have unfinished work, for the children and grandchildren, but perhaps it is unneeded. Perhaps the need is **my own**, something I desire to do. I can't speak for Ruth; her situation is more immediate and critical.*

Next Monday I will speak at the COAM session, a senior citizen's program in Minneapolis. I will comment on trust and hope in relation to health care and on "moral dramas in health care." Trust is a basic issue in health care, no doubt, and one approaches illness and death, as well as all life experiences, in a positive or negative way.

What are the differences between mistrust, naive trust and basic trust? Is there some skepticism in basic trust that is absent in naive trust? Or is skepticism an erosion of trust?

[1] Trusting one's body's own healing powers—but only up to a point, because the body is mortal and aging is a biological fact of life.

[2] Trusting the medical professionals and institutions— naively, never questioning; distrustfully, always suspicious and anxious.

Basic trust: realistic, alert, knowledgeable about human error and limits, but still confident.

Hope. What is the difference between naive optimism, despair, and realistic hope? The hopeless person gets stuck in illness Rollo May has observed. Is there a forlorn hope, so

16

*poignantly evident **en masse** at Mayo, a hope that once more*
medical measures will save one? If there is no hope of release
*through cure, what then is left? Hope for life **after** death? Does*
that help a dying person? We really don't know about life after
death, do we? Do the near death experiences tell us anything?
Why are those experiences so much alike as people describe
them?

After tests and examinations, we learned that Ruth's bone scan and
neurological exam were negative. She has no detectable cancer. Cancer will
appear again, her oncologist said, but it could come anytime from two months
to ten years. No cancer right now, so for the time being we can relax. Facing
these penultimate experiences trains us for facing ultimate ends. We are
mortals and are being put through training, like soldiers in boot camp!

How terrifying it would be if we could not trust everyone in
medical care [and in other activities]. Society cannot function
without trust.

On Christ the King Sunday, November 26, I preached at St. Paul's in
Gaylord, Minnesota, on the Luke story of Jesus and the two criminals being
crucified. In the sermon, "A Plea and a Promise," I reflected on the exchange
between the one thief and Jesus:

November 26, 1989
"Jesus, remember me when you come into your kingdom"
(Luke 23:42).
"Today you shall be with me in Paradise"
(Luke 23:43).
This passage stirs me by its stark, bare-bones quality.
Everything else is stripped away, and all that is left is a plea and a
promise. Maybe this is the essence of prayer—a plea and a
promise, honesty and hope. This is an austere version of the
gospel, the very essence. There will come a time in my life when

17

there is nothing left but to die, no rescue from troubles, no healing
of terminal illness, no liberation from tyranny, only dying, like the
two criminals and Jesus, an unworthy man honestly confessing his
wickedness and Jesus promising, not rescue but being present
with him in the "abode of the righteous dead" [or Paradise].

Isn't this what is essential—an abiding relationship in the
world to come, in the presence of the righteous, to dwell among
the righteous in the presence of God?

"I am your guest, and only for a time,
a nomad like all my ancestors.
Look away, let me draw breath
before I go away and am no more"
(Psalm 39:12, 13).

How true, Lord. We are not possessing titles to our lives.
We are more like temporary occupants, as sojourners in a motel.
No, that image removes us from land, soil and neighbors. We are
more like temporary owners of a place—like tenants, not tourists.

Generations pass—Dad, Mother Victoria, Mother Anna,
Ruth's parents Carl and Hildur, many...Ruth and I as well. We
know our lives are soon to be gone from here. Teach us to love
you, each other, our children, the truth.

Around Thanksgiving 1989 Ruth suffered increasing discomfort—
headaches and weakness in the legs. On Monday, November 27, Ruth was so
uncomfortable that she asked me to take her out of the house for a ride. We
drove to a Christmas tree farm in New Ulm to pick out a tree and then came
home through Mankato. That was a poignant time together, a tender but sad
time, riding silently together through the country.

The next day, I took her to see our family physician. He arranged for a
CAT scan in Mankato the next day. Tuesday and Wednesday were days of
suspense, awaiting the inevitable. Thursday morning, in the examination room,
our doctor broke the news. Three tumors in the cerebellum. His manner was
grave. He had already arranged with Ruth's oncologist for Ruth's admission to
Methodist Hospital in Rochester. As we left the doctor's office, the office

18

nurse hugged us. She and the others in the office knew how life-threatening these growths were.

Part II
Final Time
December 1, 1989 - April 3, 1990

Diagnosis and Treatment

We went to Rochester on November 30. Ruth was interviewed and examined by a neurologist. Her left arm and leg were subtly, not grossly, less stable than her right arm and leg, symptoms which corresponded to the location of the tumors.

> *"Any religiously significant event needs more than one telling...Through the retelling people form pervasive attitudes and outlooks about the mystery of life."* John Shea, **An Experience Named Spirit**, *(Chicago: Thomas More Press, 1983).*
>
> *The inner story, or the significance of the story, is not easily put into words. What is happening touches on the deep mysteries and will have to be told often before I get it right.*
>
> *I need to tell what has happened to Ruth and me. I must first try to capture the feeling of aloneness for I am beginning to realize, slowly, what not having Ruth as companion would be. This realization comes over me in increments, such as being in bed alone in the motel, which gives me an intimation of the loneliness that might be ahead. I don't feel grim or angry, just sad and forlorn. I am glad the knowledge comes in small doses, so I will not be overwhelmed. I hope I will not, because I must get on with my life.*
>
> *There is nothing I want more than to be present with Ruth in her suffering, to keep vigil, even though I am virtually helpless and she must now depend on those who are competent to ease her distress.*
>
> *Ruth and I are quite aware of our mortality during all of this. At our age we know our lives will soon end, and always the end comes too soon; but, as Ruth said today, not too soon if to live*

means much pain. Yesterday she said she thinks she may die, here
and soon. She said she wants to live, but not in pain.

When I returned to the hospital on December 1, after lunch and a nap, Ruth exclaimed at once, "I had to make an important decision while you were gone. The doctor hoped you would be here."

The doctor told her the largest tumor is located at the base of the cerebellum, where its growth could block the flow of blood [or spinal fluid?] and shut down the basic respiratory and circulatory functions of lungs and heart. It was growing fast. This blockage could happen at any time, and death would be instant. They recommended radiation treatments. There would be an immediate risk at the beginning of radiation treatment, because radiation causes some swelling, so to offset the swelling, Ruth would get decadron. The doctor said that the "worst case scenario" of death at any time was not likely to happen, but the medical staff needed to know what Ruth would want done. The options were to put her on a life support system now to prevent imminent death, or to open her skull and put in a drain to relieve pressure. The drain would suck out the tumor, thereby reducing but not eliminating it.

Although the radiation therapy and decadron would not cure the cancer, the treatment would give her more time. She could have anywhere from two to four months before the cancer would work its lethal effect.

Ruth told the doctor that she did not want the life support or the surgery. We had discussed her condition recently and were in agreement about her receiving no heroic treatments. She had written an "advance directive" on November 17 and now her decision was written on her chart.

The handwritten statement which follows was not put in the form of a legal living will or given to any of the doctors, including Dr. Thompson, our family physician. It was sufficient for them, at that time, to have her oral statement and a note on her chart. I talked to the doctor later and confirmed Ruth's state of mind on the matter.

*I do not wish to have a life support system continue, if there is **no hope** that I will ever be able to function on my own. I do not wish my physical body to continue to be kept alive if my mind is incapable of thought or reason or response. I wish to die with dignity with my family and with my church aware.*

Ruth and I had a good, quality conversation about facing this development. Our relationship had been characterized by much communication about some very difficult situations we had had to deal with over the years, and so we were prepared to cope now with this situation.

We discussed whether or not I should stay by her bedside all the time, because at any moment she might go into cardiac arrest. We agreed that it would be not only impossible, but might be a sign of some unresolved issues in our relationship. We looked upon the **total** picture. Every time we separated we ran the risk of seeing each other for the last time. What was important was realizing the total quality of our lives over the years and being at peace with each other, with others and with God.

Ruth was being cared for in a competent and compassionate community at Methodist. I was satisfied about that—a great boon!

December 6, 1989

*There seems to be a weakness in the Mayo system. The overall care is excellent, but for the life of me, I can't determine **who's in charge**. We have four neuro-oncologists to whom we must relate. And someone delegated one of the residents to talk to Ruth about her options. Why does the physician in charge delegate this assignment? The physician is not merely a technician; in this system he or she is a specialist with particular skills and knowledge. I want to know why the physicians think Ruth's decision is wise. Ruth thinks we get mixed signals from the doctors about her prospects. That is all right, if they would be willing to be human enough to be honest about their limitations. In our case we have experience enabling us to make our own*

23

decisions, but it must be hard for those who do not have the background we have.

December 9, 1989

Today I am thinking about what I will say to pastors on December 19 about their role in the medical care setting. As I see it from a viewpoint of a family receiving care, pastors are outsiders who are only marginal participants in the medical decisions and indeed have no role at this time. That is the perception one of the chaplains gave me of her role in this decision. Pastors are not usually included in the consultations going on among medical team members. The pastor is an outsider as far as medics are concerned. The concern of the medical team is to arrive at **medical** decisions and usually those decisions are based on medical criteria, such as physiological and psychological factors. I don't mean that all medical professionals discount the contribution of the religious professional to the patient's well-being, but it is a matter that seems to be on a different plane.

I, for one, am rather easily intimidated by medical experts, but I don't think pastors should be, because I see little evidence of spiritual care given by the medics. In this specialized context they refer such care to the hospital chaplains. But it must be recognized that hospital chaplains are not as acquainted with the personal history of the patients as their own pastors are.

In the hospital the medical professionals are marked by symbols of authority, such as nameplates on which the name and status [MD, RN, dietician, etc.] are printed. Hospital chaplains have their nameplates, too, but the parish pastors have no sign of their status [unless they wear clergy collars] although they have access to their parishioners. Their role in this complex medical drama is affected by several variables: the competence and confidence of the pastor, his or her training, the relationship with and attitudes of the patient toward the pastor, the attitudes of the physicians and others with regard to the religious dimension. The place where medical decisions are made makes a difference. In a local hospital the pastor is a familiar figure and near at hand when needed, but in a medical center away from home the pastor is a stranger and unfamiliar with the staff and routines.

December 11, 1989

In John Shea's **An Experience Named Spirit** *(Chicago: Thomas More Press, 1983), "The story is functioning religiously when it moves the mind and heart of the listener into the religious zone, into the relationship with the ultimate Mystery. In order to do this it must cut deep, stop the hearers in their tracks, grab the soul."*

Over time the story sinks in, from hearing to reflecting to acting. The story has an imperative: Go and do likewise—not literally imitating but with the same intent to do what is right in the new situation.

The inner meaning of these events in our lives can unfold only gradually. John Shea is right. I suspect I will reflect many times on them, on which are "religiously significant." They are illuminated by what I have learned from teaching medical ethics.

About prayer—I said to Ruth, "I see how **saying** *prayers is a ritual, and as such is important; but thinking that the quality or quantity of the prayers is significant might be faulty, if we assume that efficacy is dependent on them."*

What is important is living a prayerful life. So she and I pray the rituals together every day. She also prays her own prayers alone, and I have my personal rituals. "Pray without ceasing" is not the same as heaping prayer after prayer endlessly; it means living prayerfully, not just saying prayers.

Today my task is obvious—to concentrate on giving Ruth loving care. Tomorrow, who knows what it will be?

For now, I pray for her, for relief from her pain, for peace in her heart, for a sense of your presence, O Lord. Maybe Ruth will be one of the exceptions and live longer than the doctors predict. So I pray, help her **live** *as long as possible.*

December 12, 1989

"Man in his prosperity forfeits
*   intelligence.*
He is one with the cattle, doomed to
*   slaughter.*
Death will herd him to the pasture.
When he dies he can take nothing with him"
(Psalm 49:12-14).

Psalm 49 is a hard hitting song about mortality. Grim, if one has not experienced the grace and goodness of God. There is one break in the overcast of gloom:

"But God will redeem my life
from the grasp of Sheol" (Psalm 49:15).

At the last nothing of value is lost to God. In God, not in Sheol, is my everlasting home. I am embraced in God's everlasting arms!

December 13, 1989

Some thoughts on suffering come to mind for a lecture to Lutheran pastors on moral dramas in medical care.

Q. Where is the growing edge of your understanding of medical care?

A. Seeing suffering from the inside, by the side of Ruth and with the family.

Q. What is the nature of suffering as you see it from that perspective?

A. Surely it is physical pain and destruction of the body, even if pain can be controlled by medical care.

Q. Is that all?

A. Oh no, not at all. Suffering is interpersonal. Alienation surfaces between people who are not at peace. If it is so in this family of ours, it must also be so in other families. The imminence

*of death provokes crises, the smoldering embers flare into flames.
It has happened to us.*

Q. Anything more?

*A. There is also a degree of intellectual torment. There is
something irrational about illness, pain, even about the very
effort to give medical care while trying to extend life, especially
in old age where much of the effort that is spent on terminal care
may not be in keeping with humane treatment. Is death a fearsome
god who forces us to fight him at great cost? This is a profound
theological issue, made more compelling by the advances made in
biomedicine. Who is God? By whose will do we subject old
people to long periods of dying, of not really living? All this
equipment of modern medicine is so marvelous from one
perspective and so malicious from another. Is biomedicine one of
the modern successors to ancient idols, such as Malek and Baal?
The ancient issues are not dead, are they?*

Q. Whew. That's quite a thought.

*A. I'm not done. I see a more subtle and terrible pain—
separation from God, anger, inability to pray, loss of connection
with the eternal. I can't imagine a more miserable state than to
lose that connection, that communion.*

*"Out of the depths I cry to the Lord.
Lord, hear my voice" (Psalm 130:1).*

*Maybe the silence is some kind of an answer—a wall
protecting us from false, destructive ways, forcing us to explore
the darkness until we find the pressing point in the wall that turns
a part of the wall into a doorway.*

December 14, 1989

*Bitter, cold, freezing winds.
Yellow "sun dogs"—ice crystals.
White snowfields.
Bleak, barren.
All humans hustling out of the cold*

27

into pockets of warmth.

No casual conversations on malls,

*instead, curt "It's **cold**."*

Absence, outside.

Inside, flames flare up, warmth.

So it is, Lord.

Facing the prospect of loss,

I huddle close to you,

To your silent, yet embracing presence within,

and warmed by the protective human routines

and supports.

I can survive the sting of loss without freezing solid. I may get some frostbite on the surface, or numbness, but within, a flame of grace, a cleansing fire that consumes anger, regret, guilt, shame, envy.

"All flesh is grass" (Psalm 90:5).

"The dead will be raised imperishable" (Corinthians 15:52).

The phrases echo, crossing one another in the cold air of winter.

December 15, 1989

*Martin Marty's **A Cry of Absence** (San Francisco: Harper & Row, 1983) is about what he calls wintry spirituality:*

"Winter is a season of the heart as much as it is a season in the weather...Winterless climates there may be. As for the heart, however, where can one escape the chill?...Wintry frost comes in the void when love dies, or a lover grows distant, or the divine is absence...when God is silent."

He contrasts such spirituality with that of a "sunny-sider" who never seems to be chilled by the absence, by loss of love or of God's presence.

*I must seem to be a sunny-sider to others. I have enjoyed much goodness and often appear assured and confident. Am **I** honest and will I also have to go through winters when the sun is*

28

low on the horizon or hidden under a gray bank of clouds, when the days are short, when darkness covers the earth, when the ground is hardened, cold, when the air freezes all living things. Then it is indoors time, bundle-up time, a time when the presence is beyond the horizon, a time when the spirit is "on low." What then? It is "hang-on" time. Can I merely say I've got my prayers to keep me warm? Do the Psalms provide enough heat? So far I must say yes, Lord, yes. But I realize I have not yet experienced loss fully, only the anticipation of it.

On December 1, 1989, Ruth had her first radiation treatment. She was a bit scared. An escort came with a wheelchair to bring her to the Charlton Building, where the radiation therapy is administered. Wrapped in blankets and confined to the chair, she was at the mercy of others. I went with her each time—on a long ride down the seventh floor corridor to elevators, in the elevator to the sublevel, a left turn to cross the threshold to the carpet-covered floors of the Charlton. The escort delivered her charts to the desk and left us waiting. Patience, Ruth! Courage!

Eventually a technician in a white coat—they all wore white coats—came for her and brought her to the desk near one of the radiation treatment rooms. Another wait. Patience.

I did some Tai Chi while I waited for Ruth's treatment to be over. There were four or five technicians at the desk. The hospital corridors seem to be populated mainly by people in white coats, or blue surgical gowns. No wonder medical care is so expensive. The complex organization is very evident.

Soon, ten minutes or so, Ruth was wheeled out after her treatment. On her forehead was a +, like the sign of the cross, to mark the exact place for the rays to shoot at the hidden target.

Another wait by the Charlton desk for an escort to take Ruth back to her room, 7307b.

This routine went on every day for ten days. One day the total time spent was three hours because she had an appointment with Dr. Caruso, a radiation therapist, who had many to see.

Home Care

Carl, Rilla and the granddaughters, Rachel and Rebekka, arrived December 9 from Lansing to spend Christmas with us. Ruth had been released from the Rochester hospital on December 13.

I realize that specific events are connected to a larger story, with causal connections as intricate as the patterns in my brain. Along with the eventful bursts there is the steady pulse of everyday routines of getting up, prayers, breakfast, going to work, attending chapel, conversation, lunch, nap, walk, grocery shopping, early supper, McNeill-Lehrer news, a few TV programs, playing Yahtzee, going to bed.

Ruth and I returned to the morning routine we had been following for years. After breakfast, which we had around 6 a.m., we sat on our living room couch. The large windows gave us access to a wide view of the valley. We were up early enough in the winter to watch the sky change colors as the earth spins toward the sun. We recited the ritual on pages 162-163 in the **Lutheran Book of Worship** —

"O Lord, I cry to you for help,

In the morning my prayer comes before you."

Then we talked out our prayers—of thanks, for guidance. We recited two prayers from the liturgical collection and the Lord's Prayer, and then each read aloud from a book and we discussed our readings and our current concerns. We were reading Wes Jackson's **Altars of Unhewn Stone: Science and the Earth** (San Francisco: North Point Press, 1987) and Arnold Carlson's **The Holy Spirit and the Neighbor's Need** (published privately by his wife). The ritual set the tone for the day and put our lives in touch with the Holy Presence.

Because Louise was on duty during the Christmas holiday and had services at the churches in Watson, we had our family Christmas on the night of December 21.

December 21, 1989

"Have mercy on us, God, have mercy,
for in you my soul has taken refuge.
In the shadow of your wings I take refuge
till the storms of destruction pass by
My soul lies down among lions
who would devour the sons of men" (Psalm 57:1, 4).

The psalmist speaks for me. I feel beset upon by invisible negativities while the angels of truth and love are sustaining us, and God is directing the battle. Everyone is hurting in the family, with one trouble or another. We gather, a besieged family, to find solace and strength in the good news which is not a sentimental story but one that has been sentimentalized. It is a story of an invasion of the Lord of love into the horrors of Herod's world, not just a political horror but the elusive demons of disease of body, heart and mind. The Lord of love came, a tiny baby, whose birth made a woman cry, and then smile with joy.

What a wonderful moment! In the darkest, coldest day, the birth of a baby! Not the swift, overwhelming, swooping of a flock of bomb-bearing jets. It is so important, I think, to recognize the truth that God comes to us in the dark of the night, in the frigid cold of winter. He chooses to dwell in the stables of the suffering.

*We are suffering now. It is winter, cold and dark: "For unto us a child is born, to us a son is given, and the government shall be upon his shoulder, and his name will be called 'Wonderful Counsellor, Mighty God, Everlasting Father, **Prince of Peace**" (Isaiah 9:6).*

Since we could not entertain the Erling family for our traditional Christmas Eve morning breakfast, they invited us to their home for Scandinavian food, music and dancing. Ruth played the piano for the dancing, and Bernhard photographed her and gave us a color print of her at one of her favorite pastimes.

31

That week there was bloodshed in Panama as the United States struggled against an entrenched tyrant and faced the prospect of huge cost of lives, money and world respect. There is no easy way to get rid of a tyrant. We saw this also in Romania, where there was a bloody revolution against a tyrant the U.S. supported. And in our family—another kind of battle.

There are two images — that of an ongoing battle between good and evil, the bright and the dark angels, Christ and Satan; or that of a unity of all things in Christ, an inclusive community of those who were once enemies and strangers - which have a long history. Which "picture" is the truth? Perhaps both.

Before the death of Christ, war; after, reconciliation and peace. The battle has been won, yet in our family the battle goes on; so I pray for courage and strength coming from love and truth to "awake the dawn." I cannot manipulate and force a victory. What matters is that I keep on—waiting, listening—with a steadiness of purpose that I feel, and a calmness.

There is an outer and an inner story I could tell. The outer, factual story is easy compared to the inner, interpretive account of what the facts mean. And why do I choose what I include? There would be no facts to tell if there were no inner motivation. Why is Anna's death important to me? Why did Ruth and I go on trips and to the places we chose? Why did I do forums on the subjects I selected?

I am describing these days, because I need and want to remember every precious time, even the hard times, with Ruth. There is a bleakness about these days, not grim but poignant and sad. It is easier to deal with our mortality because we have the nurture of the Psalms, ritual and prior experiences.

However, when the hour of dying comes, when the bell tolls, all is changed. Objective knowledge becomes personal encounter, not just someone else's account. Such knowledge is a knowing beyond full description and analysis. It is ineffable. Only stories can give hints of subtle depths and nuances.

As I review the year, I realize that story or drama is the key paradigm. I am living in a story larger than my own. I am becoming a story within the story as I live through the fates that come and respond to them. I am not the author, yet it is I who make up the meaning of what happens. It's a strange paradox. The events are fates, and the meanings are the ones I receive from traditions which I shape and use to make sense of my fates. Life is full of interruptions, which compel responses. Even choosing not to make much of them is a significant response. I do not control what happens, but I choose what response I think I should make and that choice is often shaped by the regular pulse of my life. I am struggling now to make the connection between the regular routine and the interruptions.

*Ruth and I have entered a new chapter now. The final chapter of one's life begins when a terminal illness is diagnosed. We have the advantage of time to deal with it, as people who die suddenly do not. So we have had meaningful conversations about what this time of life means to us, a time for remembering, but without regret for enjoying our lives **now**, and not letting anticipation of what is to come cast a pall over our times together. Ruth and I have enjoyed a life of quality together. We continue to do so. The meanings of this life continue to develop. The word, mobility, seems to be an apt metaphor for our experiences.*

January 1, 1990

A new year at the beginning of the '90s.
O Lord of life, love and light, enlighten me. I put my trust in you and hope for a good year.
Serendipity, the surprising good.
Your mercy is steadfast and endures from generation to generation of those who count on you as guide and refuge and strength.

33

Ruth had some good days early in January. She enjoyed grocery shopping and rides along roads in the countryside. We drove out one day to see our daughter and her husband.

About the middle of January, Ruth's condition began to decline. She was weaker, tired and had some pain. She slept after each meal. Meanwhile I was still working on my projects, the sermon for Gary Guptill's ordination, a presentation of "Moral Dramas in Health Care," and a forthcoming forum on environmental ethics.

January 17, 1990

The question is not a choice between faith healing and medical therapy, between crude prescientific practices and the latest state of the art. The question is deeper.

When Christ is the Lord of life, love and light, what does that translate into with regard to: [a] style of life; [b] attitudes toward death and suffering; [c] scientific research; [d] the distribution of medical care; [e] uses of high tech to prolong lives of severely handicapped?

When Ruth chose a treatment option that would give her more time but rejected options that would be expensive, painful and of limited value, such factors as these affected her decision: [a] her age, nearly 70; [b] her acceptance of her mortality; [c] her awareness of the high cost, though covered herself, with implications for the health care distribution; [d] the commitment to quality, not quantity of life.

Should she have rejected the radiation treatments also, which would only postpone the inevitable, only give her a few months, and thus save the system something like ten or twelve thousand dollars? That is the hard question. The determining factor was consequences. Having more than the radiation treatments would be excessively burdensome on all counts.

Ruth is a Lutheran Christian, a participating, lifelong member of a people who have chosen to live in faith in Christ's person and gospel. She is also a modern, educated woman with

34

adequate knowledge of medical technology. She considered her age, her inevitable mortality, the quality of life, and her sense of justice which constrained her from demanding unlimited efforts to prolong her life in the context of the needs of others, such as children, for health care.

January 29, 1990

Ruth was awake at 4:30 and prepared breakfast. I awoke after five. We had breakfast of Red River cereal, grapefruit, toast and regular coffee. I had my usual six prunes. Then we had our morning prayers. We were almost finished with Arnold Carlson's book and had started "The Church in Society: Toward a Lutheran Perspective," a proposed ELCA social statement. I had my ritual meditations, and Ruth had her bath. I helped her out of the tub and gave her the morning back rub, tucked her into her blankets for her nap and turned out the light. Then I had my own morning shower and shave.

The dawn sky [at 7 a.m.] is clear, yellow on the horizon and shading to a blue green azure dome. My self awaits the dawn from on high. In God we live and move and have our being.

Ruth had not been well for over a week. She was weak but had no pain. Friday morning, while I was out, she fell, although she did not faint, and was in rough shape. I helped her check her blood sugar level on Saturday morning, because she was trembling too much to do it herself. She says she is losing weight. Her face is puffed. Yesterday her eyes were dull. She was in a bad condition all day, so did not have a very happy time of it.

It's incredible that Jane Hokanson came all the way from Alameda, California, to see Ruth and me. What a long friendship we have had! We had a good talk over coffee at Prairie House Restaurant before she came to visit Ruth in the afternoon. She urged me to consider contingency plans to deal with likely difficulties after Ruth dies.

That is putting it starkly. Ruth is even now afraid she is dying—and for good reason—but I still hope for more good days, hope that her present

35

condition is just temporary due to her cold. Even so, I know I am going to lose her and do not know how well I will cope with the loss.

Already I am getting a taste of being alone, especially when she goes to bed, which is often, and I spend the evening alone. Saturday night I listened to music, wrote letters and wept as I heard the song, "In the gloaming, O my darling..." and other old songs.

Today I must concentrate on what I want to share with North Branch people on ecology.

February 1, 1990
Rochester, Minnesota

I read two contrasting passages this morning:

"Then I looked on all the works my hand had wrought and on the labor that I had labored to do, and, behold, all was vanity, and there was no profit under the sun...Yea, I hated all my labor" (Ecclesiastes 2:11, 18).

"Therefore, my beloved brethren, be ye steadfast, unmovable, always abounding in the work of the Lord, for as much as you know your labor is not in vain in the Lord" (I Corinthians 15:58).

In Paul's letter death is swallowed up in victory. "We shall all be changed" (I Corinthians 15:51). The hope inspired by that strange event we call the resurrection of Christ. In Ecclesiastes all die, hard workers and drones. We all go the way of the grasshoppers, and whatever wisdom and quality we have attained die with us.

My view: We are not isolated individuals but members of community. In this we both receive and give. We are both responsible for giving and responsive to what is given. My story is caught up in a larger story. The last scene in that story is dying, and dying is not pretty. But I must put dying in a larger story—a rich life of giving and receiving. In dying we also are giving, giving space and place to a new generation. Our lives have been fruitful, because of the sacrifice of others. So, too, our lives, by being given, fertilize other lives.

February 2, 1990

The X ray, blood test and CAT scan revealed no change. The growth of the tumors had been stopped, but they remained. The oncologist asked about neurological symptoms, such as headaches, confused thinking, unsteadiness. Ruth told him about her utter weariness, loss of interest and weakness in the legs.

He explained the effects of decadron; large dosages of decadron give people a "high" feeling of energy and elan. As the dosage is reduced, the high feelings depart and the low mood and loss of strength are typical side effects. As the natural functions of the body resume, these side effects diminish. The decadron also leaves the large thigh muscles near the hip weakened, which accounted for her difficulty in rising from a sitting position and unsteadiness when walking.

I expressed my concern about low blood sugar and insulin reactions and my opinion that Ruth should eat more. He agreed and arranged an interview with a diabetic specialist, who advised Ruth to stop taking regular insulin in the morning. Ruth was willing, but only to do so gradually. The low sugar usually happens in the morning between nine and ten o'clock.

The oncologist's diagnosis was guarded and cautious.

Going public in the description of Ruth's illness in the Christmas letter, 1989, elicited much response. People had called, written and conversed with Ruth or me and expressed much care, love and respect, for Ruth in particular.

It was not my intention, however, to tell others in order to elicit such responses. Although we had been usually open about our family situation concerning diabetes and some other problems, Ruth and I had assumed full responsibility for our own burdens. I admired Ruth especially, because even though she had to cope with both diabetes and cancer, she had not yielded to self-pity. She was weary now with coping, just plain tired of it and occasionally angry; but she had not let it be an easy escape from fulfilling her responsibilities of household work, church duties, family responsibilities, and entertaining.

Now she could not do her normal tasks, so I had become a house husband, trying to do all the work she had done. I was truly glad to do it and also to take care of her, because I had been deeply in debt for her many years of caring for me and the children.

The chores were not onerous; indeed, I found it challenging to organize my work and learned something new every day.

Why should we share our lives with others, ever? Where is the boundary? By relating our experience of entering a terminal time, have we contributed to the quality of life for others? Does our way of facing the reality help others?

Both of us were surprised by the flood of calls and writings from our friends. We did not expect it. Maybe our surprise is evidence for the fact that getting such a response was not the reason for telling them what was happening.

I have thought and written much about life and death issues, about dying, about illness. I am aware of the subtle ways we deny our mortality. Is it better to live on an illusion of endless life? No! That is an adolescent stage of wisdom, beyond which one should go eventually. Is the quality of daily life enhanced by acknowledging one's mortality? I know, intellectually, that I am mortal, but such knowledge may not be an operational knowledge that shapes daily living. The operational basis may very well be the illusion of immortality. For instance, I may cherish the thought that even if my body dies my works will live beyond my time, significant enough for others to remember. That, too, is vanity. I will soon be a forgotten person in the normal, day-by-day world. I see the finitude of my place and attainments as a faculty member and I have had to let go of the desire to be influential in the college. This desire for immortality is such a subtle affair! I value friendships with students of the past and with colleagues enough to cherish the continuance of those relationships. Yet I have relinquished the roles in which those relationships took shape.

Last week I canceled all speaking engagements so I could be free to take care of my family duties. I enter this new chapter ready to respond to its challenges.

I believe in frank acknowledgment of our limits, our helplessness to cope with and solve some problems, and believe in freely confessing when I have done something unfitting.

Do I threaten those who are unable to do so? Do I rob them of their defenses by such open admission of mortality? I am in a quandary.

We are communal persons, so it seems appropriate to share mutual woes and joys. Is it pride that motivates someone to be utterly private about personal experiences, especially those of weakness, mortality and failure?

According to Ernest Becker in **The Denial of Death** (New York: Free Press, 1973), all heroic endeavors, human projects to attain the good and the right and immortality, are driven by fear and awe of death. They are "denials of death" in that they seek to dethrone death.

February 3, 1990

Following an evening walk in the arboretum, I was listening to a Beethoven violin concerto and reflecting on a day that had been ideal (blue sky, no wind, mild temperatures, fresh snow) remembering calls from Ruby and Marc, Mildred and Alfred, Hilda; reading letters from Crysta Wille and John Fahning; and taking a ride with Ruth past Lake Emily and over to Cleveland.

My dear Ruth was tired today and sleeping now, so I missed her companionship. But I had promised myself that I was not going to begin missing her until it was unavoidable. I was healthy, energetic, and with good **elan**. I could take life as it is.

O Lord of life, love and light, in whom I live and move and have my being, you are in the depths of my being, you are beyond me, you are the Ancient Mystery and the Anticipated Completion, Alpha and Omega. I cannot touch you. The sense of you is very mysterious, yet very intimate. Belonging to the Way, I call you Christ, because Jesus revealed you as your Yes to humanity, not to perfect humanity but humanity as we are, still stumbling, yet ever striving for the righteousness that is in us, a hunger we cannot deny, no matter who we are.

You are the merciful judge, assessing, deep in me, whether what I am doing is in harmony with mercy, the up-building love that you intend my actions to be. You sustain me. You lure me. You are the solid rock, a sure foundation, but not a fortified prison. You lead me in a changing world and through the inner changes I am experiencing.

You say to me, "Fear not; I am with you." Though I walk through another valley of death, in which I cannot escape dying and which does not end in death but new life, I fear no evil. You are with me.

I should say something about hope. Crysta Wille wrote that she believed that hope was not just thinking everything will turn out as we want it. I agree. Some of our friends express the hope that Ruth will recover and live much longer. They are happy when I report some reassuring piece of information. Well, I hope for as much time with Ruth as possible. I also hope that her dying will be easy, when it is her time to die. It may not be, however, so if what I want does not come to true, should that be reason for despair? No. Ruth exists in the eternal, in the life of God, whether she lives or dies. She has experienced in living the power and mercy of eternal God. All her life such experiences have happened.

Does my faith depend on assurances such as: When she dies will she enter another world we call heaven? Yes, if it means she

*lives and dies within the divine presence. No, if the hope is but a
dream of continuance of earthly life. "We shall all be changed..."
I exist, not just in time but in the eternal, something very real
that is not confined to my awareness or my brief time on earth.*

Yesterday as I was writing about Anna [my stepmother], at my
computer, Ruth came down and objected, "You always have to be doing
something, either writing or talking on the phone. Why can't you come and sit
still with me?" I realized she wanted my companionship, so I went up and sat.
We listened to music and then went for a ride. Maybe Ruth was reacting to
my lifelong pattern of putting my projects first. I was rueful.

February 9, 1990

*O Lord, this is a silent moment for seeing the dawning sky,
for listening, for sensing your presence, all encompassing
mystery, holy, holy, holy. This is a time for awe, for adoration, for
awakening of life, for remembering and renewing covenants.*

*My response to you is not just personal. I am one small point
of the universe's consciousness of itself. The star, or planet,
shining in the night sky prompts me to say a word, not just of
delight for beauty, and humility for a sense of the vastness of the
universe, but a word, **Lord**, a word meaning you.*

*A word of worship. I pledge anew to be an energy center for
peace and justice and compassion, especially for vulnerable
ones. May you, dwelling in me as Spirit, guide me to be
appropriately helpful for Ruth.*

The night was difficult for Ruth. She awoke at midnight, came out to
the kitchen, and began preparing breakfast. She called me. I came. I saw her
sitting in her blue robe, her wig adorning her, at my place. She had taken the
grill out and three strips of lean bacon. She said, "I thought it was time for
breakfast." She went back to bed but had trouble staying asleep so she was up
before five, prepared a waffle mix and called me for breakfast. I made coffee
and prepared the grapefruit and finished mixing the waffle batter. She tested

her blood - it was 89 - took insulin. We ate, but she was quiet. I asked her if she had pain. "A little," she said but would not tell me where or what sort of pain. During devotions she recited the prayers but did not talk about anything. I was silent after prayers for a brief time, and then she began the closing prayers again. I read from Arnold Carlson's book, but she was unresponsive to the ideas. Yesterday's lilt in her voice was gone. She was not feeling well, yet she went to the piano and played her two hymns. I could tell she was not coordinated; her playing was erratic. She struggled with her bath. I gave her a rubdown, and then she was quiet, taking her usual nap.

John Kendall visited yesterday, brought a lovely plant and told us about his son David's research in the autoimmune aspect of diabetes. There is growing evidence that diabetes is an autoimmune disease, and that there is a real, if not well-understood, relationship between mental and physical processes. Stress may affect immunity negatively. He also said that it is a time for Ruth and me to get back from this community what we had given to it over the years.

I took her for a ride to Arlington. We visited Pauline Wiemann briefly. Pauline seemed to have recovered from her bout with cancer. She told us about a woman whose doctor gave her a second course of radiation treatments for cerebellum cancer and burned out her synapses so that she is alive but not very functional. Scary! I hoped Ruth had not been hurt in that way from her radiation treatments. She had lost some of her capacities and was so slow and tired, but perhaps she would recover and get stronger.

If not—then one wonders about the therapy. We gained a good month, and that was important to her and the family. I didn't demand more than is possible, but I could pray without restraint for her recovery. So I did. "Lord, I pray that you will have mercy on Ruth. Heal her. May my prayer be an opening for her good."

Kyle and Doris brought us a meal—tuna pasta, salad, prunes, pumpernickel bread. Marian brought Ruth a valentine with an incredible tribute to Ruth. Dorothy Davis sent a beautiful book and an affectionate note. All this kindness was a form of energy for me. Ruth responded, too, but more weakly.

Dottie Davis wrote: "It's been a month since your Christmas letter and news of Ruth's cancer reached me. It has been difficult to take up my pen and respond to both of you. Tonight I got some help from a videotape shown at our Stephens ministry meeting. It is not **what** I write that will help, but that you know I care, and I care very much."

I wanted to respond: "Yes, Dottie, I also have been hesitant to call, write or visit people who are dying for the very same reason. What words to say is the inevitable issue, because we humans are so reliant on language. Your words are very meaningful, because they speak of the rich connections with you, Howard and Janey."

I noticed that people were very caring and wanted to help in some way. They brought food, plants, flowers, some physical token, all of which we appreciated, but it was their coming or writing or calling that was the most gratifying. Some had lots of words, others few words. Many talked about what they are doing.

I had learned that I needed someone to listen more than to speak. I am such a talkative one that I need to learn to listen, to give people space, listening space, so they can talk if they want to.

Ruth was not well during the day. She was very weak, yet she was determined to get up, get dressed and go grocery shopping. She had trouble getting into panty hose because she had put both legs into one stocking! I do the same sometimes getting into my shorts. No big deal. Marian invited us to tea at 10 a.m., but Ruth was too tired. I did not want to leave her. In the afternoon Ruth Gamelin brought a coffee bread and a valentine for her. We had coffee with her. Ruth listened to Ruth Gamelin chatting about various topics but did not participate vocally. She was quiet most of the time now. Was it because she was so weary, because she was no longer able to express herself or because she was withdrawing into her own inner world? I didn't know. I was beginning to experience her absence. As I lay in bed alone, I said to myself that this must be the way the surviving spouse experiences the loss of partner. I thought of Emma G., whose husband Henry has Alzheimer's disease. He was with Emma but no longer capable. So she knows what absence means, even before he dies.

43

The previous account seems stark. [It recalls] what Martin Marty calls "reflections for the winter of the heart." Winter is cold, trees are dormant, some animals hibernate, but chickadees, juncos and squirrels do not; they hustle for food. I help them with sunflower seed. I feel more akin to them than to hibernating bears. In this wintry time of my life I keep active, I read and think and write. Maybe the chill of the heart will immobilize me, but at present I am a chickadee. I take care of Ruth [hustle for her], I try to anticipate her needs, tell her I love her. I keep at some of my normal activities. I am not hibernating in grief.

In his book A Cry of Absence, Marty describes "spirit-filled piety" as that of a woman who says "praise the Lord" too much, as if compelled to show a summery, sunny spirit. After encounters with such, he says, questions come to mind: "Is the summer-style believer being honest? Will she not hit the void someday? Is the cry of absence, not heard, or does she ignore it?"

Am I being honest in what I have said and written? I am trying to be. Maybe winter has not yet come. Maybe my [spiritual] winter is mild, like the winter this year in January. Maybe I am an "autumn" person, in an "Indian summer." I know I will lose Ruth, and I experience loss in small ways, such as sleeping alone and missing her lively conversation and doing by myself the chores she routinely did. But she is still here, still alive, still affectionate. Maybe I am in October, not January. We shall see. I have wept already—a couple of weeks ago when the realization that I will lose her hit me, but as yet there is no cry of absence. For now, I have a lot of energy, I feel cheerful, I am serene [except when Ruth has a severe insulin reaction that is hard to manage].

Ruth had received so many expressions of appreciation that have been consoling and surprising, such as Marian's letter. Maybe we deprive our friends of the opportunity to tell us what they would like to say by not sharing what we were experiencing in a time of loss. Eulogies about people after they die do not console those who die, although family and friends benefit. I had been very shy about expressing my affection and regard for people who were dying. I never called or visited one of my colleagues, never talked about his illness or what he was going through.

Many people came to us in the weeks since Thanksgiving. Our friends in St. Peter have been close now, but so have long-time friends who lived away.

Which is the best way to communicate under these circumstances? Writing? Talking? Talking conveys feeling, nuances of the person that cannot be communicated in letters, but talk is ephemeral whereas writing leaves a permanent record. It seems that one should work at writing to make one's less verbal meaning communicable. Broken sentences, single phrases, even words without structure around them can communicate, sometimes more than complete, polished, expository or narrative writings.

Letters stand between speech and essays; they are more spontaneous and flowing, although they flow less evenly than polished writing. My journal writings are not sculptured, polished; they are very free. I leap from one subject to another.

February 10, 1990

As I write in my journal, the dawn light was getting brighter along the horizon across the river valley. We have enjoyed a view of the changing light and seasons through the large windows of our living room. I would mourn leaving this house! When we moved into it in May 1958, there were no trees, or only a few small ones, so the landscape was stark. We could see the whole valley and the hills across the valley. Nearly 32 years later only during the winter are the valley and hills visible. The naked branches of tall trees are brush-shaped etchings on the dawn-lit sky.

Ruth, as she usually did these days, has gone back to bed after breakfast and our usual morning prayers, readings and conversations. We just completed reading Arnold Carlson's posthumous manuscript, **The Holy** **Spirit and the Neighbor's Need** (published privately by his wife).

I found a stack of old copies of **The Lutheran** containing Ruth's published writings. I began to classify them by series and chronology. People still commented on her writings, most of which were published in the 1960s. In recent years she had written only a monthly column, Worship Notes, for the newsletter of First Lutheran Church. We also had saved many letters, letters between Ruth and her parents, between Ruth and me and letters from friends and relatives—hundreds of letters. I had organized them and wanted to save them for our children and grandchildren. Chester Johnson says that no one is a good judge of the future value of his or her archives, so he encourages me to save, not destroy, the collection. In our collection there were more women's letters than men's.

Ruth's conversations were minimal now. She says little and tires when others or I talk too much. I was not sure whether it was because she is too weary, less mentally acute or withdrawing. Time would tell. I missed her animated responses to my chatter! No one could bring me to a halt better than she could when I made some wild statement. She has stopped reading, too. Before this happened to her she was an avid reader, especially of mysteries. Each morning, before her bath, she went to the piano to play two of her favorite hymns. She also listened to classical music and hymns on stereo or radio.

I have been reading Martin Marty's **A Cry of Absence** (San Francisco: Harper & Row, 1983), which was inspired by the death of his first wife. It should help me understand the experience of absence that I am beginning to have.

It seemed important to share our experience with others. Several people have thanked us for letting them into our story. I wondered if by being so private, keeping our stories to ourselves, we do not deprive one another of participating in the deep and rich human experience.

I awoke at 4 a.m. from a dream and jumped out of bed to see why Ruth was muttering. She had awakened at three and wanted to get up. I got up, and we prepared breakfast.

I thought about the spouses [I dislike that word; companions would be better] of persons who are ill and need care. The husband or wife is affected, too, actually a participant in the illness. Frequently after a companion dies, the partner suffers illness, even dies. Perhaps the stress of terminal illness weakens the immune system, especially if the terminal period is long and painful. I resolved to take good care of myself, as well as of Ruth. I might not be able to prevent getting ill, but I could reduce the odds by proper care; so, for instance, I went for walks and meditated.

I had a hard day. I was not alert soon enough about Ruth. She had put potatoes, vegetables and meat on the stove and then had gone to lie down and had fallen asleep. I was reading the Sunday paper and was unaware of the cooking food until I smelled something burning. I jumped up, alarmed, dashed to the stove, turned off the burner, and rescued the food. The vegetables had burned. The potatoes had cooked dry. The meat was **well** done.

Ruth was staggering when she awoke and came down the hall. She was so wobbly I helped her to the chair and gave her some orange juice. She regained enough sense and strength to make the gravy as I mashed the potatoes. We were able to eat a well-done meal.

I chided myself for not being more aware and for getting as frantic as I did. Ruth had been so independent and reliable for so many years that I was habituated to leaving meals in her hands. I needed to change.

At the peace study group, I tried to explain that Ruth's current condition faced both of us with our mortality and that Ruth and I were not denying it. I decided what I said was too stark for the people. They seemed nonplussed. I needed to exercise restraint and be tactful. People wanted to believe that Ruth was getting better.

Yesterday afternoon Barbara and Steve brought us a book by Tim Hansel, **You Gotta Keep Dancin'** (Elgin, Illinois: David C. Cook, 1986). The theme of the book is that in the midst of life's hurts you can choose joy. They had found the book very helpful and wanted to share it with us. It has a very positive theme. Without diminishing the awfulness of pain, tragedy and affliction the author still stresses transcending that awfulness. I am not sure yet if it is a book about a spirituality Marty would call summery with a message, "Follow me, my prescription, think the right thoughts, and all the chill will disappear." Marty thinks many serious people are repelled by such a message. I lean toward the wintry style of spirituality, I realized. I hope I will be able to affirm life even when death comes.

February 13, 1990

I will see Dr. Thompson with two concerns to discuss: [a] Ruth's condition and what I should be ready to do. I want to ask him about the side effects of radiation when applied to the brain. Ruth is less able to express herself, considerably slowed up mentally and also less stable on her feet. Will these conditions get worse or will she gradually improve to a more normal state. [b] It seems important that my health be maintained. I must be in good health for Ruth's sake as well as my own. If she dies I do not want to be more vulnerable, as I will be if my immune system has been compromised by stress. I might not escape illness, but I can try to minimize the conditions that are conducive to it. How shall I care for my health? Continue meditating? Eat well? Walk a couple of miles a day? Keep up my own interests, even if at a minimal level? [c] I also want to comment on how important I think the family physician is as the one who is reliably present to us in our suffering. The Mayo specialists are good at what they do but are not present over a period of time, which is important for us now.

To push back darkness and chill—the winterkill of chronic illness—am I most at home in the wintry style of spirituality? I think so, even though I may seem to be an upbeat, cheerful, optimistic sort of person in my outward mein. Inwardly, I experience an austerity of heart, not cold or stern, but spare and lean, no ecstatic experiences or frolics but a steady confidence that endures through the ups and downs, the peaks and pits, which are not as sharply high and deep as they once were. For example,

48

facing up to mortality, rather than ignoring it, is a rather austere stance.

Lord, I live within your loving embrace, but it is not a womb, not a playpen, not a yard, not a "safe house." It is the world, with all its variety, which brings a diversity of opportunities, benefits and challenges that are my fate. Today I pray for the strength and patience to be true to you.

February 14, 1990

Martin Marty: "Sensible people have to make sense of their surrounding world. Even a plot about plotlessness, as in the Theater of the Absurd, is the first clue to finding a world that is not wholly random."

*Esbj: We construct worlds of meaning, but those constructions are **responses**, to what is **there**, beyond us, not necessarily visible to the eye but evident to the inner sense.*

It seems that my life is a story that is unfolding. I can't see a meaningful plot in the story. So where does the meaning come from?

[a] Patterns which are recorded in traditions, such as the Psalms.

[b] New combinations

[c] Retrospect—which allows us to see where we have been from a higher, or more comprehensive perspective, such as a lookout on a mountain road.

*[d] Revelation which is a presence I call spirit, that is mysterious, sustaining, even guiding. The meaning is always **more** than a + b + c. The meaning is one or more of a, b, c **plus** presence of spirit. This may be too abstract to be meaningful, but I have to account somehow for the experience of the **new**. My thoughts are not all-encompassing, yet they are glimpses of the all-encompassing.*

I awoke at 3:20 a.m. Ruth was awake. We got up at 3:55 a.m. and began breakfast preparations. Ruth made the pancake batter. I made coffee and cut the grapefruit. We were finished with breakfast by 5 a.m.

Ruth is getting weaker. It was very hard for her to rise to a standing position. She wobbles as she walks. I helped her stand up from sitting on the sofa. I helped her every day now to get out of the bathtub. She played her two hymns much less accurately. There is a slight slurring in her voice as she reads. I had noticed, too, a decline of interest in letters from friends, in calls and in our next door neighbor's invitation to come over. Yesterday, when she awoke from a nap, she was confused about what time it was, and she thought today was Friday.

Yesterday I spoke with Dr. Thompson about Ruth's condition. "What I see is more than tiredness. I don't think the Mayo doctors told us everything. One said she would lose some memory, but she seems to be losing more than memory. I miss her lively conversations," I said.

Dr. Thompson replied, "Ruth is not going to get better as the decadron dosage is reduced. It is hard for me to say this, but the radiation destroys normal brain cells, too, and they do not regenerate. We have billions of brain cells. As we age they diminish by hundreds of millions. Ruth's brain has been affected, as a side effect of radiation. You can expect her to become bedridden and less able to function."

I asked, "Will the tumors resume growing and if they do will they interfere with respiration and heart and will she then die rather quickly?"

"Maybe."

"Ruth does not want to have efforts to keep her from dying. She has written a statement to that effect. Recently she expressed the hope that she would slip into oblivion." Dr. Thompson put a note to that effect in her medical record.

So that is the reality Ruth faces, but this morning she still prayed for help to get well. I am sad.

I'm in touch with hospice people but haven't called on them yet. I will probably need help soon.

I talked to Dr. Thompson about maintaining my own health. I told him what I was doing to keep my health—walking each day, getting out to talk to friends and colleagues, meditation, writing in my journal, keeping a little time for projects, eating proper food. Getting enough sleep was the hardest. If Ruth woke up I heard her and became alert.

Dr. Thompson approved of my regimen.

Illness is not confined to the one afflicted, though it was centered in her. It spreads to persons who are close at hand. Ruth's illness is also mine, in that I could be affected by it. If my immune system were affected, the cancer I had in prostate and on the forehead could flare up.

People wanted to help, but they could only do so much. They brought food, but I had to tell them what not to bring. For example, Ruth did not like pea soup or bean soup and could not eat sweet foods. I need people's care, so I could care for Ruth, and I was not alone, because friends called or visited or wrote to encourage me.

February 17, 1990

My top concern was caring for Ruth. Ruth is experiencing weakness in the legs. She had not had enough exercise since the end of November. The muscles in her thighs and calves looked smaller. It was difficult for her to rise from a sitting position and especially hard for her to get out of the bathtub. I was helping her each time. Yesterday I asked her to turn her back toward me so I could use both arms [to lift her]. That worked better than the day before when I had to use only one arm. It was such a strain that I could feel the wrenching, and I think she hurt her back. She has been complaining of back pain for the last two days. I had bought a tub mat yesterday, so she would have better traction. When I spoke to Gene Lund, she said that she would bring a handle to clamp on the side of the tub. We decided to try that out. Eventually it would be too hard for me to lift Ruth because her legs would be too weak. Then, Gene said, we would give her a sponge bath.

Ruth or I need to tell Dr. Thompson about her back pain, in case it was due to something other than strain. One of the Mayo doctors said that something could be done, if the cancer migrates, to control pain.

About Ruth's mental state: Yesterday she had trouble turning the stereo system from radio to phono, something she used to do easily. Was she

51

forgetting a familiar procedure? On the other hand, she continued to plan and prepare the meals. I helped with much of it. I did the breakfast, peeled the potatoes and cleaned up after the meal. When she read, during the morning prayers, there was a slight slur in her voice and some hesitancy as if she was grasping for how to say a word. Her conversation had declined markedly during the last two weeks and so had her interests. The animated exchanges so characteristic of our conversations over the years did not occur. However, last night she watched "Washington Week in Review," one of her favorites, and Bill Moyer's conversation with a woman philosopher. She no longer read books, magazines or the newspaper, but she still read the mail.

When Hilda Powicke wrote about the hospice program in Toronto, Ruth said, "I wish Hilda wouldn't emphasize that hospice program." Her reaction made me wonder what she was thinking. Was she still thinking she would get well? Was she denying her actual decline? Not entirely. She explicitly mentioned her mortality in a conversation with the Wilkinsons last Sunday. She had not discussed it with me lately, not specifically in relation to what was happening to her.

I heard her groaning. When she awoke a few minutes ago she said her back was hurting. I decided to get Tylenol for her. Gene said she should take it regularly to ease pain.

This morning she decided not to play her two hymns or to take a bath.

Dr. Thompson had told me last Tuesday that Ruth will eventually be bedridden. I wondered if that change is already coming.

It is hard trying to describe Ruth's state of mind. She has been certainly aware and responsive, but not articulate. A dullness, if that is the right word, seemed to have come over her.

What I write in my journal describes what I have perceived. I knew I was going to lose Ruth, in some respects have already lost her—her help, her wit, her admonitions, her lively mind. She was becoming "absent." I lay alone in bed and realized that this was what I would be doing in the future. I was doing the household tasks she had been doing for almost 45 years of our marriage.

Several weeks ago, as I drove out to Bernadotte Lutheran Church for services, my coming loss struck me hard, and I wept. I was sad, but not dominated by sadness. I felt much tender love for Ruth. I wanted to provide for her needs, to respond to her calls for help, to be near her and to touch her.

We had had our talks, especially when she was at Methodist. I didn't expect her to be talkative now, but I would respond when she did talk. She had said a few days ago that she was afraid. Maybe her silence now was a protection against reality. I was not sure.

She is getting weaker. I wish she could say what she was thinking!

I talked to Gene this morning about Ruth's back pain and weakness. She suggested I call her oncologist for advice. Ruth's back hurt this morning and again this evening, all the way up her spine.

Jean Larson brought bread. Betty Gustafson brought chicken soup.

Ruth and I drove to Mankato to get One Step strips used for testing blood sugar levels. She was able to walk to and from the car.

I feel so helpless about her pain! She wouldn't take more than one Tylenol.

Tonight we watched **My Life as a Dog**, a Swedish film, much praised. I felt as one in limbo, not knowing what to expect or what to do. I was reading **Twelve Weeks in Spring: The Inspiring Story of Margaret and Her Team** (Toronto: Lester & Orpen Dennys, Limited 1986) about the Toronto hospice team Hilda mentioned.

February 18, 1990

Questions on my mind:

[1] Will Ruth improve slowly as the decadron dose decreases; will her own adrenalin kick in? Or are the weakness and pain an indication of decline? I am not sure, so it is hard to choose the best action.

[2] What can be done to control pain. Tylenol? Yes. Narcotics? Surely there are other options and additional ones. I'm going to get more knowledge.

[3] What exercises are helpful? Should Ruth exercise her legs in some way other than walking? Exercise bike?

[4] What am I to make of these symptoms: playing the piano, she is making mistakes she never used to make; tuning the stereo

from radio to phono, she becomes confused; reading aloud, her
speech is slightly slurred; in conversation and oral prayers, she is
losing thought and content.

[5] Should I encourage having visitors? Should I ask Ruth
about rationing time for such activities?

[6] Keeping the eating on schedule is hard, because Ruth
needs or wants to eat earlier than usual.

I wished I knew what Ruth was really thinking. Did she
silently think she was dying; was she pushing the thought out of
mind and still hoping to get better?

I read **Twelve Weeks in Spring** about the hospice team that took care of Margaret Fraser who had no family. The team was a highly organized effort to cover the full range of her needs: household chores and repairs, shopping for food and other items, social contacts with many friends, basic physiological care, pain control, spiritual nurture, providing music, tapes.

The difference from my situation was obvious. I was the primary person trying to manage Ruth's care and respond to her needs. What do I need? Advice about and assistance with her bodily needs and someone to help regulate the social aspect of visits. Marian was the person I needed to consult about visits. I also had needs. The Toronto team was shared by shifts. I was on the scene 24 hours a day. I needed to keep some free time for walks and my journal.

Being knowledgeable about medical ethics is like a background in my visual field, there but not in focus.

It was 6 p.m. and I was sad. A sunset the colors of the valley and sky were muted, pastel shades of violet and pink. The western sky had faded from orange to yellow. I was listening to **Mahler's Symphony Number 4.**

Ruth was lying quietly on the couch. She had not had a good day. While I was at church services she fell in the kitchen. As we were about to have the noon meal she fell in a swoon in the bathroom. I thought she was out cold, so I called Dr. Thompson. She revived and needed to eat.

Dr. Thompson came, examined her, chatted for a while and asked her to cut regular insulin to zero from ten. She promised, and I will see to it.

54

Later she discovered she had been incontinent, so I cleaned her clothes and helped her bathe. This evening she wanted to tell me something but couldn't complete her thought until I helped her by saying something about testing her blood later.

I knew I was losing her, so I was heartsick. Looking through the road atlas today, I remembered all our auto trips across the states and wondered if I could bear to travel alone. We had been such close companions for so many years.

It was not easy to determine how much time she has, but it was obvious she was weakening both physically and mentally—my dear, dear Ruth!

I resolved to call her oncologist and JoAnn Pool of the nursing service to get advice on appropriate care. I love Ruth—deeply, tenderly, I do!

February 20, 1990

I talked to the oncologist about Ruth's leg and back pain. He advised getting an X ray locally to check out the area in the back and suggested that Ruth walk as much as possible, but without using an exercise bike.

JoAnn Pool came, surveyed the bath situation and made suggestions— using a bath stool and a walker to help Ruth get up from a sitting position. The walker did not help.

I was showing signs of fatigue the next morning. I needed more sleep and perhaps some relief, some distancing from the situation.

We were up around 2:45 a.m. on February 22. Ruth tried testing her blood sugar level. Three times the tester did not work. She said, "I'm doing this too much."

"Why not wait until morning? I will clean it." We went back to bed. I lay there for a while, unable to sleep because of my thoughts. Then I began playing my game of remembering cities through which we have traveled, beginning with A, B, C.

I thought about the side effects of radiation therapy applied to the brain. In Ruth's case, it had stopped the growth of the tumors for the time being only. She gained an extension of normal or almost normal being, except that she needed a lot of rest. When the neuro-oncologists explained her options, I thought they muted information about side effects — they said there would be some memory loss, that was all. Maybe they assumed that people would rather not know the whole truth. No one at Mayo really sat down and discussed **her** with her.

How can I put it? The way the holistic perspective at Mayo works is through **team**work, with each medic having a specialty. Whatever specialty is needed in a particular case, that is given. So the medical oncologist turns Ruth over to the neuro-oncologist and to the endocrinologist and to the radiation therapists. Who knows the whole person?

But who of them knows whether the Ruth person I know would want to live on in a semistate for months in exchange for a good Christmas, a good month? We all assumed she would want to arrest the cancer, even if the ultimate cost was high.

I was beginning to see at Mayo, as I watched hundreds of people, that we all want the medical profession to save us, and they often give us added time. The cost is immense, not meaning financial cost only.

February 23, 1990

At 1 a.m., Ruth was in poor condition due to low sugar, so I got her to take some orange juice, a glass of milk and a piece of toast. At 4:30 I heard her moaning, so I checked her and found her in a severe insulin reaction. I goofed trying to take a blood test and could not move her into a position where she could drink orange juice. I called 911 around 6 a.m. because I could not handle the situation. She was out of it, so the paramedics could not get her to take glucose. At the hospital Dr. Thompson ordered an IV to get her glucose level up, and then she revived enough to take glucogon by mouth. She was so out of mind she did not remember the emergency crew coming or her going by ambulance to the hospital after she came to.

Yesterday her glucose levels were erratic—very high several times and low, too. Her eating has also been irregular. Ruth resists eating enough and also insists on doing her own blood testing and administering insulin. The doctor says I am supposed to take over, but she resists my efforts—which are not very deft I will admit. Her thinking is not clear either. She is forgetful. She has trouble understanding the blood test chart I made. She is slow in speaking and often fails to finish a sentence she starts. She was not very interested in what I was reading at morning devotions but she recited the morning prayers.

I couldn't lift her, so if she was too weak to pull herself up, I was relatively helpless to help her. Yesterday was a **bad** day!

The dietician said she would give us a regular diet which we can follow, and it would be flexible enough to include donated hot dishes.

I was not getting enough sleep when Ruth was having such difficulties, so I was feeling fatigue and realized something must be done.

Dr. Bauer released Ruth from the hospital yesterday. I expected her to be released no earlier than today, February 27, 1990. He wanted her to continue the effort to regain balance at home, to follow a plan and to report to him by Thursday or Friday.

It was an instance of dismissing a patient as soon as possible for both financial reasons and for putting health care in the hands of the patient, family and friends, where it primarily belongs.

I had to be quite firm and follow the prescribed schedule of eating, insulin, medication, exercise and rest. But could I deprive Ruth of the primary responsibility? No. I didn't want to, but the difficulty came when she had her mind set on doing something that was not according to the schedule. She had been so independent and thought she knew better than doctors and dieticians what was best, even when evidence was against her! Over the years she had been very successful in caring for her health, but low blood sugar levels in recent years had brought on crises so serious I had had to call 911 or the doctor several times.

Now was the time to change that pattern. She needed a higher sugar level. It was hard for her to change, because it meant really accepting the reality of cancer.

February 28, 1990
Ash Wednesday
"Thank God...that he is our Father and the source of all
mercy and comfort. For he gives us comfort in our trials so that

57

we in turn may be able to give the same sort of strong sympathy to others. Indeed, experience shows that the more we share in Christ's suffering, the more we are able to give his encouragement" (2 Corinthians 1:3-4).

People who suffer chronic illness are better able to give encouragement. They have been comforted, so they can give the same sort of strong sympathy to others. Also, I am discovering that because Ruth and I are suffering from this life-threatening illness, we have experienced mercy and comfort. At least I have, and therefore I want to pass on spiritual help and comfort to others.

Ruth is very quiet—not able, I suspect, to share thoughts as had been her wont. She sat silently throughout the meal with Erlings yesterday, while the Erlings and I carried on rather lively chatter. I suspected Ruth's mental processes were affected by the cancer, the treatment or the side effects. She was more confused about time and other basic matters.

She watched "In the Heat of the Night" last night but with very little reaction or repartee. She would rather nap than watch her favorite news program, MacNeil-Lehrer.

Yesterday she had a bad day. Even after I gave her morphine, she had pain in the back. She was unstable, so I had to help her move from bed or sofa to bathroom. She had to go to the bathroom often. Her sugar was in the 200s, so it was not low sugar that was the cause of her mental and physical problems.

I needed some relief. However, if it was to help Ruth get to the bathroom or to keep her from falling, the persons who do so must be willing and able, and Ruth must be willing to accept a substitute for me. It is an intimate procedure. Who wants to be seen by friends or strangers going to the "toilet?" In the hospital it is standard procedure but not in one's home.

I wanted to give her interesting food, not rigid control of menu. This was not the time for exact measurement of amounts but for a palatable and interesting diet.

If Ruth is close to dying time, the care I give is to be very loving and responsive to her needs.

Carl and Louise, our children. What roles for them? Should I invite them to a greater participation? I don't want to exclude them or deny them the privilege of helping in the care of their mother. Sad as it would be, they would feel worse if arbitrarily excluded.

I told Ruth I was going to the Ash Wednesday service and would be gone for an hour. The service was long, so I left at 7:50 before it was over. When I got home, Ruth yelled, "**Robert!** Where have you been? I hollered and hollered for you. I looked for you in every room." Fortunately she did not need anything or have a troublesome fall. What should I do? Have someone stay in the house while I am gone, someone to respond to her?

Hospital Hospice Care

March 1, 1990

Beginning at 3:30 a.m., Ruth and I had one crisis after another. Ruth was in pain at 3:30, so I got up and at 4 a.m. administered the prescribed teaspoon of morphine. [The doctors entrusted me with the whole bottle, apparently not afraid I would administer an overdose.] She had insufficient relief so she asked for a Tylenol, which I gave her.

We had breakfast at about six. After breakfast Ruth tried to move from table to couch while I was out of the room. She collapsed on her knees with half her body on the couch. She did not have the strength to lift herself. I helped her move to a sitting position, where she could take hold of my hands and I hers. Somehow we managed to get her partially lying on the couch, but not yet where she should lie. She could do no more. The pain and weakness defeated her, and she was too heavy for me.

I called Gene Lund. She came, bless her, and helped expertly to move Ruth to a more comfortable position, with her head propped on two pillows.

During the morning Ruth had to urinate four times, so each time I held her steady as she tottered toward the bathroom. I gave her a teaspoon of morphine at 9 a.m. and another after a lunch of roast beef sandwiches.

Though she protested, I gave her another teaspoon of morphine at one o'clock, because she was in pain. Dr. Bauer came about 1 p.m. and assessed the situation. He saw no reason to think she could not be cared for at home and advised keeping on schedule with the morphine.

About two o'clock she asked me to take her to the bathroom again. This time she staggered precariously and then sat down on the bathroom floor by the door. I tried to lift her, but she was too weak to get up. I propped a pillow behind her so she could rest against the toilet and called Gene. She called Becky, her daughter who is also a nurse. Before Becky arrived, JoAnn Pool, hospice supervising nurse, came by with the portable commode she had promised to bring. When Becky came, she and Becky were able to get Ruth to the bed and then onto the commode and back to bed, where they propped her up with several pillows.

During all this commotion, Ruth was groggy and incoherent. She could not complete sentences. Several times during the day she smiled at me and said, "Oh, Robert, I love you," in response to my encouragement.

The nurses showed me how to use a safety strap, a wide belt used to lift people in conditions of weakness, but I knew I could not do it alone. It took two people to move her position on the queen-sized bed. Ruth lay on the bed, half awake, while Becky watched over her and I went on some errands. I planned to have a counsel with the nurses in the evening to devise a sensible care plan. I dreaded being alone with her because I was so inept. I called Louise and then Rilla to tell them what was happening.

I made a nice supper of foods Ruth liked: chicken, broccoli, baked potato, tossed salad. She ate very little and needed my help. I felt so inadequate trying to serve her!

After supper, Gene came with a bed table just when I was trying to get the bedpan under Ruth, as instructed by the nurses; but she was too uncomfortable with that arrangement. When I tried to shift her to a better position, she tried to help but was unable to make the shift without pain.

It was obvious by now that I could not keep Ruth at home, so Gene called Dr. Bauer for permission to admit Ruth to the hospital. He gave it at once. Gene called for an ambulance. The paramedics took Ruth into their competent hands, and soon she was back in a hospital bed where at least she would be safe and properly cared for.

I had no ambition to be heroic. I had tried caring for her as well as I could, but I did not have the nursing skills. Ruth was not able or willing to accept the transition of responsibility for her care from herself to me without protest. She submitted, but reluctantly, to my awkward ministrations.

On Monday she **wanted** to come home, and the doctors thought it might work since she was quite alert at the time. But she had a fairly bad day on Tuesday, a much better day on Wednesday, but Thursday was the terrible! God, be merciful. Let her die rather than suffer.

I cried as I drove along the perimeter road of the campus, but what I felt was not grief for a loss but gratitude for a blessing, for Ruth had been and still is God's great gift of a lifetime with me and for me.

> *Yesterday my tears were like waves*
> *crashing on Nauset Beach,*
> *surging up the beach and receding,*
> *swish, gurgle, whoomph!*

So today my heart was at peace, because Ruth was being cared for properly by those who knew best and she was in a peaceful setting where supplies and equipment were readily available. At home we could only improvise and clumsily try to help Ruth. She had a new family now, the nurses who are with her. It was hard to relinquish being the primary care-giver, but it was both wise and loving to do so.

> *Lord, I entrust Ruth's care to them, who are your servants,*
> *and finally I relinquish her, so she can join that host of ones who*
> *both fear and love God and live on in God's eternal and present*
> *mercy.*

March 3, 1990

Compared with the hectic scene at home two days ago, the hospice room at the hospital was so serene and quiet. It was down the hall away from the inevitable noises at the nurses' station. Ruth looked peaceful, lying in a comfortable, clean bed and dressed in a comfortable gown. She seemed to have let go of her home place and of her lifelong cares for the children and me. She was quiet. Whatever thoughts she had were hers alone and she seemed to have

61

no need to talk. Over the past few weeks I had sensed a withdrawal from her cares and worries. Gradually she had turned over her tasks about the house to me. She had gone somewhere, beyond past times and places. She had not clung to what was past.

Yesterday I arranged with our pastors for a communion in the afternoon. Eric and Violet Gustavson were visiting us. During the lunch hour with Ruth and Louise, I realized that Louise might want to preside and asked her to do so. Pastor Fahning came in the afternoon to have the service, because I had failed to reach him to tell him of the change. He graciously yielded his role to Louise and said, "I am leaving so you can be alone as a family." Ruth's instant response was, "Oh, John, you are family, too." She would say that, not just to be polite, but because for her family was the church, the company of the faithful. Since the terminal time had begun, we realized that we not only had kith and kin as families, but also in our family Valley View friends, friends from college years who had been in touch, some friends from our high school days, former students, faculty colleagues, members of the Judson church [where I served for twelve years] and even some from the church in Newington, Connecticut, where I served as pastor in the late 1940s. In this time when family breakdown is common, Ruth and I have had the rare privilege of living in a place and a time where such an extended range of family could still be enjoyed. The rush and clamor of an urban, mobile, uprooted populace has been a distant rumble, not destroying our lives.

Excerpts from a letter not sent to Louise:

I am awed by the utter richness of your spirit and confounded by your complexity. With tears in his eyes Eric commented about what a beautiful service you conducted at Mother's bedside and what sensitive and tender care and competence you showed. One sentence I recall word for word. "She should not have doubts about her calling."

I woke up today after sleeping for only two hours again. I know I need to get a good night's sleep. I left bed, put on Beethoven's Pathetique Symphony and cried. I cried because Ruth was going to lie in her bed, no longer free, now dependent on others for everything, lie for hours. I also knew I could not be there all night. It would be arrogant and stupid to try. The nurses who are there are her primary care-givers, for her physical needs at least. They are "family" for Ruth at this time, and I am more like a visitor coming and going. She needs to see me, to have me silently nearby, of course; so I shall be there as much as possible but not always and not through the night.

So I prayed and cried, "O God, I give Ruth to you. I do not cling to her now. I want her to know that it is all right for her to leave me and to go to you. She is your child, God, she belongs to you not to me. You gave her to me as a dear companion for many years.

"Now, it seems time for her to go into your everlasting arms, to abide in your love in some new way beyond my understanding. All her life she has belonged first to you, ever since she was a little child learning from her mother about your invisible and real presence. I cannot give her the care she needs now. As Gene Lund said, 'At home we would have to improvise,' and would upset the house in ways she would not like. So I entrust her to those you have called to care for the sick and the dying and thus to you. I miss her, God, I am losing her and am alone in our house. It is okay. I accept the change.

"Ruth wants to slip quietly into oblivion, without stirring up such ado and fuss. She would like best to 'steal away,' rather than lie conscious or drowsy in bed away from home. So I ask a favor, God. Take her. I don't want her to lie for weeks, her dying drawn out. I saw what it was like to be confined when I visited Anna. Maybe you can't do anything about it, God. Maybe you are as helpless as I am to stop this. But I pray, without limits, for her peaceful departure. 'Lord, now lettest thou thy servant depart in peace, according to thy word,' for [Ruth's] eyes have seen 'thy salvation which thou promised to thy people Israel.'"

Crying and writing this has given me peace. I want you, Louise, to hear this story. It is a very personal gift to you, not a general delivery letter for all, to share this gift of peace which first came to me. You long for peace, for an end to the conflict within you. Maybe there is a door now, a door to liberty, according to this word, "He has sent me to proclaim release to the captives" (Luke 4:18). Maybe the time has come to relinquish what seems so precious to you.

Excerpts from a letter to Carl and Rilla, not mailed:

It is very difficult for you to be so far away at this crucial and significant time. You want to and need to be participants. Perhaps I can help by explaining the situation here as clearly as possible.

When Ruth's mother was terminally ill and dying at home from breast cancer, Ruth, her only child, was here in St. Peter. Louise was eight, Dan was three. I was tied down with a heavy teaching load in my fourth year of teaching.

Neither Ruth's mother nor her father asked Ruth to come home. They did not want us there, or at least Hildur did not. Hildur wanted us to remember her as she was before the disease ravished her. They both knew that Ruth had more than enough cares to handle. They thought there was not much we could do and our presence with two small children would be disruptive rather than beneficial—so they thought, as I remember it.

I realize now that people who are dying slowly as Hildur did and as Ruth is doing, gradually withdraw from the earthly scene. Those who can let go are moving to a new time and place where we cannot come yet. I think this has been going on inside of Ruth for the past month. In December she finally let go of her anxieties. Then I noticed a lessened need to call you, as compared with my need to do so. This does not mean she does not love you; she dearly loves you as is evident in what she has said to you and done for you. More recently she turned over the management of the household to me, because she has to rely on my strength and health. Last Monday she wanted to leave the hospital and go home. By Thursday night she knew she could not be properly cared for at home. Gene Lund watched her as the emergency squad slowly and carefully transferred her from bed to stretcher. Gene said there was no protest in Ruth's eyes or on her face; and she was silent. She wanted to go, I suspect, where she could be properly cared for.

I had no trouble letting go of caring for her, after the difficulties I experienced trying to improvise at home. She has been passed from her kin to another family, the nurses, who can appropriately take care of her. Please, trust me when I say they are doing so with competence and tenderness.

While Anna [my second mother] was in the care center at Moose Lake, her primary family was no longer John, Carol, Ruth and me. Her care was provided by the members of the staff who were with her every day. We still were family when we visited her but really more like dear friends who drop by for a visit and then leave.

It may be hard for you to believe that this is happening to us. Ruth and I exchange few words, but our love of a lifetime binds us together, even as we are being separated in other ways.

When I try to help her, she isn't always pleased. It is no longer my place in her life. But I can do for her what no one else can do with the same level of intimacy and do so in our times together. We have our morning prayers after breakfast, in which she participates. Last night I chanted the familiar words of Psalm 23, the Gelineau setting we know so well. I read the prayers she used before going to sleep every night. I sit by her as often as possible. I call her "my dear lady" and recite "I love you." I hear her say "I love you." But I can't take care of her or make medical judgments that are superior to those who are experienced experts. It would be wrong to try. I tried and I only made it harder for her. There comes a time to die to the old and be born to the new, a time to move from one chapter in a story to the next. As Ruth and I made good quality of earlier times, in the midst of hard challenges, so we are doing so now.

Last December you were able to be here and made a very important contribution to the story in ways so fitting to our needs. Rilla, Ruth fully trusted you to take charge of the household. She has told me how much she respects your competence and the high quality of family life you work hard to create. Having the girls here was a joy. Having you around, Carl, was very good for her because of your low-key and relaxed way of relating to her. You are very much like your mother, Carl. You are more a Bostrom Carl than an Esbjornson Carl. Because of her parish duties, Louise could not be here all the time as she so desperately needed to be. I told her, "Your time will come. Now is the time for Carl and Rilla. Their turn first, yours later."

Now it is her turn. Yesterday she was with me and was for me what she can best be—not housekeeper and cook but spiritual and pastoral presence. Her gifts of ministry are as strong as the unique gifts you both possess.

Carl, the very best and most helpful work you can do for your mother and me now is to concentrate as far as possible on your work. You need to focus on what is going on at an important moment in your life. I told Ruth about how confident, excited and in tune you are with the prospect of a position at Carthage College. She was obviously very pleased that you are having an interview.

Carl and Rilla, please trust us to do what is right for Ruth and put your minds on your current tasks. If Ruth lives, she might still be here when your spring break comes. Leave that in God's care. I can't overstress how liberating it is finally to "put all my trust in God, my hope...in God's mercy." It has freed me to accept my limits, my mortality, and my new place in the story. God can liberate you and us as well.

March 6, 1990

Lord of life, love and light, I give you this day. No, no. You give me this day to enhance with the quality of mercy the ordinary things I will do.

What is happening makes me realize that I am a character in a story written by the holy mystery writer, God. Paul said all things work together for good for those who love the Lord, but it is hard to see this most of the time. Nevertheless, there come those cracks in manifest, or paramount, everyday reality. If one is alert, like watchmen waiting for dawn, one espies a gleam of glory so bright and good that one is lured toward the crack. Then the breach closes and the gleam is hidden. Now, I know the light is there and that in other times and places the glory will break through again. Lord, bless Ruth with comfort and good care and give our friends a glimpse of glory!

March 7, 1990

Ruth said, "I don't know when I will go home."

I replied, "I don't know either." Was she thinking of Valley View, or the heavenly home imagined in hymns? I don't know.

Yesterday she stared at the sink cabinet and said, "Is that a coffin?" I said, "No, Ruth, that is the sink cabinet."

Conversations were like that now—brief, incomplete, enigmatic at times. She seemed to be slowly moving away. She showed less and less interest in what was outside of her, beyond her. She lay quietly in the reclining chair where she was placed this morning. There was a sad, rather forlorn expression on her face. She seemed content to have me sit by her, doing nothing. This morning I fussed too much, so she frowned and chided me, "Don't fuss with me, Bob." I suppose I felt I had to do something.

This noon she ate slowly and not much. I helped her once or twice, careful not to push food at her and not to urge her to eat more.

March 8, 1990

It's 2:35 a.m. and I can't sleep. Fearful thoughts come unbidden. Now I feel more at peace. I cried, not in tears but from the depths of prayer:

Lord, I put my trust in you, my hope is in your mercy. You are the author of my story, not I. Who am I to think that I should be immune from the burden of the cross. Yet you, Christ, bore the burden, so I would be saved, not from but for responsibilities.

For some reason, beyond my understanding I feel free, even though I have responsibilities I may not be able to or want to avoid. I feel gladness, Lord, a deep joy, as if at the center of my very being there is an empty space, a garden, green grass, an apple tree in full bloom, blue sky, bright sun, a day in May, light of heart. You are my light.

Last Sunday Bob and Gen Strom called from Tennessee to tell me they were coming to see Ruth and me. They would arrive on Tuesday, March 6, and leave on Wednesday. It was an inspiration to know they wanted to do such a crazy thing—inspired, Bob said, by **our** trips going out of the way between Minnesota and New England to visit them.

I decided to have a gathering Tuesday night of our friends in the vicinity who had been in college with us. We would have a hymn sing, such as Ruth and I had had for guests on occasion. I called Marian and Chet Johnson, Bernhard and Marilyn Erling, Vic and Betty Gustafson, Ponnie and Luvy Sellstrom, Bob and Evy Pearson, Frank and Ruth Gamelin. My brother John and his wife Carol were already planning to come for several days.

Tuesday morning, Betty Gustafson came to help me clean house. Jean Larson sat with Ruth while I worked. Carol brought bars and coffee bread and other foods. Betty brought bread. I bought almonds. We had cold drinks and coffee on hand. I borrowed a video camera from the college so I could show the party to Ruth afterward.

I told Ruth on Tuesday morning that the Stroms would be here, and she was very pleased. Then she said, quietly, "We can now celebrate our fortieth wedding anniversary." [Our **45th** would be on May 6. Her sense of

68

time was distorted.] It never occurred to me to make the gathering an anniversary party, but it was fitting. We were married on May 6, Bob and Gen were married on January 6, a year before we were. My birthday is on April 6, and the party was on **March 6**! Furthermore, Gen was Ruth's matron of honor and my brother John was my best man at our wedding, and both would be here.

We gathered at 8 p.m. The house looked so clean and peaceful, thanks to Betty's work. John operated the camera. When all were present and seated, I told about our courtship—which provoked much kidding and laughter. Then I played the cassette of Ruth's 1980 St. Michael's Day homily, one of her best, so her friends could enjoy that perceptive, articulate, imaginative mind of Ruth's, which we have all enjoyed for years. Then Vic led the singing of hymns, which he had selected from the black, red and green Lutheran hymnals. Bernie pointed out that all the hymns which Vic chose from the green hymnal were also in the black Augustana hymnal, which obviously was Vic's favorite hymnal.

We had refreshments, during which there was a lot of good conversation and laughter. The gathering had just the right blend of humor, friendship and seriousness.

When Gen and Bob and I had a "coffee and rolls" farewell at the Prairie House Restaurant the next morning, I asked them what we had been doing by having this party. The party was not a wake, for sure, at least not a conventional one. Nor was it only a wedding anniversary, nor just a gathering to honor Ruth, nor was it one dominated by denial of coming death.

It was a unique event. I can't imagine it being repeatable. It was as if the walls of ordinary, everyday reality had been breached for a while, and we were existing at another dimension, in which ordinary time, place, people and party formats were suspended. Maybe it was a foretaste of the heavenly feast, of a life beyond tears and pain and death. Joy, not sorrow; humor, not morbid grief; appreciation, not fear of loss—those were the moods. I was awestruck.

Later I told one of my friends that it seemed I was not the author of this celebration story, only a leading character in it, as was Ruth. There were such favorable coincidences that made the gathering possible, factors I had not foreseen. Would those **not** present ever be able to grasp the meaning I see?

Some might, somewhat perhaps. Others would not; they would remain bemused or skeptical by my interpretation.

Bob, Gen and I came to Ruth's room for their farewell. I said a prayer, choking down grief. Bob's eyes filled with tears. Gen's eyes were glistening, too, although she said she did not usually cry even if she feels deeply inside. I wept with Bob after we left the room. I told Ruth they would be back in May.

I do not know what Ruth was thinking, but she was moved and thankful the Stroms had come. I am not sure she fully realizes she will not go home to Valley View. She is not talking out her thoughts. She has gone into an inner, private place. I offer openings for conversations about what is coming, but she either does not choose to talk or is incapable of completing thoughts due to damage caused by medication or radiation or the cancer itself.

I long to talk with her about what is going on, but I will not rudely batter down the fences. I will not. I can only pray that she will not reject me, but rather is slowly leaving me behind as she goes into experiences I cannot share with her.

As I cannot go with her wherever she is going, so she cannot go with me into my life here in our home and into whatever happens in my life from now on. We who have been so close on our long journey together are now beginning to part company. She goes on and I stay. That is what parting is. We are prepared for the final parting by the "little deaths" of separation that have occurred throughout our lives.

I am being prepared for Ruth's absence by being alone in bed at night, by doing the household tasks Ruth has taken care of, and by making decisions without her counsel. I realize that I soon will begin "a life without Ruth," except that she will live in my memory, and her influence will continue to shape my life. But I will have to shape the memories and influence without conversations with her.

Each morning I bring to the hospital grapefruit to share with Ruth, more or less as a ritual reminding us of breakfasts we had every morning at home.

At breakfast the morning of March 9 she said, "I should be going home, so you won't have to bring grapefruit much longer." A little later she

70

said, "I wonder how soon I'll be able to go home." This time I knew she meant Valley View.

I said, "Your legs are too weak, Ruth. You need help to move."

"Well, I don't want to go home and then have to come back here."

Later in the morning she said, as she stared at the sink in the room, "Who is that old man sitting there?"

"Do you mean this?" I asked, pointing to the faucet. "It looks like a man sitting in a slump, like I do sometimes."

"He has long hair," she said. I could not see how she could see that, so I wondered if she was experiencing a hallucination or just noticing a likeness of shape. These are small glimpses of what she was thinking.

Tonight I am very sad about losing Ruth. I cried this afternoon when I was making the bed and observed Ruth's box by the side of her bed. Her box contained odds and ends such as a worn paperback prayer book, some candy in case she needed to counteract an insulin reaction, bobby pins, and the like. If I put the box away it was a sign that she would never use it, never be back.

March 9, 1990

I awoke at 3 a.m. with the fearful thought that a serious medical mistake, prescribing morphine as pain medication, had put Ruth where she is. If she had been heeded, when she resisted taking it, would she be better? I was tempted to fall into a guilt pit until I realized she had started to be weak and a little confused days before this was done. Temptations come when suffering loss: anger, accusing God, others or myself; guilt, the illusion that one is at fault when one is not and refusing to accept forgiveness; despair, self pity, refusing to think about appropriate action.

Thoughts on fate, coincidence and providence.

[1] Fate is what happens to us that is beyond our intentions or desires. Ruth's illness is an example of fate.

[2] Coincidence is the coming together of events and action that was not planned, but which seems to fit into a story or plot— the party with college friends, Ruth's comment about celebrating our anniversary, our wedding attendants, Gen Strom and John,

being here for the party, getting access to a video camera—all worked in coincidence but without prior plan.

[3] Providence is the belief that all works together for good, that even this fate we cannot escape is for good. In other words, we can interpret the coincidences as providential, as having a larger good than we imagined beforehand.

March 11, 1990

The sound of rain, welcome to a dry land, awakens a memory of a day on our honeymoon in New Hampshire. Because of the rain, Ruth and I stayed in bed and I still remember the sound of rain on the roof of the little red cabin and the feel and aroma of the wood fire in the small heater stove.

O Lord of life, love and light, in you I live and move and have my being. I am your creation, yet it is I who act in a complex of physiological and environmental interactions.

I rejoice in you, even now when I must cope with the loss of Ruth, my dear companion. She has not only enriched my life, but trained me to do what needs to be done!

I do not brood, Lord, in self-pity but rather attempt to carry on, already, a life in which Ruth cannot participate and cannot help to create. Help! Have mercy! Guide me today, so that I can create the best quality of life that is possible for her in her present condition.

March 11 has been a critical day. Ruth was articulate and relatively clearheaded in the morning. Dr. Thompson walked in briskly and said, "Your blood sugar was great today—147." He felt her pulse but did not ask her how she was feeling. When he started to leave, Ruth said, "Wait, I want to ask you when I can go home."

"You can go home when you are stronger," he replied. "You are weak. You need help," he continued. Then he asked me what the hospital staff had said about how long Ruth could stay in the hospice room. "I thought they said

72

she could stay here indefinitely," I replied. "Good," he said, and then left swiftly. Several days ago, when I had told him about Ruth wanting to go home, he told me he would speak to her about it.. Yesterday the opening came, and his message seemed to be that she would get strong enough to go home.

The conversation, which ended so abruptly, was confusing, because it seemed to support her hope that the care she was getting was aimed at that end. Still, I was glad I was the one to talk to her about her prospects. I knew more than he about Ruth's attitudes, how they had developed, and the experiences she had had since the beginning of December.

I reminded Ruth that I could not take care of her under the circumstances at home.

"Oh, I wouldn't want that," she said, "but I have assumed that I would get well enough to go home and that we could manage."

"Ruth, when we were in Rochester we talked about what was ahead. The doctors told you that you would not get better, that you would eventually die of this cancer. We agreed that we would make the time you had left as high quality as we could, just as we have done through the years of our marriage, even in the difficult times."

She nodded, so I knew she had grasped my point. I continued, "That is what I want now, the best quality we can make out of our situation. That is why I am glad you are here, in this pleasant room and getting high quality nursing care. You couldn't get it at home."

Then I tried to address her belief that she might improve enough so she would be able to go home. "I don't want us to delude ourselves; it is neither honest nor Christian. I want us to be realistic and do what is loving and best."

We did not talk about dying. Maybe I, too, lost the right moment. It is a very difficult situation. I could not come right out and say she was dying, not now. When she was rational last December, Ruth could deal with dying on a more abstract level, but now it is not a future prospect but a present reality, a far more difficult matter.

She was sober and quiet the rest of the day. That evening when she heard me say it was seven o'clock, she sighed. I said, "I know it is hard."

She said, so sadly, "Hard to face reality." She must have realized she was going to die and that she was not going to have another reprieve, such as she had had after leaving Methodist.

I was upset about Dr. Thompson's question about how long she could stay in the hospice room, because I thought there was no problem. When I went to ask the nurses, they referred me to the administration desk. Now I realized that whether she stays or not was going to be an **administrative** decision based on costs of coverage, not a medical or family decision. I asked what the options would be when the twenty days were up. We had the choice of moving Ruth to a nursing home or to our home, where nurses would come to help care for her.

Now I was up in the air! However, I could not be intolerable or angry, because I realized all of us, doctors, nurses, administrators, family, are relatively helpless and we bumble our way through difficult situations. We are all fallible, and medical science and practice is fallible and limited, too, when facing the incalculables of life and death. When we realize we are limited, finite and fallible, we become insecure; and when we are insecure we become defensive, uptight. Instead of being rational, we rationalize, resorting to illusions rather than dealing with reality.

When Pastor John Fahning called on Ruth while I was there, I led him, or he me, into a typical professional, academic discussion of the texts for next Sunday's sermon. We pretty much ignored Ruth until I asked her, "We've been chattering. What do you want to say?" She made a noncommittal comment. John shook her hand, said good-bye and left. I saw myself and how I have been uncertain in similar situations and have resorted to diversionary tactics to avoid dealing directly with human needs that are hard to meet. No, not hard. What is needed is compassionate, candid action that builds trust and does not delude!

This morning when I awoke, I thought, "Maybe we should 'go for it,' assume that an impossible possibility is worth every effort, based on the belief that 'with God all things are possible,'"and that not one of us can claim to know the limits of God's mercy. This is not unrealistic, because we enter the battle

74

of faith fully realizing we may lose, but at least we have given it our best shot! That realization would give **quality** *to loss. However, the main agenda for Ruth is for her to be treated with love and cared for competently, what she is facing.*

O God, your mercy is boundless and very available. I do not know its limits. I do know, or think I know, that Ruth wants more time and wants to get better. I pray without reserve for what is best for her, for quality condition and time when we can be all together next week as a family and even time to celebrate her 70th birthday on May 10.

March 13, 1990

"My soul pines away with grief,
by your word raise me up" (Psalm 119:28).
"My soul lies in dust,
by your word raise me up" (Verse 35).
"I bind myself to do your will.
Lord, do not disappoint me" (Verse 31).
Lord of life, love and light,
My petitions turn to thanksgiving and praise.
Your word has lifted me up from the couch where I wept.
Your word has lifted me up from the dusty bottom
of the hole in the ground.
I bind myself to do your will.
You do not disappoint me.

About 10:30 last night one of the nurses called me. "Ruth does not want a drink, or to be rolled, or to eat. I asked her if she wanted to talk to you, and she nodded." When I talked to her on the phone she asked me to come and said she was falling apart. When I came she tried to tell me that she was trying to deal with who she is and what was happening to her. I held her hand. I spoke softly about what she and I were experiencing, and about how hard it was when she lay alone and scared. We remembered how it was easier to talk about it last December in Rochester than now in March in this room in

St. Peter at midnight. I said Christ came to be with us in our loneliness and hurt and he also "humbled himself and was obedient onto death." I said Christ was here in the members who make up his ever-living Body on earth. Christ comes in the person of the compassionate and caring nurse, and comes to dwell in us as well so that **our** lives are his eternal presence. I said, "I am here and only four minutes away if you need me."

I put on some music—Don Shirley piano and then the Kings College Choir chanting the Psalms. I sat holding her hand as we listened, and she grasped mine tightly.

Later she asked, "When will they bring breakfast?"

"It is still before midnight, Ruth." She sighed, apparently realizing that time moves slowly for her, too slowly. I surmised that she might need to eat; she looked like she might. I called the nurse and she said she would bring toast and milk. "That is just what she likes before going to bed for the night," I said.

I kissed her good-bye, told her I was near and to call me if she needed me.

First Lutheran people may think I am a little crazy to try to preach on the theme given me, "To live is Christ, to die is gain," when Ruth and I are facing imminent death, loss and absence. Maybe I am. I pray that I may be able to do so.

*Ruth and I are walking a way we have never walked before. Though we have experienced the loss that the deaths of our parents and other elders brought, this is different, especially for Ruth. It is **her** life that she is losing. It is Ruth as I have known her for over fifty years that I am losing.*

What is distant can be discussed in theory. What is near must be felt as reality; and, as Ruth said, that is hard.

There is a solitary depth in another person that one cannot enter, especially when the other is walking down into the valley of the shadow of death. I can speak, not from where Ruth is but from where I stand, and I dare to speak because the Word has lifted me out of silence and gloom. The Word is in Paul's letter.

76

Paul was also facing imminent death when he wrote that "to live is Christ, to die is gain."

I preached the following sermon during the March 14 Lenten service at First Lutheran. In case I was unable to preach, I had asked Dennis Johnson to be ready to read it for me.

Since I am a member of the "colony of heaven," one who is within the embrace of God's presence and power, I not only live differently and have a different language, but I will also die differently.

The Lord does not prevent my death, not even an untimely death [one that messes up my plans], and not even a sudden death or a lengthy dying. The medical experts can give me comfort, can keep pain minimal, can do what is helpful for bodily care, and also for psychological consolation, but ultimately they cannot rescue me either. And their help is as available to those whose "god is the belly" as it is for me.

What is different, then about dying "in Christ"? Paul says "to die is far better," because he believed that he would then be "with Christ" in some other state called heaven. What is different? Since we are already citizens of the colony of heaven, "our outlook goes beyond this world to a hopeful expectation of the Savior who will come from heaven, to a hope of having our wretched bodies remade to resemble his glorious body." That is what made dying, not only bearable but desirable for Paul.

Nowadays people work hard to make their bodies less wretched and more hale and hearty. There is an almost perverse, addictive devotion to tanning, jogging, low cholesterol diet, the latest aerobic exercise plan, and Eastern meditation rituals.

What is the more glorious body to those so addicted? Jane Fonda's lithe figure? Joe Montana's tough, mobile body? The body of an eighty year-old man who can still finish a 10K race course?

77

We really don't know what the glorious body Paul had in mind might be. We have only hope, and that makes all the difference in how we die, even if we suffer pain, even if dying separates us from friends and family not yet ready to let us go, even if we are not yet ready to acknowledge our mortality, even if fear and anger surge up, even if dying is at the end a lonely exit where no one can follow, even if there is no vision of radiant persons to greet us at the far end of a tunnel, even if in our candid and realistic expectations we know that dying for each of us may not be gentle or sweet or serene.

We can bear to expect death, because our outlook is a larger scene and story than our earthbound, twentieth century-bound lives.

I think of heaven not as a place beyond the edge of the known universe. Jewish Christians, such as Matthew's author, used heaven as a substitute for God in the term, the kingdom of God. Heaven is thus being in the presence of God **with** Christ.

We, who believe in Christ, abide in him, as branches in a vine, as organs of a body. By grace Christ dwells in us, as our true self that yearns to love, to do what is appropriate to loving, to live joyfully and patiently in all circumstances.

To be in Christ is to be in a company, a colony, a community we call "the body of Christ." It is to be in the physical presence of people who gather to constitute the colony, to hear the Word, to help one another live by the Word.

To live is more than to eat the right food, get the right exercise, meditate by the most effective disciplines, associate with health addicts, get proper rest, avoid carcinogens. To live in Christ is to be live from beyond this perspective, to live in a "colony of heaven."

Because we are not dominated by Lord Death we cannot only face our little deaths but our final dying. We can more gladly live in an alien society, doing whatever is possible to foster good health care, clean environment of air, soil and water in the capitols in Washington, St. Paul and in local Front Street politics. We stay in the world to be witnesses of a different perspective.

Paul wrote while in prison, where for all he knew his next abode would be the chamber or the courtyard where the executioner would wait with broadax ready to chop off his head.

Executions are horrifying, and quick. But many of us will die slowly, lying awake for long nights, longing for dawn, wishing for surcease from weakness and pain.

This kind of dying is not martyrdom in the traditional sense where the enemy is a tyrannical government and its torturers. The enemy in these long deaths is more common—expensive care that keeps us alive longer and delays death only for a time.

As for me, I want to live and be strong and mobile and sane as long as possible. But it is not because I think living for 80 or 90 or 100 years is all there is.

Rather, it is because my life has a meaningful mission—to live in a Christ-like way that builds up others. I don't think dying is ever better than living, but dying is one of the chapters in our life story. And because we live in Christ and Christ dwells in us, even that chapter is a time to live with quality, the quality of mercy. If one we love passes beyond all competence and contribution to us, we grieve such a passing, but the quality of helpful love is still our concern, even loving those who cannot love either themselves or others.

It is a challenge to live from the perspective of a citizen of the colony of heaven, of those who abide in Christ, who live in the embracing presence of God, who tends us as tenderly as a mother, with the compassion of a competent nurse.

March 16, 1990

I began to wonder if I could stand it. Ruth was so sad last night. Lying quietly, too tired even to pray the Lord's Prayer with me, she looked so sad. I asked her if she felt sad. She nodded. Had she cried? A little, she replied.

In late afternoon she spoke to me. "Bob, I want you to consider..." She could not put into words what she wanted me to consider. Then she said, "I want to go home." All I could say was, "Yes, I will see what can be done, but my first concern is to make sure you are getting the best care possible and are not hurting." She nodded in reply. I could say no more, and I am hurting for her. I don't want her to suffer this kind of pain, the pain of separation from her home, her familiar place. I am going to begin serious discussion even though the process of dismissal and readmission is very complicated and we might lose Medicare and ELCA financial support if she goes home (I was mistaken about that.)

I am yielding when I probably should stand firm. I didn't have the heart last night to even say that it is best for her to be in the hospice room, because I am not sure it is. Ruth is more than a body to be kept free from pain. She is one who has more subtle pains of the heart, and pangs of hunger. I can only admit that I am helpless to erase the dilemma and ask God for guidance. When the family is together next week, I hope she can be brought home, at least for visits during the day. That may be enough to satisfy her need.

O God, I hurt for her! Please do not delay her going home, God. It is better for her to depart when she hurts so. Receive her. She is already in your presence, and I hope I can help her see that. I know, though, that she loves her human family and earth place, so it hard for her to separate your presence and place from our particular presence and place. We love what we love so deeply that we do not want to lose what we love, and we wish for reunion "on the other side."

This is my prayer for Ruth, too.

Remember your word to your servant Ruth
by which you gave her hope.
This is my [and her] comfort in sorrow

that your promise gives me [and her] life
(Psalm 119:49-56).

Oh, the irony! What promise? What life? Ruth has been an upright person, one who from childhood has tried to obey your decrees and trust your promises and worship you.

What life? Surely, now, not her physical life, which is dying, and not the life of her mind, which she is losing, and not her social relationships, which are being destroyed by her isolation and loneliness. As for her soul, the secret is in your keeping and her heart. I cannot speak for her about that.

What life? Eternal life? A life beyond her present existence "on the other side"? That is our hope, isn't it? Though we walk in darkness, you await us beyond the culvert, the dark tunnel of dying. Isn't that what people who have near-death experiences report?

Consolation is hard. What can I say and do today to be consoling? The medics can give her body comfort, and the nurses can give competent and kind attention. Her friends can visit and write to maintain some degree of affection and regard for her.

But I, her closest friend, know she needs something more. She longs for home, Lord. We have taken her autonomy away, in order to treat her anatomy. No, not we, but that mindless, merciless disease has robbed her of freedom as well as strength.

I know how highly Ruth holds the value of self-rule; she wants to be independent and knows she is helpless, under the control of others who claim to know what is good for her. And so she appeals to me, "Bob, I want you to consider..." She appeals to me, whom she has trusted. Ruth, dear Ruth, do I now know what is good for you? I am uncertain. I abhor the effect on you of your loss. Maybe you think you are betrayed after all these years. Maybe you suffer a loss of trust because I seem unwilling to accede to your longing to go home. I don't know. Is your last thought going to be, "I was betrayed by a friend I trusted?" Will you die like Jesus in that you know or think a close friend betrayed you and your other close friends forsook you and fled?

What loneliness! What loneliness!

Ruth, dear Ruth, it is not betrayal; we cannot go where you are going, not yet. That last journey is a solitary affair. I can only trust in the words of the psalmist, that God does go with you, with his hook and staff, to comfort you as you go into the valley of the shadow of death.

Can I be God's servant, assigned to go with you, never deserting you, being there for you, as were John and the women present as Jesus was dying on the cross? Yes, I can. Painful and hard as it is to watch you suffer and to be helpless to satisfy your need, I can. God give me the strength!

I told Ruth what we were planning, but she was not too responsive. When I said, "Do you still want to go home?" she was noncommittal. No wonder! I had asked her right after a new catheter was inserted to relieve discomfort from a blocked or slipped tube. Now she is comfortable and eating lunch.

The questions are practical ones:

1] Take Ruth home or leave her in the hospice room. The hospice room is convenient for care-givers, but an exile place where Ruth is held captive. Even the bars on the bed suggest a prison.

2] Bring her home for visits, or not. Would it really make her day better, or add to her burden, when she returned?

3] Should I arrange to be with her [in the hospital] more than I am?

If I brought Ruth home, I would have to accept less efficient care for her in return for more familial care in familiar surroundings. If her care becomes so difficult that she is subjected to a worse fate, then I would have a burden of guilt for bringing that consequence on her. It is not my fault! The disease was the tyrant!

This morning the birds were a choir singing a canticle to spring. I thought of Ruth's love for our house and its large view of the valley and the yard and tree strip behind the house. No wonder she longs to return! I hope she can. I am committed to doing this. I told Rilla that when my heart is serene I gain strength to deal with the situation. I feel it is right to bring Ruth home and that sense of rightness opens me up to the strength I must have.

March 17, 1990

I hoped the decision to bring Ruth home would not be too late. I had a feeling I was chasing the story of Ruth, not making it happen. Cancer is a trickster defying my reason and controls, a deceptive enemy who makes surprise attacks. Has my attention been diverted or distracted, so I was not seeing soon enough what was happening to Ruth?

When she came home I would become the "charge nurse," but not doing what the trained nurse did unless she assigned tasks to me. But I would be the one who organized Ruth's care and delegated tasks to others. Could I manage? I have never traveled this route. Should I anticipate or create a scenario to prepare for what was coming?

At 11:50 p.m. I awoke, restless dreams having disturbed me. I was feeling lonely, more so tonight than hitherto. Ruth had been calm, cogent and comfortable this afternoon. She rested, slept during the late morning after considerable distress earlier—BMs were difficult for her.

When I talked with Ruth later she said something about being able to put on a record for music if she woke up at home during the night.

I asked, "Are you still thinking about going home?"

"Of course! I've been wanting to for a week," she responded with some asperity.

I will have to pay attention to how she feels about going home by Monday. My primary concern is to make it comfortable and enjoyable for her. It might be that a visit on Tuesday when the family is here, or Wednesday, will be a trial to see how she responds. Above all, I want to avoid acrimony. We'll all be on edge, perhaps, so my serenity and strength needs to be in good shape.

The house is empty yet alive with memories of many experiences. It is in such a world of the familiar that Ruth wants to be, and I don't blame her!

She is tired of being in the hospital. Her most persistent desire is to go home. She spoke about being afraid of being left alone upstairs. She probably remembered those occasions when I went out at night, once to a game, once for a walk, when she awoke, disoriented, from a nap, called for me and got no answer, searched for me and couldn't find me. Those were distressing times even though I had told her I was going. I said, "Ruth, don't worry about being left alone if you are upstairs. Someone will always be with you."

Louise came home to help me get the house ready for Ruth's return. Carl and his family are coming from Lansing, Michigan, to spend a between-quarter break with us.

Dying At Home

March 20, 1990

Ruth's homecoming went well. Louise cleaned the downstairs room. I met for a care conference and got instructions at 10 a.m. A college crew moved the beds. Betty prepared beef stew for supper. The house was almost ready. Carl, Rilla, Rachel and Rebekka were coming.

Louise and I stripped the hospice room of flowers, cards, pictures and other personal items. The room seemed stark, although still pleasant because of carpet on the floor and pretty wallpaper. Doing this opened my eyes to see how important it was to bring flowers and other decorative items which create a less stark setting in the hospital.

I have a new awareness of the difference between women and men in relation to perception of the needs of patients and participation in visits. When men accompany their wives, the women do most of the talking; they also are the ones who bring the flowers and other things. I suspect this is due to their customary roles in the home. Men tend to delegate such care to women. I, being the active one now, am more observant and ready to provide whatever care or items Ruth needs or wants. I see no reason why men should not visit alone, or do as easily what women more readily do. Once we men get over being diffident or indifferent, we can also give tender loving care.

March 22, 1990

*How does the amazing grace come? By word, yes, and by
actions undeserved and surprising. The children's unself-
conscious play and prattle, Rilla's practical wisdom in sickroom
and kitchen, Carl's quiet, gentle presence, Louise's affection and
action, friends' concern, medical practitioners' competence, and
a robin's song summoning the dawn.*

March 21 was Ruth's first full day at home, a warm, and bright day.
After breakfast, she lay all morning on the couch, listening and watching.
After lunch she napped in bed, got up for supper and then back to bed.

I was as clumsy as a puppy! Trying to lower the rails of the bed and
move the commode, I knocked over the water pitcher, and later the vase with
daffodils, as I tried to hurry Ruth to the commode. Rilla gave me lessons in
nursing care. This was uncanny—I awoke a minute before midnight, just
before the timer went off, to give Ruth her pain medication, and she awoke me
just before her 4 a.m. medication time. I took her successfully to the commode
and back without mishaps.

One learns to rejoice in having good and timely bowel movements
when one's body is in trouble! My experience from surgery in 1961 gave me
understanding now.

Another strange experience. After the previous night's turmoil, I
thought I would be exhausted and need much sleep the next day. Not so. A
brief nap in the afternoon was all I needed, and I had solid sleep between
medication times during the night.

*I am learning new lessons in respect for practical wisdom,
quite independent of academic learning. The skills needed for
nursing the sick, and feeding a family and managing a household
are varied and not quickly learned.*

*The same is true for the wisdom of a practical spirituality. The
ways of nurturing and consoling the heart are quite different from
the academic arts of textual criticism, philosophical reasoning
and historical research.*

How different? The focus of attention is on what is the direct, fitting word or act in the world of the now, not of the past or future.

March 25, 1990

Why bother with God if, in the end of it, all that I am and can accomplish is as litter blown apart by a breeze? Psalm 39 seems to deprive me of any validity, any worth. I am dust, a puff of wind.

If God is merciful and mighty, it seems that he could and should make this life worth living. It should not be necessary to believe in God only on the basis of hope for a life beyond the grave.

Where do I stand on this grave issue?

[1] I would rather have lived, even if there is suffering, than not to have existed at all. I'd rather there be a creation, even if it means eons of great struggle rather than there be nothing at all.

[2] Quality varies as we age, so the task is to make each chapter in the story the best we can. Accomplishment in work and play, or in raising a family, is not all there is. This period when we are facing terminal illness presents another challenge, to be loving, and caring and thankful for past goodness and to be patient and courageous. And all the while recognizing we live on the grace of God.

Brave words. Would I say them if I were lying where Ruth is? I am not sure, but I declare now that I hope I can be as courageous and patient as she is!

If I had no hope of a life after death, would I say these words? Yes, I think so. I do not demand immortality as a bargaining point with God.

Yesterday, Carl and family left for Lansing about noon. It was a poignant moment of parting. I was choking with tears. Ruth said, "Don't cry, Bob." Rilla said, "It's all right to cry." Carl stood silently, yet his feelings

86

were strong. We hugged. The girls hugged and kissed GaGa. They waved as the Chevette drove off.

March 26, 1990

We are alone, in a house now quiet after all the activity of the last five days. The wooden blocks, gathered by the girls from the arboretum paths, were piled neatly in a box, saved for the next visit. They had provided the girls with much entertainment.

Ruth and I had leftover meat loaf, baked potatoes, and tossed salad. After eating she wanted to go to bed, not to the couch. I had a hard time lifting her high enough to get into bed, so the transfer was painful for her. Her legs were almost useless.

Rilla worked hard while she was here and helped much. She cleaned and organized the cupboards and foodstuffs. She rearranged the bureau so sheets could be stored there. She helped with nursing care because she had had experience as a nurse's aide.

Betty Gustafson brought soup last night and sat with Ruth while I took Meadow, Louise's dog, for a walk. Judy Douglas brought in several pieces of cake.

Ruth had a restless and painful night, so I was up several times. She finally slept.

March 27, 1990

I had a dream about a Benedictine monk who was lecturing on geometry at a conference at St. John's. I can't remember why people were so interested and why I was interested too. When I awoke I recalled my interest in the quality of space. What is "good" space in relation to the good life? An ethical concern.

Why is our living room a space Ruth enjoys more than the hospital hospice room? It is "familiar," it is ours, it is roomier, and it has an open side with a view of the valley.

Space has a sacred aspect, too. What is "sacred space"? A place set apart, where theophanies have occurred, a space devoted to the meditative life, empty of other values. There must

87

be, I think, a space that is unoccupied and unused except for prayer. When I do my morning meditations and exercise, I use the same area of the living room floor. The other day I did them in another space, and it was not the same. Why? Habit? Or is it associations and memories that make meditation space qualitatively different?

March 28, 1990

"Your will is my heritage forever, the joy of my heart" (Psalm 119:111).

I have never pondered over such a connection between the will of God and the heritage and joy of my heart. What does the connection mean? Why do I respond to it so affirmatively?

Joy, yes. Knowing and doing the will of the creating, liberating God brings a surge of joy. Doing it well—creating and loving—brings a satisfaction that is like that of hitting an ace serve in tennis or delivering a sermon well or saying just the right word to someone. There is a harmony of thought, feeling and acting that is pleasing. In other words, doing the will of God has an aesthetic component.

O Lord, whose will is at once both my duty and my delight, I "set myself to obey thy statutes in fullness forever" (Psalm 119:112).

What is your will today? I must get help to care for Ruth, especially to transfer her to and from bed. It is neither right nor beautiful for me to do it alone.

I read the psalm to Ruth. She did not respond. I do miss our conversations!

Conversation on Martin Marty's A Cry of Absence:
Marty: "Winter is more than dormancy; it is dying."
Esbj: So "wintry spirituality" is an experience like death.

88

Marty: "The wintry image forces an urgent theme on the spiritual seeker. The search for a piety does not permit evasion of the central issue of life—its 'being toward death.' Every yes hereafter has to be made in the face of 'ceasing to be.'"

*Esbj: The first wonder is that there is everything rather than nothing. **I am** is a primal thought preceding all descriptive conclusions, such as I am male, I am awake, I am hurting.*

*The second wonder is as mysterious and primal. **I am not.** I will someday cease to be. I can scarcely imagine **not** being, not being here when Rachel goes to college, for example.*

In a minor way I experience my nonbeing when I realize I am no longer an active professional colleague. For many, I have already ceased to be as such. Even in their memories I am at best a fleeting, peripheral thought. And for more recently hired faculty members, I am as one who never existed as a colleague.

*Why is this thought bearable? Is it not because I understand that my **primary** being is "hid with Christ in God?"*

Marty: "Whoever says 'God' has chosen to imply goodness and power. If there is goodness and power, why is there death or the pain and suffering that is associated with it? Did God cause death? If so, where is the goodness and love?"

*Esbj: The perennial issue, Marty. I cannot avoid it. How can I say God is good **and** mighty when I observe Ruth's suffering?*

Marty: "Why bother with a God too weak to create and sustain what matters most to every person?"

*Esbj: Which is **to be**. Ruth **wants** to continue to be, not to cease being—unless being is too burdensome at the end; then she wants to cease being. And is it that hope that "there is a land that is fairer than day" which sustains us as we face death? Just as we also say, after the winter comes spring, the fair month of May?*

Pain. I am between a rock and a hard place about giving pain medication to Ruth on a four-hour schedule. The conventional wisdom of medical practice is to give the medication regularly at low dosages to keep

89

pain under control. Do not wait until pain comes and gets the upper hand, because then more medication will be necessary to get on top of the pain again.

This morning at 4:30 Ruth adamantly refused the pain medication. I gave her doses at 8:30 p.m. and 2:30 a.m. [I had slept through the midnight time]. She said she had a headache but the pain was not so bad that she wanted relief. Ruth had always resisted using medication, or used it only reluctantly [only one aspirin at a time, for example]. When she refused this morning, she said, "I want to talk to the doctor." She appealed to a higher court, so I had to abide by her decision. It was 6 a.m. She slept. If the pain got out of control, I would feel bad because I gave in to her. If I forced her to take it, I would violate her "autonomy" and that would be hard for me. I tried to practice "weak paternalism" by describing the way pain medication works and the consequences that may occur if one does not follow conventional wisdom.

There was an alternative, as described in the story of Margaret, the subject of a book Hilda sent to me. Margaret, dying of painful cancer, chose to rely on other methods of pain control and to accept pain rather than become dull mentally. Should Ruth do the same?

The problem I faced was complicated by the fact that her brain itself had been affected by the radiation treatments and the cancer. This made it hard to attribute to morphine her loss of mental clarity.

March 29, 1990

It was a hard day but not until evening. In the morning Ruth chose to remain in bed. She ate most of her breakfast—half a grapefruit, most of the oatmeal and a half piece of toast. She accepted the pain medication at 8 a.m. along with the other medicines. Her blood sugar was at a desirable level, just under 200. We had our main meal at noon. Dr. Thompson called and apparently persuaded her to accept pain medication. Nancy, the nurse's aide, came after lunch. I went on errands. Nancy brought Ruth into the living room while I was gone and when I returned she and I had a conversation about her story. I read Grandpa B.'s "sermon on prayer" from **Cold Sassy Tree**, and in the afternoon his instructions for his own funeral. Did those readings cause Ruth to think, arouse her awareness of what was happening, or cause her depression? I don't know. The readings were both entertaining and insightful. Maybe doing them was a gentle, indirect invitation to her to think about her condition.

Later Clarice Floreen and Barbara Wilkinson tried to help me move Ruth from couch to bed. Our efforts were not satisfactory. For Ruth the process was too painful, so she was in agony. Either I was not doing the transfer properly or she had become too weak and fragile for transfer. She ate lightly. Being constipated added to her discomfort.

During the night Ruth had a bout with generalized pain about which she was helpless. "Oh Bob!" she cried. I could not take the cause of the pain from her. I cannot stop her suffering and death. I can only give her a drink of water, hold her hand, administer morphine an hour ahead of time. I could give her temporary relief.

About 3 a.m. she cried out, "O God. I don't know what to do! Bob!" She accepted the morphine I gave her at that time. This calmed her.

It was time for another assessment session to go over my abilities in relation to anticipated changes in Ruth's condition. I want to keep her at home if she can be kept comfortable, and I don't have to transfer her. It might be possible for a skilled nurse to do the transfer in the afternoon. If she wants to stay home it means she stays in bed, if **she** is willing to be confined in bed. I will need to take better care of myself, sleeping in the day if I have to be awake at night.

Ruth has submitted reluctantly to the doctor's prescribed treatment, especially to the use of pain-controlling medicine. In addition to morphine and insulin she has medication for glaucoma, high blood pressure, constipation and decadron for cancer. For a couple of days she has been increasingly resistant to the schedule of treatment I have administered, especially the use of morphine every four hours. A couple of nights ago I slept through the midnight time and so did not give her morphine until 2:30 a.m. Then I set the timer for 4:30 a.m. to get back on schedule. When I came with the medicine she closed her lips and refused to take it. I did not give it to her. She said, "I want to talk to the doctor." I promised to call him. Before eight, the next time for medication, I called Gene Lund, who reinforced the wisdom of regular administration of morphine. I told Ruth what Gene said and asked her if she would take her medicine. She reluctantly agreed. I saw Dr. Thompson at 9:30

and he ordered more frequent doses, every three hours. At noon he talked to Ruth, and she apparently was persuaded and she took the medicine each time I gave it to her.

Sometime yesterday, when I explained I was just doing what the doctor advised, she said, "Don't I count at all?"

Ah yes! She counts very much, and therein is my dilemma. She wants to have a say. She wants to count. She suspects me of siding with Dr. Thompson and against her.

It was not just that remark but her consistent attitude toward me, almost of suspicion and resentment, as if I were pushing against her own will and judgment, that makes me aware of my dilemma.

I am not clinging to having Ruth at home if doing so is no longer feasible. No pseudoheroics, Robert! Appropriate care is what you want to give.

I will have a life after Ruth dies. It would be wrong to wear myself out so that my immune system is weakened and I would get sick myself. Perhaps new activities will develop, involvement in Habitat for Humanity, for example, or using my experience to help others through terminal illness as part of the hospice team.

Conventional wisdom tells me, keep her comfortable. Yes, I agree, but does it at the same time deprive her of awareness? I am not sure. Ruth was depressed yesterday and silent about what was going through her mind. Is she confused, not really understanding what is happening to her body? She talks as if she is confused, or else she is just being very private about it. I am not sure.

I realize that generalizations, such as labels on the stages of dying, and other conventional medical wisdom do not fit a particular story. Ruth's story is uniquely her own. I do not want to trivialize it by forcing what is happening into some common plot or story line.

Ruth has always been a unique person, true to herself. Let her be now, too, O merciful God. Give Ruth serenity and strength you can give. And for me, I ask for gentleness and patience and honesty and courage to be with her as far as possible.

March 31, 1990

One of the fundamental issues, or dilemmas, in the ethics of medical care is that of autonomy - who should assume the power to author-ize, to "write the script" of medical care.

In the drama going on here in our home, now in the last days of March, there are two main characters, Ruth and Dr. Thompson. Which is the scriptwriter? I have the leading support role, an ambiguous role, because I am Ruth's main support and at the same time an aid to Dr. T. If and when Ruth and he do not agree about what should be done, I have to decide which one to support. The doctor claims to know what is best for Ruth, a claim based on his general knowledge as a trained and experienced practitioner. His instructions are specific, yet flexible as appropriate for the changes in Ruth's condition. Therefore, he has given me instructions as to medications for pain, bowel movement, bladder infection, blood pressure and cancer. He has provided me with a schedule to follow, which guides my administration of medicines. He decides how much insulin to give, when to give it and what level of glucose should be maintained. If I am to be his deputy on location, I should follow the script. Because I am no expert and have no knowledge of what is likely to occur in the near future, I must put my trust in his judgment and carry out his orders. The doctor is something like a general who plans the battle tactics and expects his subordinates to carry them out. I am like a sergeant, or perhaps more like a private doing the dirty work. As such I have direct knowledge of what is going on and where the action is taking place. What is going on does not strictly correspond to what the doctor expects or wants. Because he is not here in the trenches at 3 a.m. he must rely on my "battle station" reports in order to make changes in

Ruth's care. In this drama, if I am his support and I am confident
he knows what care Ruth needs, I should carry out his orders.

*The question would be easily resolved if I were **only** his*
support, but I am also Ruth's husband and she rightfully can claim
my allegiance. Ruth is not just the patient, an abstraction included
in a generalized model of medical knowledge and practice. She is
a unique individual, not a philosophical ideal. She has a history,
memory, fears and hopes, habits and attitudes developed over a
lifetime. Although the doctor knows Ruth's medical history,
including the way she has managed her diabetes, he does not know
as much about her as I do. I have lived with Ruth for 45 years.
While I do not know all there is to know about Ruth [every person
is at heart a mystery] I know more about her than anyone. Yet I do
not know so much as to make me qualified to write the script for
her. However, I know something that is pertinent to the drama
going on.

I know the high value Ruth has assigned to her mind, to
reason. I know the high value she also assigns to self-regulation, to
choosing for herself, even in the most intimate realms of her
relationship to God. In a chapel homily she said that no one can
have faith for me, or give me faith, not pastor or parents or even
Jesus. It is this capacity for reason, for clear thinking, that has
been diminished by the cancer and therapy—diminished but not
destroyed.

Gene Lund came to my rescue Saturday night with food. Ruth had
eaten poorly all day. Resisting food as well as medication, she was showing
signs of giving up, as if it had become too burdensome to suffer all the
trouble. Gene fed Ruth and with her usual cheery and practical ways gave Ruth
comfort.

I had an accident in the kitchen while Gene was in the bedroom. I had a
pot containing the remainder of the creamed turkey Gene had brought on the
stove to heat it a bit. I moved suddenly, hit the handle of the pot in such a way
that it tipped and spilled the contents all over the stove and on the floor. It

94

took me nearly an hour to get the viscous stuff cleaned up. Actually, not much of it was lost. I salvaged a huge helping for my supper and I was ravenously hungry. Gene helped me clean up the kitchen dishes. She is a female Brother Lawrence!

Ruth's mental confusion complicates my caring for her. I was giving her several medications after breakfast on April 1, two at a time. Usually she swallows them with a sip of water. She refused the water. She started to take them out. I said, "Ruth, take some water and swallow the pills."

"Oh, I never swallow them, Bob."

"Oh yes, you always have, Ruth."

"No, I have not!" She started to remove them again.

"Don't," I said, getting firm and tough.

"Let me talk to someone else!" she demanded. "You do things differently from the way I do." She was regarding me as she has all along, as one who did not always do things as she liked! So I called Nancy, who graciously agreed to talk to Ruth. She said something which I couldn't hear.

Ruth said, "I take the caffeine out." She was holding a cup with coffee in it.

Nancy said something.

"Oh, I guess we will do it that way," Ruth replied.

I took the phone and thanked Nancy for the rescue. She said she could tell how confused Ruth was. Ruth took the rest of the medication, including morphine, with no further resistance.

Earlier she had agreed to let me administer the medications, but she did not remember she had.

Another complication kept recurring—low blood sugar levels. This morning at 6:30 it was 38! She was clearheaded enough to realize she must eat, fortunately; so she drank a glass of sweetened milk, ate a half a grapefruit, and a half bowl of shredded wheat with banana and some sugar.

The day before her sugar level had been 69. She had been confused and refused food at first. I had been able to get her to eat orange slices and a piece of bread and then had called Nancy for help. She came, talked kindly to Ruth, and offered to transfer her to bed from the couch. Roland, her husband, and I talked as Nancy attended to Ruth's needs.

I had quite a time early Saturday morning and early Sunday morning helping Ruth after bowel movements. Cleaning up and remaking the bed involved rolling her over. I did well the first time, rather efficiently cleaning the bed and Ruth and moving her properly off and on chuck sheets. But this morning the mess was worse. Because the chucks were not placed right, the transfer sheet was soiled, so I had no way to roll Ruth over. We finally succeeded, even though I put her gown on backwards and had to do it over. She was very patient with me and cooperated as best she could.

This morning her blood sugar was 39 but she was clearheaded enough to eat breakfast. The rest of the day went well. She ate well at noon and at supper. Her blood sugar was over 200 by 4 p.m. I gave her 22 units of Lente in the morning.

We "went to church" over KRBI at 10:30. Ruth was alert throughout the service. Don Ludemann had a very fine sermon on death, based on Ezekiel's vision of the valley of dry bones and the narrative about raising Lazarus in the Gospel of John.

He came in the afternoon to serve communion to us, and he and I talked about death, in relation to his sermon, while Ruth listened quietly. She has not broached the subject on any occasion when openings made it likely for her to do so, and she said nothing now. When Don served Ruth the bread and wine from one side of the bed, she took the bread and wine and served me first, a dear and precious gesture.

One day Ruth reported a dream about a funeral service in chapel for a pastor. "All they did was sing hymns," she said. I suspect the dream is a message about the important place of hymns in her mind, and a clue to me to have more than one or two hymns at the funeral. I considered an interlude of hymn singing, with Chris Johnson at the piano. Ruth admired her sense of pace and sensitive interpretation of hymns.

I question the nursing plan that left me virtually without backup from the system on weekends. Nancy's last regular visit came from 1 to 3 p.m. on Friday, and the next was not until Monday morning at ten. I was on my own for nearly three full days. When I had a crisis Saturday afternoon,

Dr. Thompson was gone and JoAnn did not call back. I tried reaching Mary Hildebrandt. No answer. Gene Lund was in Mankato. Louise was in Watson. However, Nancy was available, though off duty, and was willing to come. Sunday morning when I had cleanup to do, I was alone and, not being an expert, I was clumsy and awkward in caring for Ruth. It was she who suffered because of the arrangement.

Barbara, a friend from Colorado, raised some questions in a recent letter. She wanted to know if we had found an understanding organization for this the final chapter in a life so rich. I wrote the following answer: The organization that understood best was the St. Peter Hospice, under the county public health nursing services. JoAnn Pool knew what equipment we needed for home care, and the kind of services nurses and nurses' aides and volunteers could give. She understood the family's need for backup and relief.

The family of friends also has significant places in the story. We would have been desolate without that support—food, letters, calls and prayers.

The hierarchical structure of the medical care system is evident in the "pecking order" from specialists to family physicians to RNs to nurses' aides. The Mayo specialists dismissed Ruth to the family physician. The family physician delegated problems of nursing care to nurses. The nurses delegated the hands-on care to the nurses' aides, and they in turn delegated hour-by-hour care to me and Louise [when she is home].

Barbara also asked, "Why does the conclusion defy any sense and only seem to bring suffering, pain, emotional agony and dreadful shared experiences? Is it fair? Does this suffering, so nearly impossible to describe, have meaning?

I answered, "We are confronted by a dark mystery, lit only and consolingly by the promise of God's steadfast presence, even when God seems absent. I am reading **A Cry of Absence** by Martin Marty. It is a consoling book in a strange way, because it links my experience of loss with the experience of the psalmists. More than anything the psalms give me the language I need now—the bleak Psalm 88, and surely Psalm 23 and 63."

She asked, "What is Ruth's experience? Does she seem peaceful enough and ready to move into a whole new something?"

I answered, "I could say a little about Ruth in December when we could talk and pray. Now I am not so sure. She participates in the liturgy of evening prayer with me. The familiar words flow, even when the ordinary sentences of everyday conversation falter in unended sentences."

There is no doubt at all in me about the comfort of a lifelong relationship with God and Christ in the Spirit as the larger context of Ruth's and my relationship. Although I am hurting and grieving, I am at peace. I have let go of Ruth. It happened one night several weeks ago. She is a gift to me, but "on loan," for first of all she is God's by baptism.

"Is sorrow breaking your heart?" my friend asked.

I answered, "No, not breaking it but deepening it. Depths of feeling I am experiencing in waves that overwhelm me. Most of the time, though, I am able to focus on giving Ruth proper care and taking care of household matters."

She wanted to know if I have made plans for afterward. I answered, "I am practicing new skills. I hope that the realization that I have a life beyond Ruth's death will help me, especially to remind me to take care of my health."

April 2, 1990

Tonight I am tired, upset and distressed because Ruth told me I was not her best friend. I had tried to persuade her to take 6 rather than 3 milligrams of morphine because Maureen said it would help her sleep through the night.

"Please, Ruth. I am your best friend, aren't I?"

"No, you are not," she said. "Why do you always go against me?" she complained.

"I am on your side, Ruth. This is something to prevent pain."

"I don't have any pain."

"That's because you are taking medication regularly." She refused the dosage, rather angry with me, so I gave up. Later she took it when Louise offered it to her.

Why did she distrust me? The morphine altered her mood, so maybe this was the shadowy side of our very close relationship, usually repressed but always there. Maybe she had felt this way about me.

When I woke up this morning, I thought about it. I knew not to take this distress as a personal rebuke. I was only the target of her distress about the disease, her weakness and loss of control.

April 3, 1990

Ruth, my beloved Ruth, my "Swedeheart," died today at 10:55 p.m. She had been agitated all evening, thirsty and in some pain. I called the hospital for advice. Dr. Bauer said I could give her 15 cc of morphine. I had given her two Tylenol after her last dose of morphine, which did not help.

I was lying in bed in the bedroom across the hall when she called loudly, "BOB."

I went in swiftly. She looked very bad, as she looked when she was in insulin shock. She moaned and her eyes stared out. She revived briefly. I told her to grip my hand. She was able to do so.

I called Dr. Bauer and described her condition. He could hear her groans. He didn't know what to do, or he couldn't or wouldn't tell me what was happening. "Test her blood, see if the sugar level is low," he said. I did. It was higher than it was the last time I had tested it. He said he would come over right away. In the meantime, Ruth began to breathe very irregularly, and her hand in mine went limp. Her lips lost color. Her eyes closed. Her breathing stopped. I knew she was gone.

Gone, Ruth, gone.
Gone home from home.
I can wish you a happy union with God
and all the saints who from their labors rest.
Ruth wanted to come home and to go home.
She came home to go home.

Earlier tonight, after supper, we had had our usual vesper liturgy. I chanted and she joined me in singing "Jesus, tender shepherd hear me, Bless thy little lamb tonight. Through the darkness be Thou near me. Keep me safe till morning light." She listened as I read the three prayers she always used before going to sleep. She prayed the Lord's Prayer with me. I sang "O God, our help in ages past" and "Go to dark Gethsemane." I gave the benediction and kissed her and said, "I love you, Ruth."

A tender moment between us occurred when I was massaging her legs and belly with lotion.

"I like your body, Ruth."

"I have a very nice body, Robert."

Ruth had a deep respect for her body. It is consoling to know that she felt that way until the end, even through the difficult time when her body began to fail to function.

My feelings are beyond my words.

I tremble with weariness.

I am aware of the absence.

I am alone in the house.

I am at peace.

So much to think about, to do, to prepare for.

O Lord, I thank you for Ruth, for giving me a life with her.

Grant me consolation and strength to meet the demands of the next few days and to find my way alone, through the dark valley where death has cast its shadow, yet not alone for you are with me.

Grant me sleep. Rest. Serenity. Strength.

Part III
Life after Ruth's Death
April 1990 - April 1991

Funeral and Burial - April 7 and 8, 1990

When Carl and his family arrived about 11 p.m. on Wednesday, granddaughter Rachel was wide awake. As soon as she came in the house, she came to me and said, "I know a lot about death. My little sister doesn't know a lot about death." Rilla had prepared her well.

When we were sitting in the living room and talking we noticed Rachel going partway down the hall toward the bedroom where she had last seen Ruth. We realized she wanted to go and look, so we turned on the hall light and went with her to the bedroom. I turned on the light. She looked in. The hospital bed was gone. The other bed had not been put back. The room was empty except for the blue egg-carton type of padding used on the hospital bed.

Rachel went in and knelt on the pad for a while and then came out. I said to Rilla later, "I am glad the crew didn't get the message about returning the bed to that room. Seeing the empty room made it evident to Rachel that Ruth was gone. I won't put the bed back. I will continue to use the other bedroom and turn this into a guest room" (a decision I changed later).

The next day Rachel wanted to go with Carl, Louise and me to the grave site and then to pick out a casket at the mortuary, so we took her with us. Later Rilla took her and Rebekka to see Ruth's body lying in the casket before the public visitation time, and she had ordered roses for each of them to lay by Ruth's body. Rachel and Rebekka were at the visitation in the mortuary the night before the funeral. They were quite curious and went often to look at Ruth's body. At the funeral the next day, they sat with their parents during the service in church and mingled easily with the people in the dining room before and after the program.

The weather was perfect, clear, sunny and mild, on the day of the funeral and on the next day when we had the committal at Resurrection Cemetery. Two days of fine weather bracketed by miserable early April weather. Providential!

101

Another sign of authorship not of our doing was the absence of Ruth's cousin Hilvie and her husband Aaron Ostrow on the day of the funeral. They were returning that night from Central America. We arranged to delay the burial and committal until Sunday, so they could participate in that service. Hilvie and Ruth were like sisters, so I knew it was important for her to be present.

Because of that arrangement we were able to move directly from the nave and the service to the dining room for a program and refreshments, without an awkward wait for the committal to take place. It was a smooth transition, involving hundreds of people. The church was filled, and so was the dining hall.

The service and program struck just the right note. I wanted the service in the nave to be centered on the Word, not on Ruth; and I must say that the liturgy, the hymns, the lessons, and the sermon were appropriate. Don Ludemann's sermon used the image of body to juxtapose Ruth's struggle with cancer and diabetes with the struggle of the Church as the Body of Christ. It was articulate, perceptive and profound.

Ruth had given no instructions about her funeral, but I knew Ruth would like to have several hymns. We chose: "O God, Our Help in Ages Past" for the opening hymn; "Blest Be the Tie That Binds" for the lessons hymn; and four hymns for a hymn sing after the sermon—"How Great Thou Art," chosen by Carl; the last two hymns Ruth played on the piano, "Jesus, Lord and Precious Savior" and "Again Thy Glorious Sun Doth Rise;" and "O Perfect Love," which was sung at our wedding. The final hymn was "For All The Saints," chosen by Louise.

I planned to preside at the program, if I could, and I did. I wrote an introduction called "Program Notes on the Service," in the form of a letter to Ruth to explain why we had the hymn sing and why I chose Marian and Dennis to speak at the program. Pastor Timothy Thoresen, representing Bishop Anderson, also spoke. The program had just the right mood, with a good mix of humorous and serious comments about Ruth. I am glad we have a cassette of both the service and the program. People said that the service and program were so appropriate for the person Ruth was, but she did not have any say in planning it.

After the service and program several friends and relatives came to our home—the Ostrow family, my cousin, Midge, and Mark from Duluth, Gene and Mary Ellen Nelson, some of my former students, Jane and Dennis Timmerman, Anita Stauffer, and others.

Holy Week

April 8, 1990
Passion Sunday

Ruth's body, her "tent," has been packed away, no more to be hugged by me, her hands no more to grasp mine, or to do her work, or play the piano, her voice no longer audible to me, or heard from the pulpit. However, I do not feel that we are separated, so at this time I can hardly think about being reunited.

Nothing can separate us from the love of God in Christ Jesus our Lord. We are joined in the eternal love and life which we have now and forever "in Christ" in whom we believe. This is very real to me, because I find myself talking to Ruth and remembering her admonitions, advice and affirmations. She "speaks" to me on my walks or as I lie in bed.

I do not feel lonely, even though I am alone. I cry, "Oh Ruthie, I miss you. I need you!" And then I remember, she is in the eternal realm, here as well as somewhere beyond my knowing.

I don't feel scared for some reason; I have serenity and strength.

April 9, 1990

In Christ Chapel at the college, four faculty members read the passion story according to St. Matthew. When John Braun recited the words Jesus cried out from the cross, "Eli lama sabachthani," [My God, My God, why hast thou forsaken me], I burst into sobs, because I remembered the last audible prayers Ruth prayed when she was alone—"O God." That is all—"O God." Then when the narrator read, "And Jesus cried again with a loud voice and yielded up his spirit," I sobbed again as I remembered Ruth's last cry, one word, "BOB."

April 11, 1990

I did not expect the continuation of conversations with Ruth! She is imprinted in my heart and memory. I should have known! We had been friends for over 50 years. We lived together for nearly 45 years. Her attitudes and values have become mine, not canceling my own but surely moderating and enriching them.

I "discuss" the day's agenda with her, and remember her advice about taking care of practical necessities and about being discreet and generous in my conversations with people.

Her voice with its tone and certain phrases, though not audible, is in my mind. Instead of thinking, I wish Ruth were here, I think, Ruth is here, in me, one with me, enjoying life with me, having her own say as I work or play or converse or think.

It is only her body that I miss, and I miss it deeply! I loved her body; it delighted me, even at the end. I miss it, with a cry of longing.

April 12, 1990

On Maundy Thursday, I went with Louise to the country church in the parish, Immanuel Lutheran. In Louise's sermon, based on the story of Jesus washing the disciples' feet, she spoke of how she and Nancy, Ruth's nurse, and Rilla, our daughter-in-law, bathed Ruth, and how that story of Jesus lifted up that very physical act of caring for the dying and gave that act a dignity and meaning so rich that she was deeply satisfied by having the opportunity to do this for her mother.

Earlier in the day I attended chapel services at which Chaplain Elvee washed the feet of a student. As I heard the story and watched him, I recalled what I did shortly before Ruth began to die. I massaged her feet and legs with lotion. The story of Jesus and my experience of doing that came together in such a way as to make the ancient story powerful, and my common act of caring more meaningful and dignified.

I have Ruth engraved in my heart and mind in this sense—
she is present in the "stacks" of memory in the synapses in my
brain and in the physical signs of her around the house. Her
attitudes and practices have been combined with mine. For
instance, I have adopted her practice of keeping the house
orderly, getting chores done before doing what I want to do. Order
is more aesthetically pleasing than mess and more practical as
well.

April 13, 1990
Good Friday

A conversation with Ruth:

Ruth: Robert, you are free now for a new life without me.
It's okay, Bob, I am not with you. Please, go on, Robert.

Robert: I can't forget you, Ruth. You are so much a part of
me that I cannot leave you in the past. We became "one flesh" and
have grown together for all these 45 years, until I cannot fully
distinguish clear boundaries between us. Even if I do things we
did not do together, you will be doing them in me. Your life
continues in me, not just as a check on me but as a supplement.
The merger is within me. Ruth, I love you and want you to remain,
not leave.

Ruth: You are a dear, dear man, Robert, and I love you. I
will try again to tell you what I mean. I do not hold you to the
patterns of living we shaped together. Those patterns developed
in part because of my physical limitations. Feel free to travel a
new way, for instance. I won't leave you, Robert. We are one,
united by the eternal life and love of God, but you are free to
create a new story. Robert, please do it.

Robert: I will, Ruth, but it will take disciplined thought and
work. I will not easily abandon the familiar ways that remind me
of you.

Dorothy Davis—Howard's widow, Janey's mother—wrote a letter about Ruth's death in which she expressed in words what I was experiencing:

I thought about you all day yesterday when you were having your memorial service. Could you really believe it was happening? After loving and living with someone for such a long time you will turn to expect Ruth to be there, set the table for two, hear her call you, and feel her beside you, all confusing and upsetting and natural. It is all so real and unreal. I feel so keenly for you. Whatever do people do at times like these when they have no faith in Christ? Let your friends "do" for you now; the aloneness is too great to bear by yourself, Bob.

April 15, 1990

I went to Easter services in the Watson Lutheran Church where Louise is interim pastor. The Eucharist was celebrated, and after I had gone to the altar to receive the bread and wine, I experienced a deep serenity of spirit. The message of Jesus, peace be with you, became very personal. I can never again pass the peace in our worship without remembering that peace, and wanting to share it with others.

Paul: "What is sown is perishable,
What is raised is imperishable"
(1 Corinthians 15:42).
Esbj: These are not shallow words, Paul. They are hints of realities hard to describe. They correspond to my discernment about Ruth. Her body is dead, that I saw; but her presence, in word and memory, is not. She is very much a part of me, and has continued influence on others.
The appearances of Jesus to the followers did not continue. He "ascended." What came to them was a new reality, the Spirit. Will the power of Ruth's influence, as I sense it in the experience of conversing with her, diminish? Will I stop conversing?

What if I were a pastor who had the task of preaching this Easter? What would I say?

April 16, 1990

Excerpts from a meditation at the "Over 55ers" luncheon on the Monday after Easter:

Knowing that my best friend, my companion of the Way, my beloved Ruth, died the week before Holy Week, you may wonder what the Easter message says to me, coming as it did so close in time to Ruth's death. Perhaps you are even asking, "Does he believe or doubt the stories and sayings connected with Jesus' death and his appearances to his followers?"

What makes Ruth's death bearable to me? It is very consoling to me, and it was to Ruth as well, that we had a long time together—51 years of friendship and nearly 45 years of marriage. We discussed this in connection with the knowledge that her illness was terminal when she was in Methodist Hospital last December. We agreed that both of us have reached the age when our demise could happen anytime, and the realization that it happens to us all became a more personal and less objective kind of knowledge. So we did not complain then or during the final stages of her illness. We decided to make the best quality of our lives during this chapter, as we had in earlier times of our lives.

Now I must tell you something about Ruth. She was a woman of faith, but it was a realistic faith. She would have questions to raise about what has happened to her and others, for hers was not an unquestioning faith. There was a strain of skepticism in her attitudes. When she prayed an intercession for someone or a petition for herself or us, she often gave a little sardonic laugh, as though to express who am I to ask God for what I want? We had time together, not only to prepare in advance for her departure, but to be together as she began to die.

But Ruth, if she were here in person, being realistic and somewhat skeptical, would ask, "But what about those wives who die in the prime of life — such as Kathryn Swanson? Or the two Gustavus students killed in a car crash last spring, dead before they had really lived a full life? Or Howard Davis, one of our friends who was killed in a car-train crash when he was on the threshold of retirement?" So many people have not had the same experience as Ruth and I had, so the fact that some of us have lived long and well does not console those who have not.

The gospel of Christ is not about living to the ripeness of old age, satisfying as that might be. Jesus did not live to a ripe old age.

Nevertheless, there is a message in the fact that since we may die at any time — it is important to make every day of life a quality time of fidelity, love, and sharing of the good and bad with courage and compassion and humor.

Furthermore, no one of us lives a perfect story. Ours was far from ideal. We had our share of troubles, especially with illness. We made some mistakes that grieved us. It has been most consoling to get letters and cards and calls in which people give Ruth such praise, but those affirmations would evoke one of her sardonic laughs. She knew her limits, her flawed righteousness, her downright sinfulness. One of the hymns she used to play was "Chief of sinners though I be, Jesus shed his blood for me."

What makes Ruth's death bearable for me and others is not that she was such a righteous woman but that she was a forgiven woman, who lived in the embrace of God's gracious mercy all her life. A central message in the Easter stories is that Jesus appeared to his disciples and he said, "Peace." Ruth and I did not feel burdened by remorse or guilt, because we have heard the gospel of peace and believed it. Jesus Christ is our peacemaker, and we are united by his word of peace.

Ah, that is nice, Ruth would respond, but what about people who have not lived in peace? What about people who die with sins unrepented, who come to the end of life bearing a load of guilt, whose grief is made more troubling by that guilt?

Early yesterday morning I read lessons for Easter with that question in mind. I came to the story of the appearance of Jesus to the despairing disciples and the message he spoke to them was "peace." There was no demand for a confession of sins, for a promise to live better, just "peace be with you." Peace is not earned, it is a gift of God, and that is one of the most consoling themes of the Easter message.

It is so liberating to know that we have a merciful Savior, who forgives us as we are. I do not say this in past tense, but the present tense. Christ is alive, present in our lives, and so the message is as contemporary as it is ancient. Christ's living presence speaking the word of peace makes it possible for me to go on living and to resume my life as a follower of the Way.

Failures do not make living peacefully, lovingly and creatively impossible, because forgiveness sets us free.

I am glad that I am not burdened with guilt and remorse about the imperfections in our marriage, or about the times I have failed to be the husband I wanted to be, or about my helplessness to do all that Ruth needed. The Gospel of Christ our peacemaker consoles me, and it is for everyone.

I must ask you to follow me as I raise a question about life after death which has been a bone of contention between Ruth and me all our married life. I must be honest with you about the way I respond to the traditional hope of reunion with loved ones in the life to come. It is a consolation to many, many people, to cherish the hope of a future reunion with loved ones in "a land that is fairer than day."

Ruth hoped for such a reunion with a longing that was consistent with her great love of her own person and of people dear to her. But she also found it hard to accept rationally, and she was a very rational person.

For me, on the other hand, it has not been so important an aspect of my Christian hope. It is not the most fundamental consolation I have from the Christian message. Whatever might come after death remains a mystery, and Paul said it well, "Behold, I tell you a mystery. We shall all be changed, in the twinkling of an eye." Such a hope is certainly not contrary to the belief in a merciful and creative God, but I have not found it either necessary or proper to base my faith on some kind of absolute assurance of reunion in a manner that I imagine it to be. I am content to leave that in the realm of the unknown and the infinite mystery of God's creative purposes.

There has been something more consoling to me in these days since Ruth died than the hope of re-union. It is the continuation of **union**.

Much to my surprise, for I did not anticipate it or expect it, Ruth's death has not separated her from me. Yes, her body is gone into the grave, beyond my touch and sight; but Ruth is present in a very real sense. Her influence remains. She is engraved in my mind and heart. We became one flesh in marriage, so there is a sense in which my body, still alive, is also hers. She lives on in me, so I create these conversations to imagine talking to her.

I do not mean that she appears visually to me or speaks audibly. It is that her perspectives, her practical wisdom, her ideas have merged with mine, not replacing my own but enriching and sometimes correcting mine. It is truly a wonderful experience, even when it evokes sobs from me.

This unexpected, continuing and lively relationship may very well give meaning to something Christians affirm, that by faith we dwell in the eternal life and love of God. Nothing can separate us from the love of God, not life and not death.

Heaven, for me, is not some remote place way off somewhere, and not in some far-off future. Heaven is a life in the eternal presence of God. We are already raised with Christ into this eternal life and love. The gospel and letters bearing the name John are very clear on this point.

This union seems particularly evident now when I worship. Ruth and I had evening prayer together only a couple of hours *before she began to die. She sang one of the songs with me, "Jesus tender shepherd hear me." She prayed the Lord's Prayer with me.*

Every time I pray the Lord's Prayer now I am praying it with her, just as I am praying it with my mother, who died when I was eight. The last act with my mother was praying the Lord's Prayer with her, and so it was with my dear Aunt Ann, her sister, who died about 50 years later in the same hospital.

The Holy Week worship services were very much more meaningful to me, because they occurred so soon after Ruth died. The liturgies of the church draw us into union with those who have died, and with those who will come after us. When we participate in worship, we are lifted up into the eternal life of God with all the saint—as the Eucharist liturgy reminds us—and our ordinary, everyday stories are raised up into the great story of God's creative and redemptive drama.

If Ruth had to die at this age, and from this illness, then what better time for it to happen than the week before Holy Week? I am glad it happened now, not earlier in the wintry time, and not later which would mean she would have lingered longer. It happened as winter is turning to spring, as new life is about to burst out all over Minnesota. She lived long enough to hear the robins sing and see the buds begin to form and the grass to become green.

Thus there were resonances back and forth between the story of Jesus and our story that gave both stories richer significance. The biblical stories are about human experiences that we have, not primarily illustrations for doctrines and theology. The story of Jesus lifts our stories up into something that transcends our ordinary limits.

Travels and Conversations - May and June 1990

After Ruth's funeral I continued my practice of writing in my journal. I have selected passages from it that relate to coping with loss and learning to live alone.

The unexpected experience of Ruth's lively presence inspired me to write imaginary conversations with her in my journal and to carry on with them in my walks. Perhaps the most important inspiration were some thoughts that I developed on the physiological nature of memory, which I have recorded in some of the following entries.

Our marriage was a long conversation that began during our student days at Gustavus and continued in our correspondence before we were married. One day in June, I read what Ruth said about my letters to her in a letter dated October 12, 1941, from Karlstad, Minnesota.

This morning Mrs. Turnwall brought my mail. I must admit I could not grasp the meaning of most of your letter. Margaret and Luverne were tickling and teasing me on both sides. Now, in the solitude of my room, I read it again and, in case you are beginning to question my intelligence, I managed to comprehend your statements with little difficulty. As usual, they gave me something to think about.

Oh, I do want to talk to you, Esbj. It is so much easier to talk to you than to write. Do you know I miss the talks that we used to have? Even if we didn't settle anything, it was pleasant just to be able to talk without having to apologize for the things you said or didn't say.

The next letter was a conversation—October 28, 1941:

Dear Esbj,

Thank you for the scolding. I know you didn't mean to reprove me, but through my own conscience you did. This is what part of your letter said to me: 'Shame on you, Ruth, for spending your time thinking about things that are past. What do you suppose God gave you all those wonderful things for if it wasn't to make use of them in the future? Do you want to be on the receiving end all your life? Of course, your college days were wonderful, but there are far better things ahead of you. A Christian is always growing and looking forward to a brighter and better future. Certainly you should have enough trust in God to know that the way He has planned for you is best. Now get down to work and stop mooning.' You are quite right, Esbj. My last weekend at Gustavus convinced me I had a wonderful time as usual, and I hated to leave; but I knew that the best thing was to leave all those things just as pleasant memories to be remembered every once in awhile. I sometimes think that women are a trifle more sentimental than men and often find it harder to adjust themselves. Dear me! Perhaps I am ascribing to all women some of my feeble characteristics!

I traveled several times. In May I traveled to Lansing, Michigan, to visit my son, Carl, and his family. Tears flowed intermittently as I remembered going with Ruth, but there were also some consoling experiences—visits with hospitable friends responsive to my need to share the experiences I have had, some unexpected discoveries that gave warrant and affirmation to my experience of Ruth's lively presence, and the confidence that I could travel alone.

My daughter Louise and I went to New England in late May and early June to visit Ruth's relatives and other friends. We visited my family in Lansing and several friends along the way. In August I visited friends in Park City, Utah. In March I went to Florida to visit friends and relatives. I "went up North" for visits in Wright, my hometown.

One of the ways I meditate is to write conversations with authors whose books I am reading. It is a way of reflecting on and giving personal response to what I am reading. This practice kept me mindful of the fact that a book is the work of a person who has spent much effort to communicate to readers. It is a form of "spiritual" reading, similar to **lectio divina** [divine reading] practiced for centuries in Catholic religious communities. It is not reading for information or to master the total thought of a writer, as one does in professional academic work. When I came upon a passage that struck me, I wrote it into the journal and then wrote my reflections and reactions to it. This practice was very beneficial during this time. The Psalms and Martin Marty's **A Cry of Absence**, which describes the "wintry spirituality," were companions before and after Ruth died.

During the summer I read Madeleine L'Engle's reflections on her husband's death in **Sold into Egypt: Joseph's Journey into Human Being** (Wheaton: Harold Shaw, 1989), and I reread **Two-Part Invention: The Story of a Marriage**, based on journals written during her husband's final illness. She provided me with a model for my own reflections about Ruth's death. I also read Peter Noll's **In the Face of Death**, his journal about living while he was dying of cancer. My journal writings reveal something of what I have learned from them, and I am continuing to learn as I read these books.

April 17, 1990

A conversation with Ruth:

> *"But I have calmed and quieted my soul,*
> *Like a child at its mother's breast,*
> *Like a child that is quieted is my soul" (Psalm 131:2).*

> *Robert: I have given this psalm only a glance and haven't been stopped by it, Ruth.*

> *Ruth: No wonder, Robert, the way you dash about. I had to chide you yesterday. You were too jumpy.*

> *Robert: Well, Ruth, since I am the only body you have, which I have promised to share with you, I will "set my soul in silence and peace," so you can enjoy some serenity.*

> *Ruth: Thank you, Robert. I do love you.*

> *Robert: And I dearly love you, my Swedeheart!*

April 24, 1990

"O how could we sing the song of the Lord on alien soil?
O let my tongue cleave to my mouth if I remember you not,
If I prize not Jerusalem above all my joys" (Psalm 137: 5-6).

This psalm expresses the sense of belonging to a particular
place, which was resonant with memories — Jerusalem for the
exiled Jews, who were so homesick and so alienated sitting "by
the rivers of Babylon" that they "sat and wept" and could not sing
songs of the Lord at the request of their captors. The song ends in
a bitter curse upon the children of Babylon.

For me, this house at 748 Valley View is such a place. If
bulldozers ever knocked it down to make room for "development,"
I would be heartbroken, too, and bitter.

Maundy Thursday, when I was in Watson with Louise in the parsonage, I awoke at 11:30 p.m. with a surge of homesickness so strong I had to exert much mental effort to stop myself from getting in the car and driving to St. Peter. I was a little boy again, on his first overnight in a friend's house down the street, where the sounds and spaces are unfamiliar. It was my first night away from home after Ruth's death. I could almost hear her calling me, "Bob, where are you?" as if she were a lonely presence there.

I **want** to be at 748 Valley View. This house is "home" and full of memories dear to my heart, memories real and glad, memories of Ruth's last days, memories of morning prayers as we sat side by side on the couch morning after morning, memories of parties, of sitting on the porch on a summer evening.

May 3, 1990

On the eve of the first-month anniversary of Ruth's death, I wept frequently as I drove to Chicago over a route I had traveled often with Ruth. Even pulling into a rest stop where we had stopped would set me off.

I cannot fully understand my feelings and experience. This sense of Ruth being with me is so strong that I create conversations with her. The worth of Ruth to me is so precious I hope to maintain the practice. Am I inventing? Yes, but the question is, "Why am I inventing this way of relating to her death?" I did not expect to have this experience. I thought that her burial would be the departure and the end, except for memories. I thought I would mourn a loss. Little did I know I would rejoice in a gain, because it seems that my love for Ruth and hers for me are going beyond where it was before her death—still growing, still creating.

I am astonished. I cry hard, and I realize that my tears are tears of joy. Yet, I also cry for loss of her physical presence. I miss her, oh, I miss her!

Lord, you gave me a great gift. I am thankful for our long life together. We made good music, Ruth and I, and I am committed to continuing this creative partnership in ways that are enriching and expanding for others as well as for me.

Glad grief—mixed with sad feelings welling up when I think Ruth cannot be here physically to enjoy this visit.

"Robert! Stop it. I am enjoying it. Remember?"

May 6, 1990

Forty-five years ago Ruth and I became husband and wife, pledged to faithful love, bonded by the prospect of becoming "one flesh."

Now, though she died, we are one, in a profound unity of love, my body is hers and mine. And she and I are still one, even though she, as body, is buried in Resurrection Cemetery. It is awesome.

I celebrate our marriage today, sad but not glum, glad but not mad. It seems to me I love Ruth most fully now, because there is a new intimacy of relationship which I experience by my "conversations" with her.

116

Yet, I weep "crinkle cries" as I remember little details from the past, and I have some big cries, too, all alone. There is a deep level of grief that I have to experience alone. I cry hard, yet my feelings are not glum. Rather than loss I experience an enlargement of intimacy—as if our love is **more** complete, rather than at an end, still growing, still maturing.

Of course, I realize I am using my imagination when I carry on the conversations with Ruth on my—or our—walks. However, who should say which is **really** more real. Everyone constructs a world of meaning. I am doing so with the rich material of a long marriage and intimate friendship.

Ruth and I did almost everything together, so why not imagine we are still doing so? We are one flesh, united by the vows and our long practice of communicating with each other. So I say, "Ruth now has my physical body as a 'site' for continuing with me." It is a crazy idea, but I am enjoying it!

On May 7, driving to Illinois from Michigan to visit a friend, I did not cry much. Is my grief already dying? No. I don't think so. My experience of loss is messy. Trying to map it into neat successive "stages" of a process only stereotypes it. I am letting it flow from my day-to-day. My conversations with Ruth were quite consoling. She said, "Robert, it is **your** idea that I continue to live **in** you now that I am not able to be **beside** you, because my body is dead. The essential 'I' lives as a presence in your mind and heart."

I responded, "We continue to **create** a life even in my present time. We are God's creating creatures. I turn from mourning a past to recycling it, using the past as material for creating a life beyond your death. Yesterday I felt quite happy and very much in love with you, Ruth."

Conversations on readings from C. S. Lewis's **A Grief Observed**:
> *Lewis: "Today I've been visiting old haunts, and I find that I do not want to go back again [to his life before his wife Joy].*
>
> *Esbj: I am thinking about this trip to New England—going back to Portland, Newington, Nauset Beach on the Cape—where Ruth and I went every June. I do not expect it to be easy. Ruth's physical presence was such an important one to her family. Maybe my being there alone will help all of us put a closing on her*

life with them. I do not want to lose them as family. I hope to keep them in my life, but I am questioning whether I can. I am even open to canceling the trip, but I don't think I will.

Lewis: "The earthly beloved incessantly triumphs over your mere idea of her. And you want her to with all her resistances, all her faults, all her unexpectedness. That is, in her four-square, independent reality. And this, not any image or memory, is what we are to love still, after she is dead."

Esbj: Aha! That is why our conversations are so significant, Ruth. They keep you from becoming a still snapshot, frozen in a brief flick of time. Your continued presence points beyond to icons of the Divine. God, you say, is the great iconoclast.

Lewis: "Images of the Holy become holy images— sacrosanct. My idea of God is not a divine idea. It has to be shattered time after time. He shatters it himself. Could we not almost say that this shattering is one of the marks of His presence? The Incarnation is the supreme example; it leaves all previous ideas of the Messiah in ruins."

*Esbj: I agree. I am persuaded to love God, as he is, not any image of him; and God is active, building, creating, rescuing, a force to be reckoned with, unpredictable, yet utterly reliable, so that life in God is **safe** even when life roars about us and we are swept off our feet.*

Ruth: Love me, not just your memories of me, Robert. I, too, am an unpredictable, yet reliable presence in your life. Now I am free, Robert, free to be, no longer held down by diabetes or cancer or obsessive anxiety. I can be a strong and loving presence for you.

I had rich emotional and perceptual experiences on May 8. Ruth was a presence, more "solid" than ever, not visually or audibly but as mind, as **being**, very much alive and active.

May 9, 1990

*Which Ruth was present to me? The Ruth who lay in bed at home, ill and dying, who smiled so tenderly at me when I massaged her feet and legs and belly the night she died? The Ruth at 21, on a May Day date on campus—young, perky? The Ruth at 31, the mother of a newborn son, or at 41, the one who had to deal with diabetes? Or at 51 or 61? **All of Ruth!** Ruth of all times. The **whole** Ruth. Ruth no longer time-bound. It was so incredible I cried and exclaimed, "I can't understand it!"*

I cried, as I drove to ELCA headquarters in Chicago, but I cried tears of gladness and joy, thanking God for such a woman and the continuing of the relationship. I felt **in love** the way I did when I was young and yet in love the way I have been in our last years. The one way, fresh, like a bright morning in May; the other seasoned, like a crisp autumn day in October.

Yes, Ruth, I'm in love with you in a deeper way than ever. Oh, Ruth, you are dear to me! I am engaged in a creative experience beyond anything I imagined. To believe that our marriage continues to develop is audacious. Even though I am now alone and must bear responsibilities for my life, you are here influencing me and giving me this joy that is free of the burdens of anxiety.

May 14, 1990

O Lord, open my lips.
Let my mouth pour forth thy praise.
How do I praise you, the all encompassing God
in whom I move and live and have my being?
By being attentive, appreciative, adoring,
loving, delighting, submitting and serving God's glory.
And, this morning, to try again to find an adequate language
to describe an experience that defies ordinary cognition.

119

*Death has taken Ruth's physical body from me. I miss her presence as a side-by-side companion. I expected to lose her to death. I "gave her back" to God. I thought death would be the end, at best an oblivion until "the day of the Lord" [a time-bound phrase that seems quite misleading in that it assumes **chronos**, time as ongoing succession]—Or merely the end of Ruth as death takes us all.*

That is not what has happened. Something else is going on, something that took me by surprise, something I hadn't even hoped for wistfully. Ruth came as a presence. Ruth is alive in me. Ruth is here, a steady, if invisible and inaudible presence, and a steadying presence.

Was it memory, a lingering energy left in the wake of her death, like echoes of a call or odors of a dying fire's smoke, something that would fade away?

*It was memory, but memory is not a disembodied set of ideas. Memory is **physiological**. Ruth is in my brain. Outward things or events or situations fire the synapses that connect her to my conscious mind. This idea occurred to me last night on a walk, and it added credibility to the belief that my body is now hers as well. We became one flesh when we consummated our commitment, but that was just the beginning, like the moment when sperm unites with ovum. I entered her brain, not just her body, and became a physical presence in her, as she is in me. Truly this makes sense and accounts for the maturing intimacy and mutual love of a long marriage.*

According to conventional wisdom, death is supposed to end this, isn't it?

*No, the companionship continues to be creative and caring, just as it was before Ruth died. How can such a state be? Well, I began to talk to her, and she **used** my voice to answer me. We began conversations.*

All rooted in memory? Yes, but memory is not static. Like history, memory is reshaped and ever-changing in configurations as new experiences continue. So Ruth, in me, and I talk over almost everything, just as we did after breakfast when she was alive. Her perspectives affect my own. I have a still powerful desire to please her, but it isn't a compulsion to remain as we were.

Ruth: Robert, you are giving me access to your continuing life and experience. I am experiencing the earth, the beautiful earth and people and events in you. We are one flesh in a profound way! I have raised the skeptical question. Isn't it fantasy, Robert, illusion, imagination? Aren't you inventing to assuage your grief?

Robert: At first I thought so, but so is the belief that your death means you are obliterated and that I must get on with my life without you an invention. *That* construction is not consoling, and it is not consistent with the facts of my experience of long association with you, Ruth, which has left its code in my brain. If I must choose between one invention and another, I choose the one that is the most interesting and the most in accord with the way the human brain is constructed. Others will hold to the obliteration fiction, if they must, but for me, I will go with what I am experiencing.

As time has passed, you have not diminished as a steady presence in my life. Last night you said to me, "Robert, I am free now to grow with you beyond the point which I had reached at my death with respect to family relations. You can go beyond me, but I go *with* you to a reconciliation not yet attained. For both of us your attitudes and actions may manifest my belief in God's inclusive mercy. What we could not attain before I died, we can attain as time passes."

The skeptic in me does not give up easily and questions the reality of this interpretation. Am I living an illusion?

C. S. Lewis's description of the presence of his wife, after her death, was so similar to what I was experiencing that I burst into tears of wonder and joy.

Lewis describes an assurance of his presence as "quite incredibly unemotional, just the impression of her **mind** momentarily facing my own. Mind, not 'soul' as we tend to think of soul. Certainly the reverse of what is called 'soulful,' not at all like a rapturous reunion of lovers. Much more like getting a telephone call or a wire from her about some practical arrangement. Not that there was any 'message,' just intelligence and attention. No sense of joy or sorrow. No un-love. I had never in any mood imagined the dead as being so...well, businesslike. Yet there was an extreme and cheerful intimacy, an intimacy that had not passed through the senses at all. If this was a throw-up from my unconscious, then my unconscious must be a far more interesting region than the depth psychologists have led me to expect.

"The dead could be like that—sheer intellects. Up to now this always seemed to me a most arid and chilling idea. The absence of emotion repelled me, but in this context [whether real or apparent] it didn't do anything of the kind."

There was more encouragement in the mail when I got home. **Three** pieces in the mail mentioned, in one way or another, the presence of someone who had died, someone known to the writer. Susie Sandberg, a nurse and former student of mine, made reference to **visiting** with a friend after she died last fall. Ann Brady's note expressed the hope that I would experience Ruth's presence; and Gloria Benson sent a statement by Rosamund Pilcher that expressed a similar idea.

I was astounded by the "coming together" of these verifications from such different sources. They are not proof. My experience does not lend itself to the test of generality, but these observations by others are clues to something possible. "With God all things are possible" (Matthew 19:36).

*Will I ever **see** or **hear** Ruth in some future state? It is an irrelevant question. I **am**, here and now, experiencing this presence. The eternal is not beyond the endpoint of the last second of time, and heaven is not beyond the last reaches of an expanding universe. The eternal is now. "In my father's house are many mansions." Well, this is my mansion and Ruth's. Both are in time and yet transcending time.*

I cannot penetrate the mystery of what Ruth may be experiencing in her freedom, but that also is consistent with what I have experienced. Ruth as always had a privacy I have rarely penetrated. Even in our most intimate sexual experience, the mystery of her being remained inviolate. She had a prayer life that was her own. She had memories and thoughts that were not shared with me.

I am very happy and at peace, yet surges of grief for a lost past overcome me. When they do, Ruth chides me, "I am in you now, Robert, in your mind and heart. Your body is mine. So, dear man, let us get on with the unfolding story."

May 15, 1990

Our conversations continue, every morning on "our" walk and intermittently. Sometimes Ruth seems to be a presence, shoulder high to my right, steady, invisible, but somehow "there," never on my left side or in front of or behind me.

*Does a person's death become ordinary to friends? I read the obituaries in the paper at a glance. Deaths **are** ordinary; they happen to everyone. Yet, the death of my wife is extraordinary to me, a major, once-in-a-lifetime event full of impacts and meanings.*

May 24, 1990
Feast of Ascension

Is my experience like that of the disciples experiencing Jesus after his death? On Ascension Day should I say farewell to Ruth, whose being now transcends time and space? How can I when she is present in my brain? I surely do not want to stop these interesting conversations.

I started Madeleine L'Engle's book, **Sold into Egypt** today, and what did I find but another warrant, or support for the experience of Ruth's continuing presence in my life.

*Conversations on L'Engle's book, **Sold Into Egypt**:*

L'Engle: "Could it be that after all these years, more than ten, Jacob still did not, deep in his heart, believe in Rachel's death? There is something in all of us that shares this disbelief, especially after we have lost those dearest to us. I still want to turn to my mother saying, 'Mother, you're the only one who knows about this...' It is a reflex that will never completely vanish. The mortal fact of my husband Hugh's death is still, sometimes, a matter for total disbelief. Many African tribes do not believe in the deaths of their members, but hold that they are still available, can be talked to, conferred with, asked for advice. Across the world and across time in the Episcopal Church [and in other liturgical churches] we celebrate All Saints' Day and talk about that great cloud of witnesses with which we are surrounded—all those, known and unknown, who have gone before us. We talk of the communion of saints, and by saints we mean not only those especially endowed with holiness, but the saints as all of God's people. This communion is the gift to us of the Resurrection. So, although the death of this mortal body is undeniable, in a very deep way we do not believe in death."

Will our conversations cease, Ruth? Will you depart, too? Will this odd, uncanny perception of your presence fade? I don't know. I hope not. I enjoy your lively presence. Am I fantasizing? There is no way of proving that I am not, and I do not particularly want to be given such proof. For whom would the proof be? Who cares whether I am imagining or not? All I can say is that these "conversations" are very satisfying, significant and real to me. Maybe there is no real barrier between eternal and temporal and my creating may be a part of the ongoing creation story.

I am forlorn tonight, far from home and the physical place which is full of you, Ruth, but you are here, in my brain patterns, and in my body which is also yours.

Coping with Loss

When I look back in retrospect on what I did during the year following Ruth's death, I see some patterns of coping that developed and that were very beneficial. The most important, I think, was writing the journal; but that alone would have been too inward-directed. I was determined to develop a regimen of household management, doing everything that Ruth and I did together. So I worked at keeping the house in order and attending to such practical matters as paying bills and answering letters, which I habitually used to neglect too long.

I decided to take up cooking. Since I had to eat, why not learn something new instead of relying on packaged foods and eating out? I was glad I did. I not only enjoyed the food I prepared better than the packaged meals and most meals in restaurants, but I also enjoyed the process of studying menus and recipes and creating my own versions of dishes. I entertained quite often, perhaps because it was what Ruth and I enjoyed doing and because I needed company.

I continued a disciplined prayer life, following routines I had practiced that combined physical exercise with meditation and prayer. In the fall I joined the First Lutheran Church Senior Choir, which was an enriching social as well as worship activity.

After Ruth died I considered discontinuing teaching at adult forums, but Dennis Johnson persuaded me not to drop out of the college's Partnership in Education program so abruptly, but rather to accept as few assignments as I wished. So I signed on and prepared only one topic, "Living Marriage within the Praying Life," and accepted only one date a month. I didn't count on extra requests for my time, however, such as preaching in Christ Chapel at the college and some extra teaching assignments at retreats and in classes. As a result my schedule filled up from October through February! It was a relief to go to Florida in March!

Coping with loss? Rather, I was living with loss. My pattern was in no sense an escape from grieving or loss.

June 1, 1990

What if our thoughts are God's participation in the universe. What if all that is exists because God is a contemplative who is observing and participating at the same "eternal moment"? What if all that is becomes nothing in the mind of God? What if the universe is one immense imaginary notion, not ours but God's?

*What if my experience of the lively presence of Ruth in my mind is an imaginary, **true** thought, a God-is-love thought?*

> *Love caused the universe to be*
> *Love came in at Christmas to be with me*
> *My life is the universe conscious of itself*
> *And the word of love made human in time and space*
> *and yet eternal.*

*My life is now at the threshold of a new chapter, not stuck in the last chapter, or all previous chapters. A life beyond Ruth's participation? It will be different. Her place is no longer an extension in space, out there, but still it is a **location**. How can that be?*

*This is a jumble of thoughts tumbling out as I try to think about being an imaginative observer-participant in God's imaginary universe—the Word made **atom**, the Word made **bios**, the Word made **human**, extended in space, located in place. Yet*

the whole of it; the whole universe sings when I sing, because I am
a child of star dust and yet that very thought is from beyond.

Beyond? There is no beyond. In God we live and move and
have our being. "Beyond" is the outer darkness—or is it the
confining, suffocating inner darkness of a heart that refuses to
accept love, or to love? Can I really reject or escape
participation in the life of God? Not according to the view in
Psalm 139.

June 5, 1990

"May I in virtue and in faith,
and with thy gifts content,
rejoice beneath thy covering wings
each day in mercy sent."

Peace, this morning, after a powerful onslaught yesterday of being lonesome for Ruth. As Louise and I traveled from Portland, Maine, to New York City I was overwhelmed again and again by spasms of silent sobbing. The lure of Cape Cod and Nauset Beach was so strong, I considered changing our plans, turning around, and going there. I was lonesome for the sea, the sand, the surf, the silence, and for companioning with Ruth in that place.

Last night I took a short break on Bill's bed before supper and cried. I talked to Ruth and she said helpful words, "Robert, wherever you are, I go, too. If you go to the Cape, I go; if you head for home, so do I."

"Do you want to go home, Ruth?" She answered, "I would like to go home, Robert." Peace came with that.

Joe and Bill were very kind to me last night by giving me space to discuss my experiences and my proposals for publishing Ruth's writings. The conversations ranged over several topics and exchanges. Bill said I should include what I am writing along with Ruth's writings.

June 6, 1990

Louise and I stopped at Genesee Abbey in Geneseo, New York, for a brief visit. Ruth and I came here several years ago, on a sunny day, the sky blue, with white clouds crossing. This time the sky was gray, a gentle rain was falling. The abbey was a jewel, even in the subdued light and rain.

I am sat in the reception room of the abbey where I could look out, eastward, toward the valley. I remembered the deep silence here last time, and I sensed it now, too. There is a ticking clock punctuating the silence so regularly it reminds me of my heartbeat and the steady passage of time.

Another uncanny instance of providential occurrence happened when I saw Henri Nouwen's **A Letter of Consolation** (San Francisco: Harper & Row, 1982), a letter written to his father after his mother's death. I took it, sat in a chair and opened it at random. I came upon a page where Nouwen wrote about the 47-year relationship between his father and mother:

"I think because love—deep, human love—does not know death, the way you and Mother had become one, the way this oneness had deepened itself during forty-seven years of marriage, did not allow termination. Real love says 'forever.' Love comes from that place within us where death cannot enter."

I wept when I read that passage, because it added another warrant to bolster the authenticity of what I experienced after Ruth died. So I sit now, consoled, tears barely dry.

June 19, 1990

In **Sold into Egypt**, again I discovered someone's experience similar to my conversations. Madeleine L'Engle said she resisted talking to Hugh after his death, because she didn't want to hold him back. Even so, she said, **Hugh spoke to her**. "I did not hear Hugh's physical voice. But I felt him, his is-ness, with me at a time when my grief was raw—all of me was aware of and open to Hugh." Hugh said, 'You know you don't want to work on **Sold into Egypt** right now. What you want to work on is that fantasy you've been thinking about.' I wrote 28 pages."

*Conversation on L'Engle's **Sold into Egypt**:*

*It is astonishing to discover once again that someone else, in this case, Madeleine L'Engle, has similar experiences and thoughts. I read a passage in **Sold into Egypt** about the cemetery not being the place of Hugh's presence; "rather, every room of the apartment in New York—and at Crosswick—is full of his presence."*

*That is just how I feel about Ruth. Her body is buried in Resurrection Cemetery. I have walked there often, but not because I think she is there. She is here at home, if anywhere. Her presence permeates the rooms of this house. She is in my thoughts, which are in my skull, which is in my head, a **physical** place for her. Her picture in the bedroom is an icon of Ruth talking to me, but it is not where Ruth is. Where is Ruth? Is Ruth alive? I can only **believe** she is, but my belief is grounded in this powerful intuition of her presence and participation.*

L'Engle: "Believing then, as I do now, deep in my heart, that God still has work for us to do, and that the reality of my father and Hugh, and of all that cloud of witnesses, is still real, alive in ways we cannot even begin to understand."

Esbj: When I think about Ruth's aliveness, she speaks of a mystery I cannot know. She does not tell me anything. "Behold I tell you a mystery. We shall all be changed, in the twinkling of an eye"—that is all I get.

L'Engle [on timing]: The occurrence of events that made it possible for her to be present at the dying and funeral of a dear younger friend prompted her to write, "The timing was so incredible that it is impossible to put it down to coincidence. Suddenly, in death and tragedy, God was revealed."

My experience of timely occurrences was such that I call them providential; such as the timing of Ruth's dying and death coming during Lent, just before Holy Week.

June 20, 1990

"The power of the wicked shall be broken,
and the Lord will support the just" (Psalm 37:17).

L'Engle: "When Hugh was dying, while one thing went wrong after another...it seemed that some malign power was playing cat and mouse all over the planet...terrorist attacks in Paris, deranged men stalking and killing young women, a horrible fire in a South African gold mine—a terrible disaster in an already beleaguered country. We seem to be surrounded by a horror and a hissing and an everlasting reproach.

The powers of darkness are at work. Another word for them is echthroi, Greek for 'the enemy,' and the echthroi, too, is fighting the light."

> *O Lord of life, I praise you.*
> *O Lord of love, I praise you.*
> *O Lord of light, I praise you.*
> *On this long day of light, I praise you.*
> *May I not be overcome by fear of echthroi!*
> *By adversity, by defeat.*

Today, as I face my tasks and surprises, may I be attentive to your word of grace, useful in service to others, affectionate, wise, and faithful and trusting.

L'Engle: "The wonderful letters I have received since the publication of Two-Part Invention have reawakened my pain at Hugh's illness and death. The letters speak affirmation and joy; yet grief that has been drowsing, if not sleeping, is suddenly wide awake. We don't 'get over' the deepest pains of life nor should we. 'Aren't you over it?' is a question that cannot be asked by someone who has been through 'it.'... During an average lifetime there are many pains and griefs to be borne. We don't 'get over' them. We learn to live with them, to go on growing...Through his pain Joseph learned how to be a human being...To be human is to be fallible. We are creatures who know and know that we know, and know that we don't know."

Esbj: And we fall short. We do what we do not like or approve of, even in our earnest efforts to do what we know is right.

June 22, 1990

"Blessed is he who considers the poor!
The Lord delivers him in the day of trouble" (Psalm 41:1).
"The Lord will help him on his bed of pain.
He will bring him back from sickness to health" (Psalm 41:3).

*Robert: Surely this view is challenged in **Job**, by the lived experience of countless people who were not saved in the day of evil or brought from sickness to health. So how can I agree, happy is the man...? Surely not by holding to a consequentialist ethical perspective which links cause—consideration of the poor and weak—to effect—reward of being saved and cured. What do you think, Ruth?*

Ruth: Robert, I can say this much to begin with. I suffered diabetes for about thirty years. Diabetes is a chronic illness, not curable but treatable with proper use of insulin, proper diet, and exercise. I was willing and able to take care of myself, except during severe insulin reactions which came when the blood sugar level was too low. Then it was you who helped me back to normal by getting me to take something sweet or calling for medical emergency help. I did not develop any of the serious side effects, such as neuropathy, bad circulation or blindness.

Robert: Ruth, you seem to be saying that you, with assistance from me and others, kept yourself healthy, not the Lord of the psalmist. This is the nub of the matter. In our time, because of medical science, we have insulin, superior knowledge of nutrition and other helpful knowledge. Knowing you, I am sure you do not substitute science for God, or medical help for prayer.

*Ruth: Faith in God and worship were central in my life, Robert, as you know; but I did not believe God would hand me deliverance in some magical fashion. As I look at it now, it was my basic outlook, shaped by Christian teaching, that was the key. I was **willing** to do what was necessary to treat chronic illness, because I so strongly believed in my responsibility to respect my own body and to respect my intelligence and knowledge of what is good. You, Robert, were considerate of my weakness; when I was unable to act, you acted, you also were motivated by what was good.*

Robert: I see this connection, Ruth. God's power is surely universal and by human effort we tap it.

*Ruth: No, Robert, you haven't got it right. The grace of God is an energy that gives us the **heart** to do what is needed.*

Robert: We'll have to continue this conversation, Ruth. Our experience of coping with chronic illness is a major moral drama in the story of our marriage.

Ruth: Please pray before you go on, Robert.

Robert: Lord, I cry to you for help. In the morning my prayer comes to you.

*Every day, I pray. Do I get help? No, **ex machina** magic. I do not pray just to get what I need, but to keep attentive to your Word, which comes, incarnate, not just in tradition of the past but in current reports and knowledge. It is a major challenge, Lord, to keep alert, because I become preoccupied with my own thoughts, ideas, and projects. I have missed some openings with respect to the poor and the weak, the traveler passing through, the neighbor's burdens. I know that being inconsiderate is not conducive to happiness. I also realize, Lord, that I have been living in a safe and pleasant environment for many years. Am I to assume [from that] that I have been selected out of millions for* special treatment? No. Is it a random affair? My good luck? No. Providence? A strong case could be made, but it does not fit the facts of life in Iran now, where thousands of people have been killed by a severe earthquake. There is no simple theological answer, Lord. I pray because I am called to prayer. I believe it is my calling to be faithful to that calling. I shrivel up when I do not pray. I become a lesser human. If my faith opens me to your power which gives me heart, I am happy for it. If considerateness for anyone who is poor and weak is conducive to happiness, I am grateful for the connection.

I dread that state of mind that causes me to be insensitive, inconsiderate, indifferent, even mean; for then I am one of those who are evil.

Love is an energy. You are love, so we believe, so you move me to appropriate action. Nevertheless, I am mortal, limited, and stupid enough to fail.

June 26, 1990

*This conversation with Ruth, L'Engle and Nouwen started after breakfast when I read a statement in L'Engle's **Sold into Egypt**.*

L'Engle: "We don't **see** those we love, but we **know** those we love; we don't **see** God's image, but we **know** God's image. It is not a matter of sight but of insight."

Ruth: I know you, Robert—to know in the sense that Hosea used it. In Hebrew the same word is used for sexual intercourse as for intimate knowledge that is not fully describable or expressed.

Robert: I remember a saying of my dad's. "'I see,' said the blind man. 'No you don't,' said the dummy." The blind man meant insight, whereas the dummy thought of sensory sight. I see you, Ruth, though you are invisible to my eyes, because I have intimate knowledge of you. You are present in my "insight." Only a dummy *would challenge me on that score. This postdeath experience of you is very intimate and strong.*

Ruth: Robert, you read from Nouwen's A Letter of Consolation last night. There were some sentences I'd like you to reread, so we can discuss them.

Nouwen: "Mother's death is certainly one of the most crucial experiences of both of our lives...A new confrontation with death is taking place...Mother's death was totally outside the field of our control or influence. It left us powerless."

Ruth: I could not stop my dying, Robert! Just as I could not stop labor when our children were born.

Robert: I stood by your bed watching you die, Ruth, totally powerless. I could do nothing but be there, holding your hand and it was so surprising. I didn't expect your death. You went so fast. I was so busy on the phone calling for help that I didn't realize you were dying.

Nouwen: "It (death) is so new and overpowering that our previous speculations and reflections seem trivial and superficial in the presence of the awesome reality of death."

Ruth: So much so that I couldn't even talk about it in the final days, Robert.

Robert: Death was so awesome, a word that has been trivialized by pop culture, but awesome it was, Ruth. The intensity of those last hours is not describable. I feel but I cannot describe it.

Conversation on readings from Henri Nouwen's A Letter of Consolation (San Francisco; Harper & Row, 1982):

Nouwen: "[Mother's] death was a definitive end, a total break that presented itself with a finality unlike any other. For awhile we kept on living as if she were gone for a time and could return any minute."

Esbj: I had that same experience yesterday. I said, as I drove to the Cities, Ruth's absence is temporary. She'll be back.

134

She's away for a while. Then I felt the blow. **She is dead.** *She is* **permanently** *gone. She will* **never** *be back. I wept intermittently all the way to Ostrows.*

Nouwen: "We even kept doing things as if we were preparing for the moment when she would appear again on our doorsteps. But as the days passed, our hearts came to know that she was gone, never to return. And it was then that real grief began to invade us."

Esbj: I've been wondering if what I have been experiencing is less than real. My conversations with Ruth and the experience of her dynamic presence—are they figments of my imagination, devised to protect me for a time from the full impact of loss? Will those experiences fade? Will I then be left bereft, overcome at last by the loneliness her death creates? Am I, at last going to be "in for it?"

I was happy to be with Ruth, so I miss her all the more now. I foresee a loneliness as Carl and Rilla move on and Louise persists in her attempt to balance marriage and career. I am in a tunnel between times of my life, and I do not yet see what the terrain on the far end will be.

Nouwen: "When we experienced the deep loss at Mother's death, we also experienced our total inability to do anything about it. I think it is important for us to allow this experience of powerlessness in the face of Mother's death to enter deeply into our souls, because it holds the key to a deeper understanding of the meaning of death."

During the last days of July, I began missing Ruth rather more intensely. For several days spells of sobs had shaken me. I am not sure why. I have been cleaning the under-stairs storeroom and found more boxes of letters. I read some of her letters. Maybe that had made my sense of loss stronger, because I realized what a rich person she was for me and others.

We had lots of rain. Everything was a deep green, the corn especially; the broccoli heads were large. A few bushes had given us several treats of raspberries. I had Christensons, Montagues and Erlings for treats, and last night I brought berries to Lunds.

I made a center-cut slice of ham, yams and broccoli for Sunday dinner, with blueberries and frozen yogurt for dessert.

Day lilies, asters, snapdragons, pansies, vincas, petunias, geraniums, nasturtiums were all blooming. Crabgrass makes the lawn ugly. On July 30 I called Linnea and Chuck Engberg in Riverside.

Ruth's article, "On Being Bored," expresses her hope of life eternal in terms of **continuing** life, not just as a detached soul, but as an embodied self who will have no time limits on exploring, learning and relating to people. She loved this life very much, so for what's left of my time on earth, I have given her my body and brain as a "mansion." It's an imaginative matter, but who knows? I may be onto something very real.

I have often said that I have learned how to be bored, while on long car trips, for instance, as we drove for miles on miles. Perhaps it is more correct to say I've learned how **not** to be bored by the activities usually associated with boredom, such as driving on interstate highways, routine housekeeping, attending lectures, listening to poor sermons.

The hardest lesson comes, as it did to Ruth, when one lies helpless in bed with death coming on. Maybe one is then too distressed and depressed and scared to be bored.

August 18, 1990

I have been exploring, arranging and reading old letters, along with working over my journals of the past year. The tendency to lapse into nostalgia is strong, so I need to listen to my own words written to Ruth years ago.

Her story and our story must be told, however, for I am committed to telling it and telling it well. At the same time, I cannot become totally absorbed in the lure of the past and consumed by grief for the loss of Ruth. That grief has become stronger, not weaker, because as days pass I remember doing something with Ruth last year or earlier. It is August, and last year she and I went to Estes Park to hike on our favorite trails in Rocky

136

Mountain National Park. Last year about this time we had the
wonderful surprise visit from Carl and his family. I choke up when
I remember those days.

> *I do not suppress sorrow's sobs*
> *They come, like squalls of rain*
> *coursing through my brain.*

But the squalls pass, and even the more violent storms of sorrow pass. I take care of routine affairs. I am learning to cook. I am getting interested again in the theological conversations going on in the ELCA and in the professional journals. The conversations with Ruth continue on my daily walks, and they are about current and future matters. I consider her influence in me as a creative, not a confining, presence that enlivens me with a different perspective, as it did before her death.

The story of life after Ruth will go on, and she will be a part of that story. This part of the story has come to an end.

Now I must move on to consider how to prepare and publish her writings, a project which I am committed to doing.

September 11, 1990

> *Today, on the road, I ride*
> *with no one by my side;*
> *yet not alone.*
> *Fret at God? Not I!*
> *Nor do I sigh.*
> *I am not sad,*
> *or mad or glad.*
> *Today, the open road away from home,*
> *will also be my way*
> *back home.*
> *Not alone, dear heart,*
> *for in my mind we are not apart.*

So we shall talk and pray,
and we will stalk our prey,
the truth.
An audacious hunt
in which we will be
hunters stalked
by an enormous,
very gentle Silence.
Awed, we will ride
wordless, for miles
made dumb
by a truth too big
to tell.
O Lord, your spirit comes so quietly at times,
like the sound of distant traffic,
not noticed but always there.
May I now give ear to the pulse of your steadfast
and loving purpose, so that my very being
echoes your eternal love.

Norma Hervey loaned me **In the Face of Death** by Peter Noll, a book by the author facing imminent death resulting from bladder cancer. It is an honest revelation of living while dying by one who chose not to have surgery or radiation because the prospects of cure were too limited.

Ruth chose radiation treatments to gain a little time at least. She continued her life-sustaining routines until the end, and her favorite activities [such as playing the piano] as long as possible. Ruth cherished life, in all details from the view of the valley at dawn to keeping her teeth clean.

We all know we are going to die, but the time is indefinite. Ruth's time was predicted to be from two to four months. That prediction made matters radically different for her. However, she did not change her life patterns. To do so would have been a rejection of who she had been all her years. We continued our normal routines, which was an affirmation of their value to us.

Noll wonders if Eric Fromm would have written anything if he had not been read. Why write at all if not to be read? I am writing, whether I am read or not. Why? Because I live the writing life; to write is a form of living, as essential as my daily walks. I write in order to be, to have an identity, to form my self-consciousness, whether others read me [what I write] or not.

September 14, 1990

Today I am in Lansing, Michigan. I missed Ruth last night, especially when we [Carl's family and I] crossed Jolly Road. The Red Roof Motel is on Jolly Road. We stayed there when we came to Lansing the first time. Such are the little things that evoke memories.

Peter Noll makes me think about solace. It does not remove the pain, the tumor, the shame, or whatever. So what is consoling? What does it mean?

Ruth received solicitous care and attention, and she appreciated people's efforts; yet she had to endure the pain alone. Even I had to leave her. Sometimes I fussed too much over her. It would have been worse, though, to be neglected, abandoned, deprived of loving. It is love we need, even in our pain.

September 15, 1990

As I face the empirical reality of death, Ruth's already and mine in the future, what no longer makes sense? What should I give up?

I have given up the attempts to "have influence," although I am still tempted. I haven't given up running off to present forums and have too many scheduled in the coming season. I should give them up next year. Time is too precious to spread myself over innocuous appearances in various places. Habits are strong, though.

For what, then, do I want to use my time? Friendships have moved up on my list of preferences, maintained by phone, letters and visits. Writing has become a top priority, even though I may never publish my writings. [By writing] I create a world of meaning for myself—prayer and worship, as its own reward, not as a means, however.

*Confronting death, a **known** final reality, I face the question of the divine reality. Which is my god? Death? Does death drive me, or does God lure me? God is not an **empirical** reality, as death is. God's reality is seen not directly but in the man or woman of conscience and compassion; a person like Mother Teresa, utterly devoted to care of the dying and accepting her re-election [as Mother Superior] as God's will [though against hers]; or Farasani [South African Lutheran pastor] surviving torture and remaining a man of prayer; Jesus, deserted by friends, tortured and executed by enemies, feeling forsaken by God.*

*As I examine my own reasons for believing in God, one surely is that there have been men and women through the ages who are **free** from the tyranny of death and from fear of those who use the threat of death, because they have given God their ultimate devotion.*

Another reason is surely this: in me, a yearning, a longing, a thirst, for God, and a sense of wholeness that praying gives and of diminishment when I neglect praying.

September 17, 1990

*Ruth wrote about "Being Casual" [**The Lutheran**, October 21, 1964] What would I say if I were in a conversation with her about it?*

Robert: Ruth, we can be casual when nothing seems to be at stake [and when we have time on our hands]. We can amble in a leisurely way until something life-threatening faces us. Ruth, dying was no casual affair for you. You did not amble along that final road into the dark valley.

Caring for you was not casual, either. It required vigilance, alertness, deftness, practical compassion.

If being casual means being careless or indifferent, I could not be casual in my role as your husband caring for you. The time was too short, too precious, to be an ambler.

Now, even cooking calls for order, discipline, and skill. Eating well is not a casual affair; snacking on just any convenient food is casual, but not healthful eating. Sooner or later snacking is boring and tiresome, very repetitious. Cooking calls for study, knowledge of a variety of ingredients and equipment, imagination, and dexterity. Cooking is anything but a matter for being casual.

Is there no place for being casual, for ambling, for carelessness and indifference? Let's explore the places for being so. The time after a meal when we can sit down and do nothing, talk without any serious purpose.

After a strenuous, creative activity, such as preparing and delivering a sermon or a lecture.

Making love is best when one is casual, not concerned about performance, not serious about achieving some climactic ecstasy.

There is a casualness about loving people, in friendships; for one must be indifferent about impressing them and carefree about making out with them.

Being casual is the kind of detachment we need if we are to remain free from the tyranny of ideals [being successful in attaining the peaks].

Being casual is a counterpoint to being caring and creative.

Facing death, maybe, calls for a final casualness, or detachment, about living longer—not resignation in resentful submission though.

September 17, 1990

A conversation with God ... imagined:

God: I will not forsake you, even if it seems I am doing nothing to help you or lead you.

141

Robert: You are that faithful, are you? So you expect me to **trust** *you, even when circumstances do not warrant trusting you, even while in the pit. Why?*

God: Everything rather than nothing. That is creation. Would you push me to say it would be better **not** *to create anything rather than to create what a cancer or a manic-depression or a genetic defect or a child-snatcher can spoil?*

Robert: It is wrong and arrogant for me to think that my ideal world would be superior to your world. Still, I ask, is mercy unavailable to some? Nothing of value is lost to you, a theologian once said. Yet some are lost. Does that mean that the lost ones are not valuable to you?

God: Jesus said, I am the shepherd who seeks the one lost lamb; the host who invites the unwanted, undesirable street people, the physician who heals the sick. He said that my mercy falls on the just and the unjust, as rain falls on all.

Robert: Some are lost, remain lost, God, homeless, suffering unjustly. You can't get out of that one, God.

God: Your notion about me is that I am a benefactor with endless resources available to any who plead properly. Are you satisfied with such a picture of me?

Robert: I am led to such a view by what I read in the book believed to be your word. Deliverance **for the elect**. *It's in the book, God. You can't deny it.*

God: The book is not god, Robert. If you think so, you are guided by your wishful yearning about me.

Robert: Am I to ignore the advice about asking in faith and believing in your promises. Why pray if praying does not save?

God: Save from what, Robert? Praying saves you from the pit, the pits of distrust and its killing chill.

An imagined conversation with Martin Marty about his book, **A Cry of Absence,** *as preparation for conducting a retreat for seminary student interns and their supervising pastors.*

Esbj: Marty, winter is an effective image for us who live in the temperate zones, but I imagine dwellers in the tropics would not relate to it.

Marty: What would be a comparable image for hot climate people?

Esbj: How about rain, for the jungles; and aridity and heat for the deserts? Both humid and dry climates are found elsewhere.

Marty: The psalmists used aridity; the dry and thirsty land where no water is—in Psalm 63, for example.

Esbj: Being dried up is surely an image of a sufferer, and humidity is debilitating. Sweating in pain, for example, and dehydration are conditions of suffering. Could one say that the human spirit suffers in cold sweat or in parching thirst? Is human suffering illuminated by such images of physical distress?

Suffering in human relationships—do these relationships dry up, does love shrivel under some conditions? Or do they get too soggy, too damp?

What about one's intellectual good? Do we not experience times when creativity dries up, when the heat of living is too much for us, so we can't really think straight?

Your book is about the relationship with God, because the Psalms are about what happens to that relationship in times of suffering.

Marty: Yes, but you must think about the situations that result in suffering.

Esbj: Poverty, pain, crippling illness, violence, alienation, rejection, confusion, loss of meaning.

Marty: Absence is a heartfelt condition—the winter of the heart, a time that is cold, bleak, dangerous for the spirit.

Esbj: Like the emptiness on the other side of the bed, where one's mate once lay. In times of crisis, people wonder where God has gone. One can experience the absence of God more fully if one has experienced God's presence. Some people apparently have not experienced the summer of the heart, a sense of God's presence and reality. If I try to evoke it, I get blank looks.

Marty: You identify the experience of God with life at its best. I am suggesting there is another way of meeting God, in the loss of the meaning of our symbols of God, the loss of confidence in miraculous cures and quick solutions, in emptiness, rather than fullness.

Esbj: Why do we need to practice silence, emptying ourselves of pseudoassurances, like preparing for the real absence? You seem to be saying that God is truly present in the experience of emptiness, the cold snaps of winter. Enough for now.

My life seems like a seven-corner junction where I must keep an eye on traffic from six other streets: preparing for a forum, caring about family situations, household management, preparing for the interns' cluster retreat, letters, continuing work on Ruth's story.

September 29, 1990

A conversation with Ruth about punishment:

"I was punished, punished by the Lord, but not doomed to die" (Psalm 118:17).

Ruth: Was cancer my punishment? I was punished by it, doomed to die, not live. Was it the Lord who punished me?

*Robert: I find that hard to assert. If all cancer patients are being **punished** by the Lord, that makes the Lord a sadistic tyrant, or like one. If all forms of physical suffering are the work of the Lord, the Lord is a monster!*

Ruth: Either the psalmist's understanding of God is wrong, or I don't understand punishment. Maybe we should discard the term altogether.

Robert: Perhaps. Doing so, though, doesn't eliminate physical suffering that is indeed very punishing. Could we say that punishing is not meting out pain upon someone for wrongdoing?

Ruth: Wrongdoing is punishment in itself, so punishment is not arbitrarily applied.

Robert: Hold it! Are you saying your cancer is a result of your wrongdoing? That is a dubious connection.

Ruth: Environmental conditions created by human abuse could be a cause of cancer, so cancer becomes a punishing effect of human abuse. Chemical abuse, such as caused by smoking, may affect people who do not smoke, for example. The innocent are punished with the guilty ones, or by them.

Robert: There could be a genetic factor, too, and surely you are not personally in the wrong, even if you are the victim of deleterious genes.

Ruth: It seems that physical suffering is inherent in human life, not imposed. Innocence and guilt can be used only if we are talking about what we do or do not do when we can do something either good or bad.

Robert: We aren't even able to do all we see we should do, because we are limited in knowledge, strength, and time. We are mortal beings, Ruth; surely that is not our doing.

Ruth: We should do what we can, even so, Robert. I believed in being dutiful.

Robert: To avoid being punished? Because you were afraid?

Ruth: Yes, I think fear of harm is a powerful incentive to do what I know is right.

Robert: What are you afraid of, Ruth?

Ruth: One of my earliest fears was losing my parents. I think I believed that if I were a good girl I could prevent that.

Robert: It apparently is common for children to feel it is their fault if something bad happens to a parent. You were taught to fear God so you could have assumed that it was the Lord who would punish you if your parents were harmed. Surely your relationship with God matured beyond that.

Ruth: Yes, but I doubt we ever erase all childish ideas. We tend to regress to them when something bad happens. Punishment. Maybe the punishment the psalmist means is alienation from the Lord.

If I attribute the suffering I endure to the Lord's deeds, that puts me in direct conflict with the Lord, because my deeds are done to preserve and enhance my life, whereas the Lord's would seem to be to destroy and diminish my life.

Robert: That makes no sense, and you know it. God is a creating God, not a destroying God, so why would he maliciously destroy what he values? The Lord's will is not to destroy but to deliver.

October 8 , 1990
Willmar, Minnesota

I entertained seven guests last Saturday evening at a "light" supper. I had spent virtually two days choosing the menu, cleaning house, shopping, and preparing the food. I made errors, due to inexperience, and spent too much money. I chose a California-style menu because Eric and Ellie came from California, Craig lives there, Bob goes to the Bay area for study and research tours, and the rest have visited. There was lively talk about California life, its weather, population, pollution and politics. I had a centerpiece of zinnias and vincas on the table. The menu was Oriental. I attempted making a pate of yellow peas, lemon juice, white wine, chives, a touch of cream and water; it was too dry. People began to arrive while I was still trying to get it right. I was still in a T-shirt, the kitchen was a mess. Eric brought a bottle of California wine, so I served it. The eggdrop soup was ready, and two of the guests had not arrived. I called them. They were unclear about the time, probably because I was. We started on the soup, which was delicious and plentiful enough for seconds, which was fortunate because I hadn't made enough of the stir-fry main dish. I misjudged the quantity, so the helpings were too skimpy. I tried making a refrigerated fruit dessert with a meringue topping—tasted good, looked awful. [I was too naive to realize that meringues are very hard to make.]

There were nine around the table. The conversation was animated and fast-moving from topic to topic. It continued apace in the living room. Most of the guests participated. No one made a move to go home until eight o'clock. Louise cleaned up the dishes after we moved into the living room and then joined us. Ellie insisted that I sit in the rocking chair as far from the kitchen as possible.

I want to remember this, my first attempt to entertain for dinner. I learned something. It is very difficult to be both Martha and Mary. Ruth usually took the Martha role of getting the meal on the table, and I greeted and entertained the guests. [We shared preparation and cleanup in varying degrees.] An idea guiding our entertaining was hospitality, not only by providing food but freedom and space for good conversation around the table or in the living room. I learned also how costly in time, energy and money entertaining with a meal can be. No wonder Ruth had to slow the pace as she got older. I must be more cautious.

I also learned something about myself. I plunge into an interesting task **before** I am sufficiently prepared or experienced. I take chances. I did so whenever I launched a new forum topic. I agreed to teach the ethics and medicine seminar before I knew enough about biomedical issues. I tried new ideas in my classes. I learned by experience. I was never so fully prepared that I made no mistakes. So on this occasion I entertained **seven** guests and prepared a meal I had never made! I must be more deliberate and cautious. I missed Ruth, her work, her caution, her advice, her instructions. Will I stop entertaining because of this experience? No, but I hope I will be wiser.

October 9, 1990
St. Peter, Minnesota

The ache of lonesomeness is **raw** at times. Ruth is on my mind or near the edges of my attention often as I work or drive. Yesterday I saw a woman walking toward the Erickson store. She was dressed in a blue jogging suit, and looked much like Ruth from a distance. My spontaneous thought was, "Oh, Ruth is alive after all." My next thought was, "She doesn't walk with Ruth's stride." That is how hard it is for me to believe Ruth is dead. I still want to please her, want to hear her praise me, such as for making soup yesterday. And I hear her voice from within my memory, "I do, Robert, I do, from within you, where I am in your memory." And I answered, "I don't want to forget you, Ruth, ever."

October 17, 1990

In the winters of the heart there are "January thaws," moments of relief, the promise of spring. Is there not some value in the winters of the heart; in the midst of suffering are there breaks in pain? Winter—being sin-sick? Losing a sense of meaning? Absence of God? Failure? The Psalms expose the nature of suffering and express a wintry spirituality that emerges in suffering? Am I comforted in my suffering by reading the Psalms? They express my feelings honestly, the full range of them. They provide the resources of spirit I need. They move me toward living and dying in the presence of God. They express the dark side, the shadow side of the self and the community.

October 18, 1990

A wave of grief about Ruth surged over me last night on the way to choir rehearsal. The weather has turned wintry—cold wind, gusts of rain. Suddenly without warning, I thought of Ruth lying in her grave, all alone on this cold, wet night and I bawled. This is irrational, I cried. Ruth is not there! Why do I feel so sorry for her? Was it **my** loneliness that caused me grief? Maybe, but I felt bad because I couldn't be with her to comfort her, provide warmth for her. There is something desolate about winter. I think I am going to miss her more in winter during those long nights alone.

November 26, 1990

Yesterday I collected Ruth's winter clothes, so I can give them away, as she wished. Sweaters to Lutheran World Relief at church, suits and skirts to the regional treatment center. Shoes? I don't know where to send them. Is it hard to do? Not so hard. My grief comes in unexpected surges, triggered more by memories than her things. I could make it hard, if I let self-pity be my motivation. Or I can make it a creative and constructive action consistent with what Ruth and I decided to do with what time we had left. As I enter now on the anniversary of her final days, I could get sucked into a bog of grief, or I could be inspired by my life with her to tell the story in a candid way.

December 1, 1990

A year ago Ruth was in Methodist Hospital having neurological examinations, and hearing the diagnosis and recommendations for radiation. Now I am editing the story, without destroying the raw, direct language of the journal.

Thanatos came today. In it was an article, "Hints for Handling Holidays." Some observations in it:

Many bereaved families dread this season of holidays. It is normal to have anxieties and fears about it.

Remember, there is no right or wrong way to respond.

Others may not understand your decisions, but that doesn't make your decisions wrong.

Your emotions will be more volatile during the holidays.

Communicate your needs to family and friends.

Choose which activities and rituals should be observed; drop some.

Be gentle with yourself.

You can't run from reality.

Plan ahead; listen to your heart. Do only what feels right to you.

Change some of your routines, such as the time of gift exchange.

Light a candle on the table for the person who died, or an ornament for the tree, or something on the grave.

Get help with cleaning, cooking, mailing, decorating.

Find a listening partner if you need to talk.

Realize you can change your mind.

What I am doing:

Sending a Christmas message to friends, including one of Ruth's Christmas writings and a letter to Ruth from me about Christmas.

Getting gifts for Carl, Rilla, Louise, Rachel and Rebekka.

Having breakfast with Erlings on Christmas Eve morning or whenever.

Putting up a Christmas tree—during Advent, and Advent candles on table.

Entertaining friends for breakfast.

Writing in my journal.

Accepting all invitations to parties.

I don't **dread** Christmas, but I am missing Ruth's involvement. I included her in the Christmas greetings. I am thinking of going to the same tree farm for our Christmas tree as last year.

December 2, 1990

Esbj: Death...God. That is the ultimate choice as to who is Lord. Death is a visible reality. God is not. But a people of God and persons who choose to believe are irrefutable pointers and very visible. I choose to believe rather than evade believing. I choose to believe God is the invisible form of energy that is strong enough to refute the dominion of death.

The thought of life beyond death seems also compelling. I wonder if it is irradicable. Do I really entertain the hope of joining Ruth in a life after death? And do I do what I think would please her, because at a deep level I believe she sees and appreciates it? At a deep level is not the idea of another life as irrefutable as the idea of God, unprovable, yet persistent? If so, why? We long for completion of a life cut short. Why? Is this longing related somehow to divine purpose?

150

Every day we go on living, even when we know we are going to die. Ruth knew she was going to die, yet she brushed her teeth every day. It is one of the most poignant memories I have.

Our [American culture] world may be terminal, too, if the economy collapses and we lose in the Middle East. The U.S. is not invulnerable, yet we go on living, preparing for Christmas celebrations. I bought a tree yesterday at Nelson's tree farm where Ruth and I bought one last year.

God and death, both mysteries that defy human knowledge. Our concern is life in the face of death; knowing we are going to die, how shall we live? I live, not only in the face of death but in the presence of God. What I know of God is the human, Jesus Christ. God is love. Love is a reality that death cannot destroy. If I am willing to love, I pass over from death to life. Everything is reversed. I no longer live in the grasp of death; I die in the clasp of love. I spend the rest of my life loving, and this helps me discern what is important: do the loving act, which is a challenge because there is no blueprint. Loving involves me in a story, ever dramatic and unfolding.

December 31, 1990

*I am sad. I miss Ruth **very much** tonight, New Year's Eve. I realize how profound and beyond words or even tears sadness can be. However, it is different from feeling sorry for oneself. I don't feel put upon or think I have been unfairly treated. Sadness is qualitatively different? How so? A loss? Yes. No. Sadness is just the way human life is at this point. Something fine, beautiful, and lovely comes to an end. The flower fades, becomes dry, turns to dust.*

*I love Ruth, perhaps more than ever. Strange. She gives me, still, a richness I couldn't possibly earn. I cannot **do** anything for her, love her in an active sense. She is not here **by** my side. She lives in my very active mind; in memory and imagination she* *is an active influence, arousing in me a desire and determination to live in a way that would please her.*

This is an analog, in human terms, of God's aliveness, presence and influence. I want to be pleasing to God, to cause "joy in heaven" by the manner of my life here on earth. Soon 1990 will be past, in eight minutes to be precise.

I am at peace, Lord God, sad, deeply sad but at peace. I feel no need to cry for help from any of my very good friends; yet, I need them, for I do not survive in isolation. What seems good is that I can make others feel good, give them pleasure.

Happy New Year, God!

January 1, 1991

I think back to a year ago, when I prayed, hoping for a good year. Was 1990 "good"? I lost Ruth. My troubled children are facing uncertain futures. What can be "good" about such a state of affairs?

There were some good developments and experiences. Friendships, old and new, flourished. My health held up, and I think I am wiser, more mellow. I have a confidence in my capacity to survive difficulty, if I remain in communication with God. There are opportunities for useful work, for the joy of working. I wonder at the great experience I have of Ruth being still actively present and relating to me, in creative memory and imagination.

I hope for a good year, and I expect more challenging lessons in how to love you and others and myself and the earth, our home, more appropriately and enjoyably.

"On that day I will fasten Eliakim like a peg in a secure place. On that day the peg that was fastened in a secure place will give way. They will hang on him the whole weight of his ancestral house, the offspring, even the material possessions. And then the peg will give way and the load that was on it will perish" (Isaiah 22:24-25).

I was startled by this passage. I know that it is dubious practice to apply Scriptural words so directly to the present, but the passage seems so realistic about my situation.

Eliakim is a symbol for anyone, a parent, an executive, a president, a pastor, who carries the burden of power and resources and on whom others are dependent. Is it a wise saying to state that a day comes when the burden is too heavy and the "peg" will give way and the load on it will crash? Is the day coming when I, a peg, too, will collapse under the weight? I know I cannot "save" my children or anyone else that concerns me.

January 5, 1991

A conversation with Ruth:

Robert: Shabbat, Ruth, a day of release when I am free to be with thee! I usually walk to the cemetery on Saturdays, and we have a long talk on the way back. Today it is too cold, so we'll talk at home.

Ruth: A day off, Robert? You need to do a washing and other neglected chores.

Robert: I will, I will, but first a visit with you.

Ruth: I am delighted you open the gates of your mind and let me out, Bob. I want you to consider...

Robert: Oh, oh! That admonition is coming again. What now do you want?

Ruth: Consider not traveling as much as you planned.

Robert: Why? We always tried to get away from the bleak, cold depths of winter for a brief time.

Ruth: Yes, Robert, but you had me as company and I shared the driving. And we weren't staying with friends and dependent on them as you think you will be.

Robert: Yes, true. I am planning on flying, then renting a car, so I would be independent; but my purpose was primarily visits.

Ruth: Our purpose was to travel, to be detached from all ties during the trip. Visiting friends was incidental and not the main reason, as it is in your plans.

Robert: I need friends. In a sense, friendship has become a favorite leisure-time pursuit of something I value.

Ruth: Well, that's better than going on a cruise, or some other leisure time activity, like fishing. The problem, Bob, is that people have routines and hosting friends can be quite disruptive of those patterns.

Robert: I learned that on a visit where I stayed a week. It may have been annoying to have a person around that long. People feel obligated to keep a guest entertained. I don't want that.

Ruth: Your plans take too much time. You haven't had enough time as it is to work on your journal project, which you want to finish by May.

Robert: True, and I am busy teaching this month and next. I'll have to devise ways that keep my involvement less complicated and reduce preparation time. And I have settled on what to present in the forum on the Psalms at Grace Church.

Ruth: And you needn't do a lot of research for the Mt. Olivet retreat on environment. Jim Gilbert's theme will be appreciation and your's responsibility. Apply love, Robert, as paying attention and being friend to nature, love as the universal bond.

Robert: My, my! You are being very helpful this morning, Ruth. I have to keep my anxieties under control.

Ruth: You are doing well, Robert. Flow with the same light-hearted, friendly exuberance of your style at the forum at Normandale.

Back to your travel plans. Another thought, Bob, from Edgar Carlson who told you to get to your writing. "There's not that much time left," he said. You are not immortal, Robert, and may not stay healthy as long as you think, so simplify your life, be frugal, do what is most important.

Robert: Ah, Ruth, that's the crux of the matter. Travel is costly and time-consuming and tiring.

*Ruth: Consider going to Lansing—you **need** to visit the children—and to Lindsborg for Palm Sunday; and drop the Florida trip, Bob.*

Robert: Well, I'll think about it. There is a limit.

Ruth: Entertain friends at home, not big parties but twosome lunches and breakfasts.

Robert: Something easy to do. Good! I am nearing a decision about travel.

January 8, 1991

*Based on readings from Bernadette Roberts's **The Experience of No-Self: A Contemplative Journey** (Boston: Shambhala Publications, Inc., 1982):*

Bernadette Roberts: "The stillness of no-self would hold fast against the most terrifying and unknown machinations of the mind. I learned that without any feelings to back it up, the mind is absolutely powerless to effect a single thing. At the same time, it became obvious that the stillness and silence of no-self was indeed a marvelous and irreversible blessing."

Esbj: Bernadette, your observation fits very well the experience of grace. When I realize a loss of moral capacity, when I discover that I am helpless and inadequate to meet a moral demand, I experience dread, or to use Paul's language, "the wrath of God." My will is absolutely powerless to effect a single thing; my dread immobilizes me; I am in bondage. At the same time, in that utter loss of self-righteousness I become wonderfully free because of grace, the righteousness of God who does not reject me. Once experienced, that blessing of forgiveness is not reversible. Life goes on, including its burdens of moral responsibility, but it is a new life. God as demanding judge responsibility, but it is a new life. God as demanding judge disappears and a merciful grace suffuses my being and doing, the flow of life-as-it-is.

January 12, 1991

"You turn things upside down!
Shall the potter be regarded as the clay;
that the thing made should say of its maker,
'He did not make me';
the thing formed say of him who formed it,
'He has no understanding'?" (Isaiah 29:15-16).

*I am reading Isaiah as my nation moves to a brink, an abyss, a sink in the sand. A mighty machine prepares for battle against a large massed army, a "righteous cop" against an aggrieved people. Which is stronger, the sense of outrage evoked by injustice, or the **iron** will of the armed soldier? The affluent nation protecting privileges, or the angry nation suffering oppression?*

Isaiah, son of Amoz, you taught a "Word of the Lord" when you wrote, "Woe to those...who rely on horses...because they are many" (Isaiah 30:15). And "In returning and rest you shall be saved, in quietness and in trust shall be your strength." And "For the Lord is a God of justice; blessed are those who wait for him" (Isaiah 30:18).

Wait for the Lord? That's the walk to Munich, that's appeasement. Waiting? We've waited long enough. Trust? We trust that our will to fight is God's will. Oh people! Do you not remember when an armada was wrecked by a storm? Do you not know that an army can sink in sand? You think that if we wait longer the tyrant will get stronger and the cost of ousting him greater.

If that is your concern, why did you not think of the conditions of wrong that condensed the rage that awaits your sons and daughters now? *Why was your war not waged against the unjust takeovers of rich emirs? Why have you not paid the price of justice? Do you not realize yet that those who do not pay a just price for peace pay the terrible price of war?*

Remember Hitler and the horror; remember Vietnam, steamy jungle of horrid memory; remember Dachau and the vengeance of Versailles; remember oppressed Jews; remember uprooted Arabs. Oh Jerusalem, where is your peace?

I know I am venting frustration on the eve of entry into war, because warriors are set on doing battle and cannot be deterred. Where should one go who objects? Into a cave? Out to a desert place? Should the prophet become the priest standing with comfort for the warrior and his family, sharing their fears, outrage, shame, pain? Should the great lines be spoken when he is speechless? Should he become the chaplain of consolation?

The day of silence has come, a time of quietness and trust. The Muslim warrior dreams of paradise. What dreams do the western warriors have—nightmares of death and hell? Hopes of heaven, beyond tears and pain and terror?

Where is heaven? Where God is, and is God present to those who call on him in the midst of their ordinary lives? In our prayers, do we turn the potter into clay to be manipulated into shapes we desire? Is God the instrument of personal attainment?

The radical overturning of human aspirations is in the gospel of Jesus Christ, a God who enters the arena, the hearth, and the heart and lifts human life into a union with God, a peace that passes all understanding.

January 22, 1991

I prepared to speak in Kay Wold's class on the work of an ethicist in relation to health care—exposing moral phenomena, demonstrating the way we think when we are ethicists. We are all ethicists when we think about our actions, about what we ought to do next. We are historians when we think about what we have done, what caused us to act and what the consequences of action were.

We become ethicists when we ask, "What ought we do?" We ask that question when something happens or is about to happen that compels us to make a decision or a choice.

I awoke this morning. I had a choice. I could have stayed in bed a little longer, or even all day. I got up. Getting up in the morning is the most fundamental moral act I make every day. All the rest follows. I choose to live healthily, to act to enhance my life, to do something beneficial for others. To be or not to be is the fundamental issue in moral experience.

Should one write a "living will?" What is a living will? Who should prepare one? When? Why? In order to make a justifiable choice about whether or not I should prepare one, I need to know what it is and why I in particular should have one and when I should make one.

1. What is a living will? A living will is a legal document in which a person states what kinds of treatment they would decline if they should become damaged by accident or illness so badly that they will not recover and cannot make their own decisions. They can make them ahead of time in a living will.

2. Who should prepare one? I should, because such a fate could happen to me as much as to anyone else. Even if I were 23 rather than 73, I should have one because accidents and illness resulting in a terminal condition can happen to young people as well as old.

3. When should I do this? While I am healthy, of sound mind and clear about what I would want to be done if I should not be competent to make decisions about my medical care.

4. Why should I do this? That is the question that leads me to convictions I have about my life. First, to make decisions about me easier for others who would decide for me. Second, a sense of justice prompts me to reject expensive care for myself, thus using resources that might better be used for others who would derive more benefit. Not only would my dying be properly facilitated, and thus suffering diminished, but others who have to deal with me would benefit by knowledge of what I choose.

Two fundamental issues are involved—what good and whose good. If medical technology does more harm to me than good when I am in a terminal and unconscious state, then it should not be employed. If I am unconscious and out of it, I may not realize I am suffering; but others see it and should be given the benefits that come when care is terminated so I can die. Just keeping my body alive is not enough. I am more than a body; I am a conscious being, a thinking being, a social being. Would prolonged and expensive care for me be to my good?

Respect for persons is a basic belief influencing me, my own person and others as well. And a sense of justice, too, makes me ready to accept limits of treatment so that others may enjoy treatment that will do someone more good.

January 25, 1991

Reading my journal written a year ago, I see that I wrote very little about Ruth's illness. Perhaps she was still feeling well enough to function normally. She prepared meals, went grocery shopping, walked in Lund Center a few times.

I had other concerns on my mind—preparing a sermon for Gary Guptill's ordination and a chapel homily on Kai Munk.

Now I am busy again. I lectured yesterday in Steve Chew's class, Psychology 101, on "elderage" and Wednesday in Kay Wold's class on medical ethics and in the ministry class, Religion 101, on "egonomy" [self-centered life, ruled by self-interest] as compared with autonomy, hegemony and theonomy. Next Sunday I have to give a forum on "Living Marriage within a Praying Life." Coming up are leading a forum on "Coping with Parting" at First Lutheran and in February teaching Garrett Paul's religion classes and participating in a men's retreat with lectures on ethics and ecology. No wonder I have so little time to work on my journal!

January 29, 1991

Hezekiah thought, "There will be peace and security in my day" (Isaiah 39:8). King Hezekiah had recovered from an illness, boils treated with figs. He was feeling very confident, so he showed all his treasures to a Babylonian delegation. Isaiah saw that the visit really was a spy expedition and foresaw the day when Jerusalem and Judah would be conquered by Babylon.

Hezekiah's short-sighted view is common. Oh well, as long as there is no trouble in my time, I should not worry. Maybe it is impossible for people to think and act for the future. Each generation has to cope with its own times. My generation is not up to the challenges of a global environment and economy. Bush easily leads us into a costly war. "Some will suffer," an expert said on the radio this morning, but the U.S. economy will absorb the cost of war. It is resilient and huge. Why can we so easily agree to a war and just as strongly oppose any government efforts to better education, protect the environment, control crime or reduce poverty?

January 30, 1991

"He redeems my life from the grave" has several meanings. Reprieve—recovery from illness or injury—is one. Comfort—strength to face our mortality and not flee from it and be consoled in the time of our dying—is another. I hope Ruth was comforted! Life after death—the audacious and transcendent hope of a new life in heaven [the presence of God], the Resurrection—another meaning we give to reprieve."

The first two are matters of record. The last is a hope, rooted in the sense of the value of each person and in trust in the mercy and power of God.

What was it that enabled me to survive the loss of Ruth, and other losses as well, and may enable me to say life is worth living even as I am dying?

Ruth was not my "center of value," not my "god." Losing her, therefore, was not tantamount to losing ultimate value. My marriage and family were not my religion. I belong to a larger family, those who give the Lord glory and laud and honor. The worth of my life was not finally based on having Ruth. The worth of my life was not tied up totally in her presence and giftedness, so her death did not leave me utterly devastated. The phrase, oft repeated in Isaiah, "I am the Lord, beside me there is no other," is a truth for me in a time of loss, much as it seemed to be for him in a time of national defeat.

Isaiah's conviction expresses in his writings that Israel was called, chosen, to be a light to the nations, coming at a time of national disaster, not national power and prosperity. In a sense, Judah, the nation, died when the Babylonians conquered her, but the faith in the destiny of the nation survived. My faith seems to have survived, too, in this time of loss.

Also, helping me to cope with loss is the realization that I have not really lost Ruth. She is very much alive in my mind and affections, in her personal imprint in our house, as a major character in my life story for over 50 years. We shared common traditions and common interests. Communication was not cut off by conflict. Compromises were reached, sometimes painfully, but peacefully accepted. Ruth is **physically** present in the synapses of my brain. Associations connecting her with things, places, music, events bring her out of those physical stacks in my memory and I can almost hear her say, "Now Bob, you had better..."

I don't think this is so odd. Others have told me they have had similar connections with people who have died. What I have done with this sense of presence is to invent conversations with her, imagine what she might say about situations. I am coping with life in such a way as I imagine would be enjoyable to her.

I also regard my body as hers, too, so I care for it for her sake as well as my own.

Belonging to a community of friends enables me to cope with loss, too. The key to unlocking this source of strength is the willingness to let people into the story of loss. It seems better to do this than to be so private and proud, as if weakness, frailty and failure were disgraceful. It seems that people want to be a part of the story of loss, not just of celebrations of success. They need to be involved in times of trouble.

Writing a journal during those days of Ruth's final illness helped me immensely, because it makes a story out of significant experiences that would easily be forgotten. Writing the story has enhanced the quality of my life.

What a poor human world we would have if no one wrote stories! It is especially important to record the painful experiences, because they are the ones most likely to be suppressed and forgotten. I kept as honest a record as possible.

Telephone calls to and from friends have been a boon. People convey such tender affection by the tone of voice, as much as by the words they say. I do not wait for calls. If I feel a need to talk to someone, I call. Now I am using the phone to keep in touch with people I know are going through terminal times, because I know how helpful such calls can be.

Furthermore, I think it is important to have a life-style and interests that are possible and desirable for the surviving partner. In some ways I am more free to do what was not easy or appropriate while Ruth was alive. For instance, Ruth suffered anxiety attacks when traveling by air, something I am now free to do. At the same time, I must keep doing what she did for us, such as cooking and managing the household.

Are any of these suggestions "exportable" to other people? Circumstances vary, such as when death is sudden, or comes at an earlier time in life, or when a parent or child dies, or when a marriage is a mess.

Acceptance of limits—finitude and failure—as a part of the human condition, rather than denial of them, is an immensely important key to coping with loss. Ruth and I prepared ourselves over a long period of time by disciplined attention to the biblical traditions and steady practice of the rituals and liturgies of the church. Especially helpful are the Psalms, which express the full range of sorrow and joy. The psalmists teach us to number our days to gain wisdom, to walk humbly with God and to rely on his steadfast mercy. Our worth is not based ultimately on our success, strength or long life.

The reality of God's presence, power and love is more, not less, evident in times of loss, because we discover we still want to pray, even though we are going to die.

"Those that sow in tears and sorrow

shall reap with shouts of joy" (Psalm 126:6).

In the American way, reaping comes in retirement as leisure time to travel, live in sun cities, play golf. Yet, I sense a restlessness, a feeling that one must keep busy and be recognized, or life becomes painfully empty. Some elders keep working at what they have always done, because it is meaningful for them to do so.

There is another way of thinking about reaping. We have a rich harvest of experience to share, not just one's work but one's life. If one is willing to go to the field of memories and reap, and then declare a feast, which shares and celebrates a life, one will find meaning and satisfaction in the "reaping time." I can reap my life and share it in writing, teaching and hosting.

Design for a forum on coping with loss
I. Losses that cause grief

1. Death of a family member.

2. Losing positions of productivity, power or influence, and parenting.

3. Losing health, strength, sanity, mobility.

4. Losing intimacy with spouse, friends through divorce or alienation.

5. Loss of life's good sense of purpose and substance.

6. God seems to depart at times into some remote place of silence and absence when we need comfort the most.

II. Loss in relation to seasons in a human life

1. Preparatory time [sowing in spring] in schools. What are the pains young people suffer? Failure in school, not being accepted by peers, losing key games, being benched by a superior player, being dumped by a girl/boyfriend, not getting into graduate school, crippling injuries.

163

2. Participatory time [adult life]. Untimely death of spouse or child, loss of job, being bypassed in promotion to another position, financial loss, loss of status in a community due to serious mistakes, crime.

> *a. Pervading sense of emptiness, of the yawning pit, the void, loss of dignity in a crippling illness, changes in religious practices, loss of the familiar rituals, "the winter of the heart" as the spiritual condition of those who suffer losses.*
>
> *b. Loss of mental health, addiction, being excluded or shunned, rebellious children, conflict with neighbors or relatives, deterioration of neighborhood, making it less safe, having house burglarized, being mugged.*
>
> *c. Shattering of conventional faith by difficulties, loss of moral integrity.*

3. Parting season (elderage): Loss of physical attributes, such as hearing, sight, mobility; retirement from work that has been a major source of meaning, dDeath of one's spouse, realization that a marriage died years ago.

III. Creative responses to loss.

1. Preparing ahead of time.

> *a. Learning from "little deaths" all through life.*
>
> *b. Meditating on finitude and mortality, the fact of limits, not just failing but sinning.*
>
> *c. Praying, putting all of life into context of God's presence.*

2. Facing loss when it comes, rather than avoiding it.

> *a. Writing.*
>
> *b. Using the wintry psalms of lament and other psalms.*

3. Gaining and maintaining life after loss

> *a. Sharing one's story.*
>
> *b. Teaching children, the young people.*

c. *Doing something new rather than clinging to
the past.*

February 14, 1991

*Happy Valentine Day, Ruth! I open the door of memory to
let you out into my present and active life. We are "one flesh" and
death has not extinguished you. I love you each day and rejoice
that you are so much in me, at one with me. I have lost your
physical body but not you, for you are in my story. You have
shaped who I am by your friendship, your love, your admonitions,
your encouragement. I still need you, so I invent these talks.*

*I do not bemoan my loss but continue to create a new
chapter in my life, and to learn to live alone, travel alone, pray
alone. I seek companions, yes, as lunch guests here or by phoning
and writing; but no one takes your place, Ruth. You are the
special person in my life.*

*I love you, in some ways more than ever; what I mean is that
I realize now, more than ever, the strength of the bond of love.*

*Ruth's death is illuminated by her faith in God and the
central place of Jesus in her life. Last year, Lent, Holy Week and
Easter were the liturgical setting for my experiences of her
suffering, death and new life. That setting provided the deep
meaning of my experiences.*

*I wonder what being married to another woman would be
like—an adventure? I have no one in mind, and no need for such
an experience, but the imagination stirs. I am enjoying the depths
of my marriage to Ruth, just as staying at home can enrich love
and understanding of the familiar, whereas travel gives
broadening but not deepening experiences.*

February 16, 1991

*Teaching students in a classroom takes a lot of thought and
energy. When they don't understand a writer or the teacher all at
once, teaching becomes a delicate act of diplomacy. A teacher*

becomes an ambassador speaking faithfully for the author and yet sensitively aware of the reader, who may be defending his or her own intellectual, moral and religious territory.

Communication should not aim at unconditional surrender, or be a delivery of unconditional, nonnegotiable ultimatums. A tough teacher may get students to study hard, in order to get a grade, but they may remain inwardly resistant. They will cover up their rebellion with bland faces and eventually discard all that the author and I offer. I must not rob students of their sense of worth, yet I must challenge them in such a way that they will want to learn something new. The challenge fascinates me.

Richard Mouar's thoughts on the sacrifice of Jesus lead me to realize that survival is not the ultimate; sacrifice is. Women know it, in giving their bodies to a man and to the risk of birthing a baby. Men know it when they go into battle to defend a people and a territory. Life given for life. Even vegetables, fowl, fish and beast are sacrificed for my sustenance.

The Christian gospel is consistent with this pattern of real life. The Lord who is for all, in all, beyond all, does not impose on us something he did not endure first. He loves unto death, and that is very powerful. I am moved to pledge my life, not as the price for an ultimate good, but as a gift for the attainment of that good.

Thoughts about Desert Shield. Justice and peace will not be gained by high-tech might. They are lost, not gained. The Lordship of Christ challenges any tendency to yield to the dominance of a nationalistic faith, which demands unconditional loyalty and support of the effort to subdue Iraq.

Truth is the first victim. Respect for persons dwindles. Peace is postponed by growing enmity. We sacrifice our most precious asset, young men and women, and rob another nation of its most precious asset as well.

February 21, 1991

On the TV war:

It is sobering, indeed frightening, to observe how soon a population can be persuaded to change opinion from or to opposing the war to or from supporting it—accomplished by repetition day after day of the justifications and the visual aspects of preparation.

The justification of the war is oversimplified.

*1. Saddam invaded poor, helpless Kuwait—the big bully! The foe becomes **one man**, just as Hitler did in World War II. Forgotten are the thousands of sons of Iraq mothers who do the fighting, get killed and maimed. We must not see them! We, the people, must not be allowed occasions for sympathy. The foe becomes a vague shadow but highly personalized in Saddam, and about him Bush can use nasty language, like kicking his ass.*

2. We are fed numbers instead of scenes of carnage. Bombing raids are called sorties. Antipersonnel bombs that tear bodies apart are not mentioned, nor are cluster bombs, which are equally lethal. The propaganda hides anything about what war does to people and their habitations. Twenty thousand already killed!

3. American servicemen and women are featured in human interest stories designed to raise sympathy for them. We depersonalize the enemy and personalize our own troops. We have to do so, or we would feel very badly about what we are doing to sons and daughters of mothers!

I feel utterly antagonized by the man who is our president. He was vicious in his attitudes and attack on his opponent, Dukakis, in the last election by allowing the use of TV to ridicule him. So he employs the same tactics now, using inflammatory public language, such as kick him in the ass and cruel hoax— surely not designed to foster any real effort at diplomacy. An article avers that Bush has made the war a personal battle against

167

Saddam; however, it is not he who will walk out to confront the foe in a shoot-out. It is our boys who will face death.

The mission is to remove Saddam, destroy his military machine. As we do this, we wreck the country.

The boys over there want to get at it. I can imagine their disappointment if the war were canceled. The troops have been conditioned and trained for battle. The build-up has reached a momentum that is moving inexorably toward the ground war. Quick, bloody, costly—but not for generals or Bush.

For what reason? To stop the tyrant? Well, we haven't gone to war against other tyrants, some of them worse than Saddam. For national interest, apparently...oil in the Gulf region. I have heard that plans to do what we are doing have been in existence for years.

February 24, 1991

If I stop praying, I die. Some light within grows dim; the world loses its allurement. As a fish out of water loses color, so do I when I do not pray. I get dull. Everything around me looks dull. I am tired, and when I am tired it is hard to be lively. Nevertheless, I get up and say yes, yes to life, yes to God, yes to engagement.

On February 23, the last day of a men's retreat at Mount Olivet Retreat Center, I awoke with a headache after a fitful sleep. I was overtired from a busy six weeks of teaching, so weary that my brain rebelled. I could not prepare a lecture for the morning session, or think coherently. So I went for a walk and I had a wonderful experience.

The sun was almost at rise. The air was clear, crisp, near zero. The ground had five inches of fresh snow—light, fluffy snow. I walked the trail to the marsh and the island. The crunch of footsteps on the snow was the only sound. I stopped walking to listen. There was complete silence, such as I rarely experience—no bird songs—no barking dogs. I walked and stopped again. This time I heard a crow cawing and a chickadee chirping and a whistle of a bird I could not identify. Then silence. From the Psalms I heard, "My soul waits in silence." I walked. I stopped. This time I heard added voices—the drumbeat of a woodpecker, the caw of a pheasant, the chickadee. The bird world was coming alive.

If I had been unwilling to stop, to listen, I would not have heard those sounds. I went back to the dining room for coffee and conversation. I was relaxed, and I knew what I would share with the men. I shared the prayer I wrote and I described what had happened to me that morning. I told them about my experience as a resident scholar at St. John's Ecumenical Institute in 1973, and we talked about Sabbaths and prayers. I shared some passages from Brian Swimme and Annie Dillard, a potpourri session. My morning experience of silence was a moment of grace, a memory of what freedom coming with grace means and of the value of stopping to listen in silence to the still, small voice of God. The voice of God and the voice of nature become one with the voice of a man!

February 27, 1991

Specialization, says Wendell Berry, gives people warrant for withdrawing from responsibility for everything but their narrow specialty. Control is a totalitarian idea, one that discounts or ignores anything that is not subject to control, and leads to the belief that such control is possible on the grander scale of man's relationship with nature.

We have a generation of soldiers who were conditioned by playing video games, trained in simulation machines, learning to relish accurate hits, with no attention to human bodies, to carnage. I feel no pride, only outrage, because the administration and Pentagon relish such control over the press and the public. An outrage flares in me and bursts through my pen because of the arrogance and the pride of the powerful along with the susceptibility of the people to their control. I feel no pride in my record of protest. It is a private, not a public act. I suspect I believe that protest is futile, so that means I also am controlled! Criticism of the administration is considered nonsupport of the troops.

To destroy another human being, one must be either crazy or utterly convinced of the wickedness or worthlessness of someone. Any doubt undermines that certainty. Criticism is a dangerous subversion of absolute loyalty to absolute controllers.

February 28, 1991

Should pilots not be given a tour through the areas they have blasted to see the dead bodies at the other end of their transaction, the human corpses, not just burned out tanks?

The general said we will never have a body count of people killed. Each U.S. soldier killed will be brought back in a body bag and treated with due respect. Enemies will be dumped into a common grave, depersonalized disposal.

We are thinking about victories. Not who but what, which tanks, missiles, and other devices, did the job. War is mechanized and dehumanized. We forget that in a Third World country the front line is manned by peasants, ill-trained and poorly equipped.

Allies versus Iraq. Rich, developed countries against a relatively poor nation. A one-sided victory that will only intensify hostility.

Robert Bly distinguishes between love of the state and love of country. I think the state, the U.S. government, is not worthy of love, especially when its policies hurt the country. I will not love the state. It is always "Caesar" demanding total allegiance. I despise boasting by George Bush and his generals, about this one-sided victory in a war they think will be studied as a model for years to come. A model of what? How to defeat a poor, developing country governed by an oppressive elite? Who will pay for this war? Our grandchildren. Why not let Mobil Oil, Texaco, Amoco, rich Texans, big money capitalists pay for it? They wanted it, I didn't. A bitter taste? Yes, I have a bitter taste about this war. I am not proud of a people so easily swayed, of this country's war mentality, created by a mass media.

170

It seems the modern worldview is a product of merchandising. We have been sold a false world, based on economics and values and desires that are fantastical, a world in which millions of people have lost any idea of the materials, the disciplines, the restraints and the work necessary to support human life and thus have become dangerous to their own lives and the possibility of life. We see a people out of touch with growing food, working the land, slaughtering animals for food; and protected from cold and heat, wet and dry. We create, at huge expense to resources, an artificial environment for concentrated commercial activities. Can we ever recover a sense of naturalness and keep our comforts, too—warm or cooled houses, variety of foods? We must not discount the cost to environment and grandchildren. We deplete the former and deprive the latter.

March 3, 1991

*Excerpt from a letter to Lena Lindberg about Bernadette Roberts's book, **The Experience of No-Self**:*

I sense a peace of mind, a serenity of spirit, so I do not search for reasons to understand or refute Ms. Roberts's ideas. It is as if I have entered a vast silence, so complete that it makes the distinction between silence and speech irrelevant. If all is silent, one can hardly speak about silence. I am on the edge of that silence, aware of it, able to talk about it. It is as if ahead of me, almost surrounding me, a luminous fog, made so by an invisible life beyond and in it.

Whether or not I have experienced the no-self state remains a question. I don't think I have, but I think I have a glimpse of such a state as a realization that having a self is unimportant when I am in communication with God and that nothing can separate me from the love of God in Christ. The eternal is all; we are one in the one God.

The force of that truth struck me after Ruth died when someone spoke of the hope of reunion with her and I realized we were not separated by death, because we have our being in the eternal life and love of God.

I am still a distinct self, occupying space and living in a specific time. I write and the writing is an event in space, as on this page. Yet I seem also grounded in what Roberts calls the no-self. I am—stripped of all specific qualifiers, such as a man from St. Peter, retired, etc.

I sense no restless striving to attain the no-self state; I am content to be as I am. Maybe this is the aging process, a shedding of self that is natural, if unimpeded by avid desire to cling to the past.

I was impressed by Roberts's account of conversations with a friend who thought that we experience "a change of consciousness that is reserved for the final years, the last stage of life, getting ready for a new existence."

I am shedding concerns these days, career-oriented concerns, family-oriented concerns. I no longer feel I have to "make it." What goes on at the college and in the lives of my children is not really my affair, and I have very little power to influence what goes on. It is not that I am uninterested in or indifferent to what is going on. It is that I am quite free of anxiety in regard to what I should do about what happens.

March 7, 1991

Being here in Palm Bay, Florida, without Ruth is a rather poignant affair, causing some "crinkly cries" as I recall scenes where we were together, such as hiking the Atlantic beach, driving to Cape Canaveral and going to Lenten services at Peace Lutheran Church.

This morning on my walk I carried on one of my imaginary conversations with Ruth. I thrive on them. Will they ever cease? Only if I decide I don't want to continue them. And that seems unlikely.

At this time of my life, what is going on? Am I at a threshold of a new day, the beginning of a new chapter? Or am I merely a movable field of star-born energy? If so, who is the author, reflecting as I am doing? Is Ruth's urging that I stop doing so much a deep sense of destiny? I am not seeing yet what will be the pattern of my life. The past year was transitional, and the momentum of a familiar pattern kept me going on the speaking-teaching routines. I can only wait and see what is coming.

March 15, 1991

This morning, as I drove to Orlando to catch my flight, Ruth and I "talked" about love.

Robert: I love you, Ruth.

Ruth: Love is a complex affair, Robert. How do you love me?

Robert: As my very best friend, in that wonderful exchange of equals.

Ruth: I can't give you anything now, Robert.

Robert: Ah, true. But you gave me so much that I have an inheritance to draw on for the rest of my life. You gave me practical wisdom, steady faith, sense of humor and cautious reminders.

Ruth: Agape—giving love without thought of return. You can't give me anything now, Robert.

Robert: I know. But this is the way I see loving you; by caring for myself, my health, my body as if I am caring for you.

Ruth: You are reversing the rule, "Love your neighbor as yourself," by loving yourself as if you were your neighbor. Is that it?

Robert: Yes, yes. I'm the only body you have. You are in my brain. I also love you in the sense that I delight in you.

Ruth: Oh, Bob! How can you say that? My body that delighted you is gone.

Robert: Of course it is, but I imagine it. I fantasize, recall you, your laugh, your eyes, your knees, your trim hips. My fantasies are not as delightful as having you at my side as we walk, ride or lie in bed, but they are delightful—and even erotic!

March 17, 1991

Suddenly, like the rain or snow squalls of a breezy March day, grief comes these days. Seeing the sign for Highway 129 here in Lansing, Michigan, I remembered a moment from the past as Ruth and I were coming into Lansing from Toronto.

"Robert, why are you taking this route **around** Lansing?"

"It's quicker than going through the city." But it wasn't. And Ruth was right. The belt-line highway went too far west.

Remembering that time, I sobbed silently while sitting next to Carl. He did not notice and I said nothing. My face crinkled silently. How quickly a life goes! Yet how rich while it lasts. I cherish every memory, so the loss is not emptiness, and it gives a reason to cry gladly. Ruth is still a lively presence. I mourn because she can't be here to enjoy our ongoing experiences.

"Ruth, you would have been delighted by the service at Bethlehem Church yesterday, sitting with Rachel and Rebekka, who behaved so well, seeing Carl and Rilla singing in the choir procession, being in the lively adult class, hearing a fine sermon and singing familiar hymns."

March 21, 1991
St. Peter, Minnesota

First day of spring.
What birds will sing?
Foggy, following thunder and rain.

I'm home, glad to be home, aware of Ruth's subtle presence here and in my heart and mind. I miss her very much more when I am traveling than when I am home, perhaps because the companionship was so close on trips as she sat next to me and we conversed. Now, riding alone is a lonely experience and sobs suddenly surge up.

174

March 22, 1991

*We are surrounded, battered, swept along by outer change. The inner self adapts, adjusts, survives, but too often does not undergo any deep transformation. Change refers to adaptation, without necessarily involving any **newness of being**. Transformation implies new being, a new creative energy flowing from the center which acts with creative power upon surrounding events.*

I wonder, has Ruth's death been an event that changed my situation without transforming me? It's hard to assess myself. I believe I have not just reacted, but responded in intentional ways to change my perspective and ways of living. At any rate, I believe in making responses when change comes. I hope I will be able to face my own final end with as much courage as Ruth did. She was scared and sad but did not stop praying.

March 24, 1991

I was in bed with an annoying and debilitating cold. I missed the solicitous, tender, practical care Ruth gave me when I was ill. I remembered being ill with a virus in January 1969, after we came home from Santa Barbara, California. I had a high fever and was weak and depressed. While Ruth was at work, I felt very lonely and so paced to the window to watch for her coming at noon and in the afternoon. When she appeared around the corner, a strong delight and gladness flooded me. I needed her, and realized how much I valued her as my dearest companion. No swinging woman's figure will come down the street, no car with her driving home, only lively memories to stir longing and gladness.

Epilogue

The following journal entries were meditations around the anniversary of Ruth's death, and at a time when I was hospitalized with pneumonia.

March 31, 1991
Easter Sunday

I am keeping the Easter Feast by listening to Bach's Easter Oratorio, a wondrous, strong music expressing the strange and surprising experience of the victory we call Resurrection.

I am coping with pneumonia. During the night I listened to "Jazz through the Night." Then I got up, put on my blue bear sweatshirt and made a cup of Swiss Mocha coffee, ate six prunes, and chose to reread Madeleine L'Engle's **Two-Part Invention**, as a ritual act of remembering and rejoicing in our marriage. These are the anniversaries of Ruth's final days, and it is very essential that I use this seclusion for remembering and writing.

I am listening to Bach's St. Matthew's Passion, deeply moving music and poetry. Reading the recitative about Joseph of Arimethea begging for the body of Jesus reminded me of the morticians coming for Ruth's body after she died.

> At evening, hour of calm and peace,
> was Adam's fall made manifest.
> At evening, too, the Lord's redeeming love;
> At evening homeward turned the dove
> and bore the olive leaf as token.
> O beauteous time! O evening hour!
> Our lasting peace is now with God made sure,
> For Jesus hath his cross endured,
> His body sinks to rest.
> Go, loving servant, ask then it.
> Go, be it thine, the lifeless Savior's Body.
> O wondrous Gift, a precious holy burden.

So I wrote:

> Dear, dear Ruth,
> At evening your breathing also ceased,
> and then your suffering, too.

At evening, like a dove, you homeward flew,

And I said good-bye to you.

Your hand went limp, you said no more.

Your body sank to rest.

Your head lay there, so still

that once was so full of wit and thought.

They came, the Josephs of our town,

to tend to your demise

with care and solemn sense of death.

I watched them take you away,

O wondrous gift of God to me,

A precious presence gone.

I remained, alone, to pray

as you did every day.

April 6, 1991

*In the hospital from April 2 to April 6 recuperating on IV from
pneumonia:*

I am feeling the loss of Ruth intensely. I am alone. The house feels so
empty, silent, dead. There are no household noises. It is warm outside, so even
the furnace is silent. When I came home from the hospital this morning the
house felt empty, silent, as if it had been left suddenly by its people. Usually
when I go away I put the house in order, so when I come back it will be clean
and picked up. But I was too ill to do so when I went to the doctor last
Tuesday and then to the hospital. The Easter lily Lunds gave me had two
wilted blossoms. The bed was unmade, and the books I had with me were still
piled on the bed. One of the plants had wilted from lack of water. There were
little piles of clutter here and there. I've never before felt so strongly as now
that Ruth is no longer here; a very odd, surprising sensation of absence.

The onslaught of pneumonia has made me feel weak, tired, so I am
vulnerable to depression.

For some reason, April 3, the anniversary of Ruth's death, felt like
the end. All year since she died I have been remembering her final year. Now,

177

remembering seems over in the sense of reliving those times. I wonder if the conversations will cease, too. They have been a wonderful and consoling, if imaginary, way for continuing the relationship.

Now I feel desolate and sad in a different mode, which I am having a hard time describing.

People have been attentive, today as well as when I was in the hospital. Chet came for me, took my checks to the bank and mail to the post office. Marian invited me for a lovely lunch. Betsy Paul brought me five balloons with "happy birthday" on them. Louise called twice. Kyle called. Betty called and will bring bread. There were cards and interesting notes from other friends and family. As usual I am overwhelmed by their kindness and generosity. Such attention ameliorates loneliness.

Then the time comes when no one can be what Ruth is to me, my very flesh, my heart's companion. It's her voice I want to hear. It's her body I want beside me. It's her laughter, her tender care I need.

At the moment, however, it seems I need to let the full force of absence sweep over me.

O Lord of mercy, I believe that I live within the embrace of your eternal love, and this unites me with Ruth; but I feel alone, Lord, alone.

Maybe being ill, alone, makes me more aware of Ruth's absence. Of course, others help, but in the moments of distress, before help comes, I am utterly alone, and will be when illness comes again. I am glad Ruth was not the survivor who would be alone without me. I am grateful that I could be her companion at her end time. Oh, Ruth, I miss you so much!

I made the bed and lay on it for a while to rest.
Snatches of memory came back:
Ruth standing at the sink and preparing supper, visible from the yard where I was working. Now the window is empty.
Ruth walking home along Valley View after work. Now, no one comes.

Ruth napping, on her tummy, in bed next to me. Now, only an empty space.

Ruth playing the piano. Now, silent keys, untouched.

Ruth sitting across from me at breakfast, eating pancakes with small dabs of syrup and butter on them. Now, no plate there, no breakfast talk.

Absence. Not as poignant until now. Why now?

The grief is almost nauseous. It could become a malady if I indulge in it, wallow in it.

Even so, I must describe this experience as it happens. I wonder if it will be permanent. I know Ruth is in my memory, a physical presence there and my very lively companion whom I imagine talking as we walk. We shall see.

8:55 p.m. Distractions to fill the empty place:

A letter to a friend.

A bite to eat.

Folding and putting away the washing.

A call to John and Carol.

*I can't keep **doing.***

The utter silence remains. I am in an empty place. I feel reluctant to start a conversation with Ruth. I wonder why. She is no more dead than she was a year ago, or last month.

Will I be able to stand this new loneliness? Will it pass?

April 7, 1991
Anniversary of Ruth's Funeral

*Wendell Berry says in **Standing by Words** (San Francisco: North Point Press, 1983), "The source of our poetry is the idea that poetry must be used for something, must serve something greater or higher than itself. It is a way to learn, know, celebrate and remember the truth...as Yeats said, 'To bring the soul of Man to God.'"*

I agree with Berry that the desire in such poets as Dante and Milton was not to be famous but to be worthy of the subject and to please God. Such was the use of their poetry.

This passage is a message to me about my work on Ruth's writings. I want to be worthy of them, see them as serving a purpose beyond her, and beyond themselves. Working on them is a way for me to learn, to celebrate, to remember the truth, and to bring the human soul to God.

So I pray, Lord, make me an instrument of such worthy purposes, not to glorify Ruth but to see her as your work. I feel strongly the desire to accomplish this work, so I beseech you for strength and firmness of resolve to do it.

What a rare occurrence Ruth's death is—its timing, its setting, the opportunity for conversation, for coming to terms with her dying. My sense of Ruth's value is so strong it nearly overwhelms me.

Where does God fit in? It is absurd, isn't it, to think God arbitrarily rescues someone, or as arbitrarily abandons someone else?

I read **The Lutheran** articles on the resurrection of Jesus while I was in the hospital. They affirm the Resurrection as the indispensable foundation of the Christian faith. "If Christ had not been raised, your faith is in vain." They assume, it seems, a literal revival or resuscitation of the body, in some mysterious, unique way. The body was there; and then it wasn't there. He appeared. He vanished.

*Are we to believe that **once**, only once, God reversed physical death; thus, in principle, destroying its power to claim us as the final and most powerful reality? This "intervention model" reminds me of how oppressed nations might have hopes for liberation raised by the intervention of a superpower to rid a country of a tyrant. I can't believe God is as undependable as a superstate government which intervenes only when its own*

180

interests are at stake. If God could do so once, in Jesus' life, why not for all? If not for all, why not at least for those, who like Jesus, strive to live a righteous life in faith?

Well, being revived after dying is not the point at all. Jesus really died. Either he did or nobody really dies. Ah, but I forget that Jesus was no ordinary human; Jesus was the Son of God, Divine. His resurrection is God's resurrection, the sign of God's victory over death. The sign that death does not end it all. We live toward God, not toward death.

Jesus' presence is a physical reality, not in his particular body but in a body of believers who remember the truth, who celebrate his life, who practice what he did. We are to live in and for God; that is what I believe. I would be something other than what I am if I were not a member of that body, the church, the communion of saints.

O Lord, I am as puzzled as ever by these stories and ever subject to doubt as I suffer the force of death. I am tottering a bit right now, staggered by the loss of Ruth. I pray that out of the depths I will be able to cry, and that my experience may be used to good purpose for the sake of others. I pray for the ones who are also staggering under loss—Emma, Marian, Bob and Elsie, Louise, Karen. Be their strength and source of serenity. Use me, if you can.

I tend to personalize God as if he were a potentate, when actually I pray to connect with the pervasive presence of God's lively love; I, too, am depleted for the moment.

This quiet Sunday morning, so unrushed, was the kind of time Ruth longed for. So often we were so rushed—by services to attend or lead. Maybe, in some other mode of being, she is enjoying the Sabbath rest in a lively, creative and peaceful manner, maybe in the stillness of this house. Maybe she is not absent at all, just quiet.

It is evening now after a lovely, warm day, with white cumulus clouds, bursting buds, singing birds. I put the Easter lily on Ruth's grave, then

181

drove out to Lake Washington to Connor's Point, as Ruth and I did once last winter. I listened to the tape of her burial service. In church this morning I sat next to Betty A. who lost her husband a short time ago. I had to remain seated during the alleluia and the gospel, because I felt weak and I pulled a chest muscle when I coughed.

This afternoon I searched for the photo of my cousin Lorraine and me, as flower girl and ring bearer at Aunt Ann's and Uncle John's wedding. I want to send it to Lorraine for an anniversary party. I looked in Ruth's albums and saw photos that illustrate times in her life story. I also found in a looseleaf notebook letters she wrote to her parents from January to March 1941. I found one describing the concert of the Minneapolis Symphony. She said very little, only, "I went with Bob." Only that for the first really big date we had!

I am not wallowing in my sorrow, but I am not evading it either. I may as well experience it head-on.

Part IV
Reflections on the Moral Meaning of Terminal Illness

Dear Zoe,

You have been on my mind lately. For over a year I have been reflecting on the experiences described in the journal, trying to make some meaning out of the experiences that could be shared. I remembered your letter written to me shortly before Ruth died in which you posed some questions. I read them and my brief, unfinished answers again in the April 1 journal entry. I was too involved in caring for Ruth to finish them and respond to your letter. Now I have the time and enough distance from those events to do so. You may wonder why I have chosen you among so many, since I hope to share these reflections with others. You have a special place in the story.

One day, almost twenty years ago, you came in tears to my office at the college. A friend dear to you had just died. You entered my life at a time of your grief. Years later, a few days before Ruth died, you came into my life at the time of my grief by way of the letter. At the time you wrote it, your mother-in-law had a tumor in the brain, as Ruth did, and was dying, as Ruth was. Our grief, yours then and mine later, and the fact that Ruth's final days and those of your mother-in-law a month later were happening at the same time, bind us in a special way. Common experience of loss binds me to other friends as well, but you are special in another way.

You joined me in the ethics and medicine seminar I was teaching in a common effort to understand the moral aspects of medical science and practice. Maybe that experience was not on your mind when you wrote to me, but the questions showed that you had more than ordinary understanding of the situation I was facing. Perhaps a teacher may be permitted to believe that you learned something in that course. The questions probed to the heart of the matter—the experience of Ruth's suffering and my sorrow, the organization of care to which we had access when we needed help, and the meaning of the experience of suffering. Now they help me to focus my thoughts on what is important.

However, the questions were not the kind you and others would ask in that class, not academic questions calling for scholarly answers. They were questions from your heart to mine, questions prompted by the situation in your family as well as mine. The questions are another bond between us. Answering them, then and even now, in the academic language of ethics, expounding on such matters as "ethical process," or the difference between "teleological" and "deontological" theories, is not appropriate. To do so would be like a doctor answering questions of a patient with the technical medical terms a specialist would use in letters to a patient's family doctor. My knowledge of ethics and theology was relevant, but the style and language is inappropriate. My reflections in recent months have made me realize the value of the tools of thoughtful analysis of moral experience gained in the study of ethics.

I want my meditations to be meaningful to you and to others who were students in that seminar and to strangers whose only bond to me is the common experience of final time, particularly for other husbands whose wives have had breast cancer.

What have I learned?

Terminal illness is not just a medical matter; it is a moral affair.

Humans are not just biological organisms or social animals; we are moral persons who feel strongly about experiences, think about them, question, form ideas and beliefs in our search for meaning, transform our longings into dreams, and make significant decisions.

The relationship between patient and physician is a dynamic moral drama happening at center stage in the complex medical care system.

That system is an organization designed to attain important human objectives, including distributing medical services and supplies to those who need them, advancing medical science and practice, and training professional practitioners. As such, it has a mixed record of accomplishment and failure when assessed by the criteria of fairness and frugality and commitment to the whole person.

184

The capacity to cope well with the fates of illness and death and to sustain the effort of maintaining health and providing medical care must be renewed by energy sources from beyond medical science and its system. The energies are spiritual, not technological or political or economic.

The questions you raised cannot be answered merely with facts and technical knowledge. They are moral issues about value and duty and religious questions about identity, destiny and ultimate reality.

What will be exportable, of value to you or others from what I have learned? Everyone's experience is in many respects unique, but there are also features that are common, if not universal. Others, too, have had experience with illness; by sharing we may learn from each other how to cope with such challenges, especially those that come at the end of life.

Final Time as Moral Experience

George Forell used a vivid image about moral decision in his book **Ethics Of Decision** (Philadelphia: Muehlenberg, 1955). It serves me as a parable about fate.

It is night. A man is in a boat that is slowly drifting toward a roaring waterfall. This man, who is wide awake in his boat, cannot escape making a decision. It is true that all his choices may be ultimately meaningless. He may start rowing madly and still be carried by the currents across the brink to his destruction. He may do nothing at all and the current may wedge him against a rock and keep him safely until daybreak. Yet this man does not know which is the proper decision. The current is carrying his boat whether he likes it or not. He cannot ask for time out while he makes up his mind as to the possible alternatives. There he sits in his boat, and everything that he does or does not do is committing him. Not to make a decision is also a decision. He cannot escape his freedom; he is bound to be free.

Fate is a word for those experiences we do not expect, plan for or want. Fate happens to us. We do not design fate. We do not desire much of what fate brings to us. Sometimes our fate is a pleasant surprise, but not always. Surely Ruth's diabetes and cancer were not desired fates; yet they happened to her. Her illnesses and her death were not fates I desired for my life either, but they happened to me. Your friend's death at a young age and your mother-in-law's death were ineluctable. They could not be avoided or escaped. Such fates mean we are not in complete control of our lives. No one is, not one. Ruth could not stop her dying. I could not. Physicians could not. Final time comes for all of us, sooner or later. It is our human fate to live in the face of the prospect of death.

However, we are not entirely helpless. We also have the fate of being moral beings, not just creatures of biological and social development. We are aware of the past and the future and can see more than one way to act. Even when we react to biological drives and social pressures, we also are able to think somewhat reasonably about our reactions, if not at the moment of decision, surely before we decide or afterward.

Thus our fate is also to make choices. We cannot escape, even when we would rather not have to make decisions. We often fail to make the best choices; we get ourselves into trouble because of them; we have choices about fate—to deny fate, refuse to see that we are aging, or dying; or to fight fate as enemy on the assumption that we really are in control and only temporarily out of control, that if we fight hard enough we can regain control; or to face fate in appropriate ways; to say, yes, this is happening; and no, I am not in complete control; and yes, I can act to modify that fate if I am courageous, candid and creative. This is our fate, even in the shadow of imminent death, even during final time. Peter Noll's journal makes this very evident, for he made significant choices — not to have therapy that might not work, instead choosing to live as fully as possible while in a terminal illness.

I think my work in ethics helped me understand fate, not as just blind chance, but as challenge, as moral challenge. Ruth's final time was a moral experience. This was apparent to me and helped me understand the situation more clearly. Experiencing the threat of imminent death and having time to think about it gave me an opportunity to test this assertion. While there were strong biological factors affecting my behavior and Ruth's and social influences on our attitudes and actions, we could not suppress our need to think, to talk, to write, and to pray. We humans are thinking, meditating and praying beings, even when we are losing both physical and social values. Surely this was the case with me, as the journal shows; and Ruth also, though she was dying. She was so, for example, when she said, near the end of her life, "It is hard to face reality;" and in spite of her difficulty with communicating by that time, she was able to join in the prayers, even during her last hours.

This does not discount the influence of biological necessities or social needs. Our capacity for thought is dependent on both physical capacity and social influences. However, we can think about those influences. We think, we imagine, we describe, we plan, we fantasize; we borrow the language of our culture, but we use that language creatively to express our own experience. We also moralize. We have a need to evaluate and judge attitudes and conduct.

Reviewing the story of Ruth's final time I saw six situations in which decisions had to be made that were significant and which are examples of moral experience.

[1] When Ruth discovered the lump in her breast in August 1987 in a motel in Billings, Montana, on our way to a vacation in Rocky Mountain National Park, she decided to delay telling me about it. She was the sole actor on the stage.

[2] When she told me, I became a character in the drama, affected by what was happening and having an active part in the decision. We decided to whom we should go for help. I called my friend for advice; we decided to take his advice and go to Mayo Clinic for medical care.

[3] If the biopsy revealed that the tumor was malignant, Ruth decided to give approval for surgery in the same operation and to follow the post-operative care ordered by her physicians.

[4] When she learned in early December 1989 that the cancer had spread to the cerebellum, Ruth decided to accept medical judgment about her terminal illness and what to do about it, and I concurred.

[5] When her condition became severe at the end of February 1990, I made decisions about where Ruth should have care and about who should take

187

care of her and how to do so—with the advice and consent of others and taking her desires into account.

[6] Facing the prospect of life without Ruth after her death, I made decisions about what to make of my life after she died on April 3, 1990.

During these experiences, neither of us ceased being moral beings when we suffered conditions that hurt us and kept us from normal activities. Living in the presence of someone who is terminally ill and dying, I could not escape what was happening, no more than I could escape the air I breathe. I had to respond, for even doing nothing is a response of a kind. This is the way it is for all of us. Even if you and I choose to do nothing but stand there, our decisions have moral meaning and consequences. Your fate, as well as mine, is to be able not only to react but to respond, not only to do something or not, but to think about what we do.

The Meaning of Responsibility

We who are recipients of medical care, and that includes medical professionals who also get sick, or injured and eventually enter their final time, have responsibilities, not just rights to claim. That is what I see now, in retrospect.

What does this mean?

One tradition of ethics describes responsibility in terms of establishing goals, formulating plans and attaining the results we believe are good. There is a technical term for it, teleological, but the important fact is that some people live by the assumption that they can maintain control of their lives by doing this.

Instantly comes to mind the old adage, "The best laid plans of mice and men..." The assumption that we can attain and maintain control of our lives by having a plan to follow is questionable in the light of broad experience. The plan Ruth followed after her mastectomy did not result in controlling the cancer.

Another tradition fosters the idea that the responsible person is one who is loyal to tradition, abides by principles, follows the book of rules. That also has a technical label, deontological. This tradition fosters conservative responses to fate, even when one's fate is to deal with dynamic changes, such as we have seen in the biomedical revolution and its impact on health care. The traditional principles of medical ethics and the rules on which they are based have been severely tested by the developments in medical technology which can be used to keep terminally-ill people from dying. The basic principles, such as nonmaleficence (do no harm), veracity, beneficence, justice, sometimes are in conflict. It may be harmful to be candid with a patient about a condition that may be terminal; and to do everything beneficial for some patients may mean depriving other patients of adequate care, and thus justice suffers. This is not a new issue, for Jesus had a conflict with his critics about whether honoring the sabbath or doing mercy should have priority.

A third alternative has been discerned by H. Richard Niebuhr and described in his book, **The Responsible Self: An Essay in Christian Moral Philosophy** (New York: Harper & Row, 1963). This is a rich and complex position, so my attempts to give a simple explanation will fall short. We humans are capable, not just of imagining our futures or being loyal to our traditions; we are capable of **response**. The word response comes from a Latin root word, **spondere + re**, which means to pledge back to. This position describes the ability and readiness of humans to be able to do more than react to change, to assess change, to understand change as a challenge. Behind the word is a tradition of making covenants, promises, oaths, vows; but there is more than conformity to rules involved. A person informed by this way of understanding moral life sees life as an ongoing story in which he makes creative moves in response to the challenges that come, who sees his life in relation to a larger context, a more comprehensive story.

This position is similar to one called situation ethics, which also calls upon one to size up dynamic situations and to act appropriately, not just impulsively or out of sentiment or impulse. However, responsibility entails both respect for tradition and creative thinking about the future. Membership in community and working in systems of law and structure are essential, although not absolute. There must be a point beyond the system where a person or protest group takes a stand, and it is a point that transcends both plans and principles in a relationship to what one experiences as ultimate and unconditional.

You may see, from the journal entries, that my view of responsibility comes closest to this one. For me the life task is not that of an architect and builder who designs and completes a plan by the end of life; nor is my task like that of a gardener who fosters a natural, organic growth toward fruition. I see life as a story, a large story, in which I have an active part in shaping it but do not control it. Life is not just dynamic, it is dramatic. It can be comic or tragic, and usually is a poignant mixture of both sorrow and happiness, success and failure. The task of such a story-oriented life is to be engaged in the story, making moves whether muddling through or brilliantly adaptive, that are in the story itself. I see myself, not as the controlling author but as a responsive actor whose distinct experience and character affect what happens.

With this in mind, you will understand better, I hope, my comments on what shaped Ruth's and my actions in this story of final time.

Terminal Illness as Part of a Long Story

Dear Zoe,

You asked me why the conclusion of a life story must entail suffering, emotional agony, and dreadful experiences. Final time is a relatively brief episode in a long story, at least for people who live the typical life span of threescore years and ten. Ruth and I had enjoyed a rich friendship, beginning during our college days—most of it within our marriage, which lasted for 45 years. The moral experiences we had during final time have connections with past and future. They are not isolated events.

The six situations calling for decisions were linked together in a developing story which began before Ruth got cancer and continued after her death.

This was not the first time illness had beset us. Before I was ten there were four deaths in my family. My grandpa Swenson shot himself to death, either by accident or deliberately. A cousin died in infancy. An aunt died in childbirth. And my mother died after five years of trying to recover from tuberculosis. My father died of heart attack when he was seventy-three. My second mother, Anna, died in a nursing home three years after a disabling stroke. I believe those experiences prepared me for Ruth's illness and death.

Ruth's mother died of breast cancer when she was sixty, her father died of heart attack when he was sixty-nine, and two of her aunts, sisters of her father, had cancer. The presence of cancer in her family suggests that genetic heritage was an aspect of Ruth's fate.

Ruth made a decision long before the story of her final illness began that had very significant consequences. She chose not to have regular mammograms and relied instead on occasional manual examinations of her breasts. This was her response to the prospect of getting breast cancer in the future.

In 1992 about 180,000 women in this country are expected to develop this disease, and of that group about 46,000 will die from it. Mammograms can detect cancerous lumps as much as two years before manual breast exams. Women who find lumps early have a ninety percent survival rate.

Would Ruth have discovered the lumps early enough to forestall her death if she had chosen to have mammograms? I don't know. The odds might have been in her favor if she had chosen to have them. However, medical opinion varies and fluctuates about the value and safety of mammograms; currently they are regarded as safe and useful.

Ruth's prior decision about mammograms illustrates how past events influence the future. Consequences come, but we cannot predict what they will be with certainty or control the effects of our decisions.

Two earlier experiences with illnesses affected our responses when Ruth developed terminal cancer in that they set a pattern for us.

After Louise, our first child, was born, Ruth suffered a depression so severe that she went to a psychiatrist for help. She was especially troubled by the sense of God's absence in her life. The psychiatrist's response to her description of how she was feeling was to tell her she was too religious and advised her to be less conscientious. She refused to continue with him. She realized that psychiatrists could not cure her of her depression. It was her responsibility to deal with her condition. They, or their writings, might be helpful, but they could not help her if she would not assume responsibility for her own health. Then, as well as at the end of her time, my place was with her to do what I could to help her. We read books and articles, we talked, we muddled through as best we could. Her recovery took time. It was hard work.

191

She had to force herself to go to church, to be in any gathering of people. She persisted. Eventually she came out of her depression and the sense of divine presence came back.

The pattern of that experience is evident, as I see it in retrospect, in our response to the next challenge. When Ruth was about forty she became diabetic. She took primary responsibility for maintaining her health. She did not become dependent on physicians or me, except when she was in need of counsel or support in times when she was not capable of self-care. Managing diabetes must be a personal work. To monitor and keep in balance exercise, insulin dosages and eating the right foods requires discipline which cannot be imposed by someone or entrusted to someone else. Doctors can provide generalized information, but only the person knows her own body well enough to care for it properly. There were times when Ruth had insulin reactions so severe that she needed my help to come out of them. I have lost count of the times that I had to force her to eat something sweet because she had lost her judgment. There were times when her reaction was so severe that I could not help her. Several times I had to call our doctor for help, or 911, such as the incident in Palm Bay described in the journal.

When Ruth was beset with cancer, the same combination of making use of medical professionals, taking personal responsibility for care and having my support is evident in Ruth's story.

Two minor incidents happened recently that started me thinking about the way particular moral experiences are not isolated events but have connections with responses to past events, and have impacts on the future as well.

One morning before breakfast my granddaughter Rebekka came from her bedroom. "Grandpa, I don't feel good. Let me lie on the sofa." She had an upset stomach, had vomited, and was carrying a bowl in case she did so again. Well, I was sitting on the sofa doing my routine morning meditations. Now she wanted my place and attention. Her parents were sleeping downstairs. Why should I take care of the child; that was **their** responsibility, was it not? I had my own agenda, important to me. Having grandchildren in the house was pleasant much of the time, tolerable at other times; but this, was this not asking too much of me, to take care of **their** child and to give up my place to

192

her? I gave my granddaughter the sofa, got a blanket for her and a sheet on which to lie, and ate breakfast.

My granddaughter's illness and request were not something I either expected or wanted at that moment. It is a simple illustration of moral experience in which I had to make a choice.

I connected this action of mine with the news I had heard the night before about a marriage breaking up as one of the partners decided to separate. I thought about our marriage and why I stood by Ruth during her final time. What if her illness had happened during the busiest, most productive years of my life rather than now near the end of our lives? Would I have been willing then to stand by, to do what I have done? Would terminal illness have been too much for me, so that I would have said, "Let someone else take care of her?" Would I have split, because marriage had become more of a burden than a blessing? Was I in marriage only for what I could get out of it, whatever I wanted? Was there a limit beyond which I could not stand firm?

I realized that Ruth's terminal illness was just one chapter in a long story of our friendship and marriage. Caring for and standing by Ruth during this time was a continuation of that story, a story replete with moral experiences.

I saw in an instant what was at stake because of the juxtaposition of these two incidents. We so often want to get out and away and we say, "I don't want to do it. Let someone else do it. This is too much. I'm not going to put up with anything more. Good-bye." We want to get out from a situation that we think is too much for us. Deciding to get out or to stay is at the heart of moral experience.

When Ruth wanted to come home at the end of her time, I knew what I must do, and wanted to do. The issue was not whether or not it was my duty to care for her at that time. It was whether or not I could care for her appropriately. That has been the question all our married life. We love each other, yes; but what action was appropriate as a practical expression of that love? Who would do what? If the garbage containers are full, who should empty them? "You do it, Ruth; I'm too busy." Yes, yes, I will admit it. There were all too many times when I relied on her to do something, when I ignored obvious tasks, expected her to do them.

When Ruth entered her final days, I went with her as far as I could go. I had an option—to abandon her, let someone else take care of her, to judge that this was too much to expect of me. I did not even consider that option. I chose to stand by her and take care of her as best I could. I realized that I **wanted** to do so more than I wanted to do anything else at that time, even though I surmised that I was not up to doing it adequately, that it was a challenge too great for me. My commitment to stand by Ruth and take care of her was made many years ago. When I married her I lost the luxury of options. A friend made that point to me years ago when he said, "Only people who have not made decisions and commitments have the luxury of considering options." I made a vow to Ruth, in the presence of God, a presiding pastor [her father] and in the presence of friends and acquaintances to be faithful to her, "in sickness and in health...until death doth us part." Vows can be broken, of course, and commitments canceled; but they are very solemn affairs linking us to one another and also to many people in family and friendship circles and congregations of faith, and to God.

Our marriage had endured over many years in which we coped with difficulties that strained our commitment to each other. We had survived them, even those that seemed at the time to be more than we could bear. In our last time together, the bond was strong. I had the option of abandoning Ruth only in the abstract, not in real life. The habit of faithfulness was too strong; my love for Ruth, and hers for me, had become so sturdy, so satisfying, so subtle and so supple that the loss coming with abandoning her to others would have been more intolerable than to lose her in death. This history of shared difficulties and delights prepared us for this final time.

Zoe, I realize that my reaction might have been different if I had lost Ruth in her youth, as you lost your friend; or if care for her had lasted so long or had become so difficult that I was too worn-out to continue. That has been the case with friends my age whose partners have had long and anguished final times. I do not tell you about our story to impress you with an example to follow. It is merely one man's story, with which others can make comparisons.

This meditation on our marriage reminds me of an important word in ethics—character. The word comes from a Greek word which means "to engrave." It seems that past experiences, including our upbringing and previous actions, develop characteristic ways of responding to challenge and change. Character, however, is not carved in stone but in pliable humans prone to make mistakes. We are "characters" within a dynamic story in which we must continue to made decisions, some of which are not very sound. The biblical word, repentance, illuminates the need for frequent assessment. Coming from a Greek word which means change of mind, repentance is a recurrent act in the moral life.

The Experience of Terminal Illness and Death

Dear Zoe,

One of your questions was "Why does the final chapter of a life so rich come to its conclusion in suffering, pain, emotional agony, and dreadful shared experiences? Is it fair? Does this suffering, so impossible to describe, have meaning?"

My answer was brief. We are confronted by a dark mystery. I need to say more now, something about the experience of final time. There are aspects of the experience of terminal illness and death that elude description and analysis by any single person. Surely this is so when one tries to describe another person's final days. I could only watch from a distance as Ruth suffered, as she drifted down the stream into the valley of the shadow of death toward the falls. Her dying remains an impenetrable mystery. She went around the corner alone, not just at the moment of her death but in a sense every day. She did not or could not describe her experience; perhaps because the experience of dying is too personal to be shared, or so overwhelming that language fails.

The journal writings were about my experience of Ruth's death rather than about hers, but my experience was a dying, too, in that I had to see her leave me and could not prevent it. I died one of the larger of life's many little deaths in the sense of having lost someone I cherished. Indeed, we die daily. The past recedes, and the unknown future approaches; and that daily dying is, if we stop long enough to meditate on it, a deep experience that can excite dread and delight, fear and pleasure. There is the pain of loss and the pleasure of new births into something richer than we could have imagined.

Terminal illness and death are an intricate combination of experiences which can be described from aesthetic, scientific and religious, as well as ethical, points of view.

There is an aesthetic aspect to it. I don't mean that death is beautiful; it usually isn't. But it has a power that both attracts and repels. It is so powerful that it compels our attention and interest, just as a fine work of art does, by its ambiguity and complex combinations of perceptions. It is so rich that we can only use indirect language of the poet or storyteller to describe it as such. What language can I borrow, what colors can I use, what music can I sing, what parable can I tell that would capture it?

There is a physical aspect that can be described. Our senses are involved. We can discern when a person has died by what we see, hear, touch and smell. I could see Ruth's decline and the physical effects of diabetes and cancer. I knew when Ruth was really dead and gone. I felt her hand go limp. I saw her eyes become empty. I heard her breathing stop.

Medical diagnosis describes what is going on in the human body. It is possible, for example, to determine sugar levels in the body which have marked effects on how a person feels and acts. The experience we had in Palm Bay illustrates this physical, measurable aspect of an illness. Illness and death are measurable, discernible, something scientists can describe—well, up to a point. Their description, while essential and helpful in making decisions about what to do, is also limited, no matter how detailed the exam and the autopsy.

Terminal illness and death are religious experiences, too. Ruth's final illness was most surely. Her experiences moved us to face our limits and to make a judgment as to the final reality with which we must come to terms; they confronted us with the holy, timeless mystery, stirring wonder and awe, tempting us to despair, to cry one last cry of unbelief and defiance, or luring us to profound trust in a mercy that is eternal, not bound by time and place. Facing them presented us with a choice between faith and unbelief, between believing death is the final lord of life and believing there is a Lord of life and death. We were moved by them, to think about whether there is something else other than this short, often painful human experience.

Humans have more than one way of thinking about their lives. As historians or scientists we aspire to describe ourselves, others and our world as accurately and fully as we can. As artists, musicians or poets, we work to capture those aspects of experience that cannot be described but can be expressed with beautiful and meaningful art forms. As religious beings we compose prayers and creeds and theologies to clarify the experience of the holy, the sacred, the relationship with the Divine.

Ethicists look at the same experiences from another perspective, related to and provoked by **moral** experience. Ruth's terminal illness and death and my experience of loss were not just a medical story; they were a moral affair as well.

I am using the word **moral** as a descriptive term for an aspect of human life we all share in varying degrees. I am not using it as an evaluative word that approves of behavior, as when we judge someone to be moral because they behave in acceptable ways. The word **morality** is derived from the Latin word, **moralis**, which means "of custom." Morality, the system of customs, rules and routines of a society, usually regulates human action. Morality is a means of keeping moral distress at a minimum. In that sense these rules, customs and routines are like rules of health, which keep pain and physical or psychological distress at a minimum if we obey them.

Most of the time our actions conform to the social conventions, routines, rules and expectations of the social systems in which we live. Much of our behavior is customary. These social regulations are necessary; they make life together possible. Although we make many decisions during a day, we do not generally think about them, do not ask ethical questions. We are willing to "fit in." I suppose we realize that life would be intolerably chaotic without regulations that make it unnecessary to stop to think every time we act. Most regulations are quite useful and so we don't have to expend a lot of energy in perplexity, wondering what to do.

However, morality comes about as a consequence of moral experience, not as its cause. Rules do not create or control the dynamic flow of chance and change. Ever so often we face the unexpected, unpredictable situation in which we must decide what we ought to do.

The fundamental plot of medical stories has these basic scenes:

1. Something painful or puzzling happens to someone; something one neither can understand nor alleviate by oneself.

2. The hurting one goes to a doctor, and he or she examines the patient and offers a diagnosis and proposes a treatment.

3. The patient accepts the diagnosis and agrees to the treatment.

4. The story ends, happily if the treatment succeeds in alleviating the condition, or sadly if the treatment fails.

The plot of moral stories has a structure, too, that can be found in many if not all experiences.

1. An inescapable fate. Something happens to a person that makes a decision inescapable.

2. Matters of significance. The decision is about matters of significance to ourselves and others and our environments.

3. Conditions of uncertainty. The decision must be made even if one is not certain about one's motives, the means to employ, and consequences.

4. Risk. Thus decisions entail risks for ourselves and others, risks of error, failure, even of sin and evil; and also prospects of something good giving us satisfaction, even delight.

Moments of Decision

Dear Zoe,

I am writing about Ruth, but it is my experience, not hers. My part in the story began in a motel in Rapid City, South Dakota, on our way home from the vacation in the Rockies, when I wanted us to decide whether or not to register for a conference on rural life at St. John's University. I remember clearly Ruth's reply.

"I don't think we will be going, Robert." Then she told me about her discovery.

That was the moment of ineluctable necessity. I was now the man in the boat drifting toward the waterfall, although the roar was hardly heard. My wife had a lump on her breast. I would be affected by whatever was going to happen, and it was the moment when I became an actor in a story which I did not want to happen.

There are many poignant moments in the story of Ruth's final days. One of them was her discovery of the lump on her right breast that July night in a motel in Billings, Montana. It must have been a very disconcerting experience. The planned sequence of events starting with a decision to go on the vacation trip was disrupted by a fate she neither expected nor wanted. She needed to know what was happening in her body.

Ethicist Daniel Maguire helped me with analysis of moral experience by the use of a set of what he calls "reality-revealing questions." It is "ethical heresy," he avers, to neglect any one of them. In **Death by Choice** (New York: Schocken Books, 1975) he writes: "The bane of ethics is incompleteness, and incompleteness is the product of unasked questions....Morality is based on reality."

What is going on? She could not determine by manual exam alone whether or not the lump was malignant or benign. Ruth needed expert medical diagnosis. Surely one of the major advances in the practice of medicine is the revolution in the power to diagnose such diseases as cancer. Sooner or later all of us become aware of a condition that poses a threat to health and life, and that awareness shakes us into the realization of our vulnerability and intensifies stress. We experience the fear of knowing and sometimes postpone finding out what is going on. Is it better to be ignorant than to know? I would say to know is better, even to know we are going to die.

Why did she delay action? Did she feel "in her bones" that her fate was fixed? Had she heard the sound of the waterfall? Surely she must have been concerned about her physical health. Maybe she dreaded what she would learn. Her mother had died of breast cancer, and two of her father's sisters had had cancer, neither of whom had died. She may have hoped that she would survive as her aunts had and not die as her mother had. Maybe the discovery was a blow that triggered her anxiety, which was for her at times compulsive. Perhaps she did not want pressure from me to go home at once and to the doctor. I can only speculate about such motives.

Although her health and perhaps her life were at stake when she delayed action to get medical care, she chose to wait so that I would have the vacation free of worry. Her decision illustrates one of the major and common moral questions we all face and often when we have to choose between our own good and someone else's; or, when we want to please or help more than one other person, we have to choose which of them to serve.

When illness or injury happen to us we normally are most concerned, perhaps even exclusively so, with our own welfare. This does not mean, though, that others' welfare is not also at issue. For example, a whole family could be impoverished by decisions to provide expensive care designed to save or prolong the life of a comatose patient. Ruth said she wanted my vacation to be undisturbed. She wanted to spare me the impact. She chose my good.

Motives are never as unambiguous as our stated reasons make them seem to be. However, I believe the reason she gave was genuine. Convictions, not just coercion and compulsion, are motivating factors when we must make decisions, and Ruth had strong convictions. Her decision to give me the benefit of an untroubled vacation was consistent with her vows made years ago when we were married, the commitment to love and to cherish which she made in her marriage vows. Ruth had hesitated for months before saying she would marry me, but when she made the commitment she was faithful to it. Love meant more to her than desire or mutuality; it meant what Christians call **agape**, which motivates one to act for the good of others even at risk to one's own immediate or future benefit. In his book, **The Moral Choice** (Garden City, New York: Doubleday & Company, Inc., 1978), Daniel Maguire calls attention to "our mysterious tendency" to be willing to suffer and even to die for person-related values; or at least to admire those who have the courage and opportunity to do so. And such persons will do it, he contends, even though there may be no assurance of good consequences for oneself or others.

There is an ineluctable tension between self-preservation and self-sacrifice in moral experience. Maguire implies that this readiness to give ourselves could show up in just about anybody, not just persons committed to the agape ethical tradition.

One might have a dispute about Ruth's motivation and offer the view that she too easily adjusted to the social role imposed on many women of her generation, namely, that their duty was to give themselves to their children and husband. That there may be a mixture of conviction and conformity in Ruth's action at this time must be admitted, but who is to judge with absolute certainty? I choose to put a most charitable construction on her action.

Ruth apparently believed it was her duty to make the decision to delay action. She did not give me a chance to share in making the decision at that time and place, even though I would be affected. People who are affected by a decision or action should usually not be denied some say in what is decided and done. This is a significant moral issue that frequently comes up in medical care situations.

Ruth was the sole actor on the stage at this time. I can only imagine her thoughts, her feelings. What a lonely and fearful time for her! Moments of decision are usually lonely times. Each of us must make the decision about our own response to situations. That cannot be delegated, not even to God.

As soon as I knew about her discovery I became a character in the story, but could I, a man, possibly understand a woman's fear of breast cancer? No, but men have a comparable experience when they get prostate cancer. I suffered such an experience. One weekend in August the condition became so severe that urination was impossible, and I suffered agony for seven hours on a trip to Iowa City. A week later in Mankato, the night before surgery in a room with a man of seventy-five who had just had surgery for the second occurrence, I faced the prospect of cancer. I heard in the distance the soft roar of the waterfall. Four days after the operation, the urologist told me that there was cancer but a very low grade, virtually benign, and that it would not alter the normal life span of a man my age. The sound of the waterfall receded and is only a faint whisper I hear only when I feel an unusual pain and my fear of cancer returns. I, too, live not too far from the valley of the shadow, where the waterfall is around the corner of the canyon, invisible but ineluctable.

We are all mortal. Like Peter Noll, we have to make a choice when we realize our personal mortality, whether to live until we die, or shrivel up in a living death while we are alive.

Curable, Chronic and Terminal Illness

Dear Zoe,

I said your questions challenged me, but perhaps you are getting more of a response than you expected or wanted!

There is much one could say about the phenomenon of illness. Indeed, there is a vast literature and a complex medical science and practice system that studies, explains and deals with it. My thoughts are rather simple, I suspect, especially as experts see them; but they are mine, based on experience.

Our family's experience with illness taught me to see the distinction between curable, chronic and terminal illness and to recognize that the organized response to each must be appropriate. The care involved in each is somewhat different, and the difference is morally significant.

There are illnesses that are curable and injuries that are reparable. Ruth recovered from her depression, although it lasted for several years. Depressions that are related to trying situations usually can be treated. The human body and mind have the capacity for healing. We do recover from injuries, infections and mental illnesses.

We have a responsibility to learn to listen to and respect our own bodies and minds, so as to give the natural healing processes the best climate for working. We help our bodies to recover if we do what keeps anxiety, fear, guilt, shame, anger and hate from dominating us. We help our minds to stay healthy if we take good care of our physical health. Ruth took steps to recover from her depression and persisted in the effective tactics, even though they did not work at once. Among them were walks, playing the piano, and praying. To be responsive to and act responsibly toward my own body were very important while I was caring for Ruth and after her death.

Medical professionals can be important aids to us when our illnesses and hurts are more than we can manage on our own. They can provide us with information from their fund of knowledge, with medications, such as antidepressants for mood disorders and antibiotics to assist the immune system in the "battle within" against infections, with recommendations for changes in our life-styles; and, perhaps most important of all, they can be an encouraging presence giving us assurance of recovery.

When Ruth was treated for cancer in 1987 there was the possibility that surgery and medication would check cancer. She hoped that the medical intervention would be successful. She took proper measures herself to contribute to that end.

Chronic illness is permanent; it won't go away. One's first responsibility if one has a chronic condition is to accept it, not as a foreign invader to be fought but as a native. Chronic illnesses often have a genetic basis and thus are an aspect of one's very being. They are manageable but not curable. People who have them can learn to live with them. If they fight against them, as if they were an enemy, or ignore them, they lose.

Diabetes is a chronic illness, inherited, with a genetic base, and it resides permanently as a part of a person's life. The image that helps a diabetic is not that of a warrior fighting to win, but of a diplomat negotiating workable treaties, not just once but again and again. The responsibility of a person with diabetes (as with other chronic illnesses) is to live by the rules of the treaty; in the case of the diabetic it is to respect and follow a proper combination of diet, exercise and the use of insulin. One can live well for many years, but even if one does so, there is no guarantee that difficulties will not occur. And many cases the disease brings death too soon.

Ruth had diabetes from age forty to the end of her life, but she did not die of it. There were times, however, when her condition was volatile, disruptive and hard to manage, and life-threatening. Diabetics live with the prospect of imminent death if they do not take care of themselves.

Medical assistance is important to a person with diabetes, or other chronic illnesses, in several ways. The experts have accumulated a lot of knowledge about how the disease affects the body, what causes it, and what can be done to control it, information which the affected person needs if he or she is to manage it.

Ruth learned and our family physician realized that she had personal knowledge of her body and its processes that made her the world's number one expert about her own diabetes and how to manage it. No one could experience it as directly as she, and no one could manage it for her. If she would not have eaten properly and promptly to prevent an insulin reaction, no one else could act for her. If she had been negligent about exercise or careless about the use of insulin, she would have been in great trouble.

I could be a support at times when she lost control, but I could not be with her all the time. One time I came home from classes to find her unconscious, so I had to call for assistance. The prospect of something happening when I was not with her was a cause of anxiety.

Anxiety and depression are related. Although Ruth's depression was cured, she suffered from chronic anxiety, a condition that had to be managed by proper offsetting actions to prevent it from becoming a deep depression or an obsession. Anxiety aggravates physical illness, and is intensified in turn by physical illness. Persons who have a strong need for control over their life situations seem to be more susceptible to anxiety, and loss of control can result in being paralyzed emotionally. This happened to Ruth on occasion, but for the most part she managed well.

Terminal illness cannot be cured. It brings to an end one's earthly existence, which ends in death. In a sense, we are all, at all times, terminal; we are mortals living in the face of oncoming death. Someday, you and I may hear the dreadful words of a terminal condition that will not pass, and then our hearts will cry and our minds will say, "It can't be true, not for me, not yet. I'll show everyone that my time has not come, not yet." We then decide to go all out for recovery, seek a second opinion, pray, go to healing services, think and meditate positive thoughts. Sometimes it works, and sometimes even doing nothing works. So, if we do get seriously ill, we decide to "go for it," as we say. We see ourselves at risk but not yet terminal, so we do all that is possible to recover.

But what if it really is the final time, as it was for Ruth, who loved life so much? We come for a scheduled appointment and walk down a corridor to an examining room and hear the death sentence. We become the boater moving on a swiftly flowing river toward a waterfall. The sound of the falls gets louder as we come closer. What does one think and do when one knows one is going over the brink soon? What does one make of the time left?

One day you will enter that canyon, too, Zoe, and so will I. There is no exit; and then we must choose whether to be angry, defiant, and full of gloomy despair; or in humility, let go of what is behind us and walk around that last corner into a darkness we cannot penetrate. I watched it happen to Ruth; I know it will happen to you and to me sooner or later. No one escapes.

Time and Place As Moral Facts

That night in Rapid City we did not know what was to happen. We had to find out. I became an actor in the story, one with power to affect the next decisions. Who should become involved as actors in the story at this time, where we should go and how soon? When we stopped at our son's home in Vermillion, family members had their say and urged immediate action. We did not consider going to a pastor or a faith healer or to rely on prayer alone for guidance. Ordinarily we go to our family physician for medical help, but this time we did not go to him first. Because Ruth had diabetes and was concerned about the consequences of surgery on her condition, she wanted to see specialists. We considered the University of Minnesota Hospital in Minneapolis and Mayo Clinic in Rochester, which were within one hundred miles of our home. The distance was not prohibitive, as it would have been if we had lived in northern Saskatchewan where Ruth was born or in Tanzania where we once planned to go as missionaries. Where we lived in relation to major medical centers was a significant moral factor.

We decided we needed advice from someone more acquainted with those medical centers than we were. My call to Randy Beahrs brought him into the action. I decided to take him up on his standing offer to be of assistance when I needed it. The call was an event to which he had to make a response. He chose to help us, and at this point in the story he had a brief but important role. My friend's action brought medical care-givers at Mayo Clinic into the story. They arranged for immediate access to the clinic. Those who did the diagnosis and performed the surgery had important roles because of their knowledge and skill. When they heard my friend's request, they had to decide whether or not to accept Ruth as a patient.

When Ruth could get into the clinic was an important factor. Gaining immediate access to these experts and a service we value also was a factor influencing the decision. We were anxious to get attention as soon as possible.

205

At Mayo Clinic, and others like it, time is valuable. Everyone who comes needs time with the medical staff and a place for care. The clinic schedules appointments and, if necessary, places for medical care in a hospital. I observed during our several visits to Mayo the elaborate system of distributing time and space as we moved from one floor and desk to another for Ruth's appointments with several specialists. We had to fit into the system, to await our turn.

Someone told me recently that people have to wait for months to get an appointment at Mayo, so I wondered if we were violating the system of distribution. As I look back on our experience I see several points of access into the medical care system.

The first was through the emergency service. When Ruth had an insulin reaction so severe that I could not take care of her, I called 911 in Palm Bay and we had immediate access to care. That was also available in St. Peter when her condition deteriorated at the end of February.

Second, when a life-threatening condition develops and a person should be examined and treated as soon as possible, the system provides for such situations by finding a time for an appointment as soon as possible. Mayo made arrangements for Ruth to be admitted shortly after we came home.

Third, Ruth needed and received routine checkups every three months. For routine medical exams, the usual appointment system serves as the gate of access, and such appointments are made months in advance.

It seems that the medical system is not so rigidly structured that it cannot respond to special needs.

Which good and **for whom** are recurring issues in moral stories. Our primary concern was for Ruth and to get for her the best care. This issue confronts us in our personal situations, and also in the vast and complex social issues of distribution of goods and services in the public sectors of society.

The next moment of decision happened in the surgeon's office, after Ruth had the necessary tests preliminary to treatment. It was a situation in which consideration of consequences, another factor of moral significance, affected her decision. A biopsy was necessary. She had to decide whether to have surgery at the same time, if the tumors were malignant. She could have the option of waiting until she knew how serious the situation was. When the surgeon said that if she didn't have surgery she would probably not live very long, she decided to have it. Her decision was based on estimates of future consequences.

The sound of the waterfall became noticeable again. When Ruth went into surgery, she imagined that she might die. The fact of mortality was no longer theoretical or a remote possibility.

The consequences of the decision were a mixture of good and bad. The mastectomy disfigured her. There was malignancy in some of the lymph glands. If the doctor anticipated further metastasis, he gave no sign of his opinion. His tactic was to be optimistic about the consequences and the recommended treatment; she would receive no chemotherapy or radiation treatments but would take tomoxafin, the recommended drug, and she would come for checkups every three months. Final time had not yet come. There was still time to live before she drifted into the valley of the shadow of death and heard the roar of the falls.

The Question of Value

Dear Zoe,

Think about what states of yourself give you delight and what states are dismal and dreadful. Think about why, every day by getting up, you choose to live rather than to die. The experience of living in the face of death, of realizing that one has only a limited time, has a force driving one to think about what is truly important in one's life.

To be or not to be is the most fundamental moral issue each of us must settle, and we do so every morning when we get up and decide to live. Ruth loved life. For her living was delightful, a pleasure she cherished, even though she had serious illnesses to contend with.

The medical intervention gave us more time to enjoy life. Life from August 1987 to November 1989 was a mixture of good and bad. It seems we cannot have a purely good life, or be fully in control. Her diabetes was "brittle," in spite of her discipline, as the episode in Palm Bay shows. There were family problems that caused anxiety and alienation, but also reconciliations inspired by the Christian commitment to forgiveness.

On the other hand, she and I had many enjoyable times. Ruth was healthy enough to enjoy eating, walking, going on trips, even hiking on the trails in the Rocky Mountains and walking on Nauset Beach on Cape Cod. There were parties on the porch with friends with whom to enjoy raspberry treats from our garden and lively conversation, and the grandchildren to enjoy in Michigan. There were concerts and plays and lectures and games at the college, and daily worship in the chapel. We traveled, putting 36,000 miles on our car during the last year before her terminal time—trips to Colorado, Florida, New England, Michigan, Arizona and northern Minnesota. Our spiritual life flourished through daily practice of reading aloud from the Bible and other books, conversing, singing and praying. Usually we did this early enough to watch the sun appear on the horizon across the valley and enjoy the pastel colors of a predawn sky. It was a full, enjoyable life, even if marked by troubles.

Which good? She loved her body. Her life was in her body; without it she would have no life at all. Not even those vicious diseases, diabetes and cancer could destroy that love. Only a couple of hours before she died, she told me she loved her body, as I was massaging her legs. Her love for her body motivated appropriate behavior. She took care of herself as best she could and as long as she could. For years her careful management kept diabetes from destroying her life. Negligence would have had bad consequences. It would be comparable to a boater in a canoe either paddling irregularly or not at all as he heard the sound of the waterfall in the distance.

There is more to a good state of being than physical health, mobility, strength and other such qualities. We humans are social beings, so we value relationships that are affirming, affectionate and accepting of us; we want to give and receive friendship, love; we enjoy convivial occasions. Illness can reduce that kind of value very much, for various reasons, so we want to be healthy, strong and able enough to enjoy social life.

She valued her friends; especially important to her was the visit of our friends from Tennessee, and that they valued her enough to drive over seven hundred miles to visit her for one more short day. I was moved by the joy of friendship, too, when my friend Jane came all the way from Alameda, California, to visit us for a weekend. Our friends in St. Peter, especially those who live in our neighborhood, were like family in the support and love they gave us. My reason for taking trips after Ruth died was to visit family and friends, not to go sight-seeing. I valued your letter, an expression of your friendship.

We are more than social beings, however, so the question of value must be related to other aspects of self. We are also intelligent beings, thinkers, who value meaning, who create ideas, art forms, beautiful and useful things. If illness drains our ability to think, if it affects our brains so much that we cannot communicate—as when someone gets Alzheimer's disease, or a stroke, or goes into a coma—we lose something precious to us. Her fate was a threat to the meaning of her life, another important human value. When something bad happens, we are forced to think about what life is all about. Sometimes events are so sudden and random that we must decide whether there is a blind, heartless fate that is finally at work, or some more meaningful purpose.

There is another aspect of value that is more subtle but very strong, and that is that state of being we call wonder, or reverence, or awe—something so powerful and compelling that we engage in acts of worship.

When we look for the best medical care, these aspects of the good state of human being are important bases for judging that care. It is not enough to have only physical care, even if that is the best in the world, when that care ignores these other needs we have. Our original decision to choose Mayo Clinic was a matter of value, based on its reputation for providing excellent medical care, something we valued highly because of Ruth's need.

Elegance, Wholeness, Balance and Detachment

Dear Zoe,

There is another aspect of the experience, which Daniel Maguire's reality questions help us to describe. The question, "why?" calls attention, not just to what causes brought the effects [diabetes, or cancer, etc.] but also the question of motivation for our actions. There is mixture of causes for decisions. Sometimes circumstances allow us precious little freedom for choice. There seems often to be some degree of coercion and of compulsion in motivation. We yield to the pressure of others' opinions. We are to some degree driven by compulsive inner feelings and memories. However, convictions also influence our attitudes and actions. They are more than views we hold as a matter of opinion. They are beliefs that possess us, and sometimes they are the decisive motive for action.

While I cannot claim that the decisions Ruth and I made were always carefully reasoned from conviction to action, those beliefs were powerful enough at least to modify our actions.

That November when Ruth's condition was deteriorating I was giving lectures on moral dramas in health care for the Cooperative Older Adult Ministry in Minneapolis, and one of the lectures was on the question of value. I presented elegance, wholeness, balance and detachment as guides for decisions about to which values we might aspire to attain in our attitudes and actions.

Elegance. Ruth's decision was influenced by the intention to maintain the best possible quality of life during her remaining time. I use the term elegance for this goal of high quality, because it points to the aesthetic element in value. One could use the traditional term, highest good, or excellence, too.

Wholeness. The principle of wholeness expresses the intention of attaining an inclusive good state of being alive—including physical, social, mental and spiritual conditions. The choice of radiation treatments had beneficial results that stand up well when we consider the principle of wholeness. Although the treatments did not extend Ruth's life longer than anticipated, the treatment gave her a few good weeks, opportunity to enjoy her relationships with the family, to enjoy the holiday season at home and to continue familiar routines that we cherished as long as possible. We enjoyed a relationship with each other that I would characterize as elegant, something beautiful and good, because we were able to continue our lifelong conversation even in the threat of losing each other. Of course, there was a decline toward low quality as Ruth's condition worsened, but the treatments gave her time to enjoy life a little longer.

In her "living will" statement Ruth disclosed the value she placed on her intellectual life, her family and church. She did not want to be kept alive on a machine if her mind was incapable of thought or response. She also

210

wanted to die with dignity, her sense of personal worth undiminished; and in the company of family and church.

Ruth wrote a letter to her college classmates in January 1990 that is a statement of values she affirmed. It deserves a reading and some comments.

It was the second week in December. I had just arrived at the Mayo Clinic with a diagnosis of brain tumor in my cerebellum. What a shock to me! That night I was lying in my room all alone looking out at a Christmas star that was twinkling on a nearby building and was trying to absorb what was happening to me. I began reviewing my life from its beginning. As I did so I thought what a wonderful life I have had. I was baptized into a church that has never failed me but given me continuous support. I have lived in a family where love abounds, and through all the difficulties of life we have been present to each other. Bob and I in particular know the joy that comes with a shared life. I have had childhood friends that are still friends. I went to a college where friends have become lifelong friends.

So many of these friends have contacted me and speak to me with such love it is as if we had never been apart. It seemed to me as if love and prayer came flowing into our home in a tangible form. The radiation treatments were helpful, so I was able to go home and be with family and have felt fairly well.

Another wonderful advantage for us is that we are only 100 miles from one of the greatest medical facilities in the world. We do appreciate medical expertise as well as prayer! The staff of Mayo was wonderful to work with.

Something wonderful happened to me that I think deepened my spiritual life. Our pastor came to see me, and we spent an hour together discussing how we viewed our faith. Then he said, "Ruth, I have brought communion. Would you like to have it?" I said, "Why, yes, I think I would." So he set the table up with the elements. He brought out the service book and began the words of that ancient communion ritual. As soon as he started, something came over me. A sense of transcendence came over me. Time stood still, and I was no longer Ruth Esbjornson. I had entered that great community of the church that has been using the ritual for thousands of years and has preserved it for the consolation of us all. It was as great as any of the wonderful moments I have had in my life. Of course, I am hopeful that the treatments are going to continue to be helpful. Meanwhile, life is a blessing and still wonderful.

The range of values she mentions expresses the principle of wholeness. She mentions relationship with people, with family, friends, with me; her religious life in a community that has given her support all her life; the experience of transcendence. The instrumental value of ritual, connecting her to a great community that transcends her and her immediate company of family and friends; the inherent value in doing the ritual, apart from which the experience of transcendence did not happen.

Balance. One of the errors in moral life can be corrected if we take the principle of balance as a guide. The principle of balance keeps one from taking extreme positions on features of medical practice and health care. It is not either physician or patient having responsibility, but both. Medical technology and personal health care are not polar opposites but used together to obtain therapeutic aims. Too much emphasis on technological fixes causes neglect of attention to the natural healing processes. In Ruth's case, diabetes is an illustration of the need for balance between diet, exercise and insulin. Major clinics and local hospitals are both important in the medical care system, and this was evident in our experience.

It is also a perspective enabling one to accept the reality that there is a time to live and a time to die; indeed, that process of living and dying goes on all our lives, as we suffer losses and make new gains.

Detachment. This principle helped me to accept losing Ruth. It is a matter of letting go, of not clinging desperately to what we value, of realizing that the treasures of our earthly existence are subject to loss [where moth and rust consume and thieves break in and steal]. There come many times in the course of our lives when we suffer loss, and the fear of loss can become a great burden that prevents us from appropriate action.

The biblical tradition again and again reminds us of our mortality.

"As a father has compassion for his children,
so the Lord has compassion for those who fear him.
For he knows how we were made;
he remembers that we are dust.
As for mortals, their days are like grass;
they flourish like a flower of the field;
for the wind passes over it, and it is gone,
and its place knows it no more.
But the steadfast love of the Lord is from everlasting to
everlasting" (Psalm 103:13-17).

The dilemma of human existence is that we are mortal beings who are at the same time conscious of our mortality. In his book, **The Denial of Death** (New York: Free Press, 1973), Ernest Becker points to the poignancy of this condition.

A person spends years coming into his own, developing his talent, his unique gifts, perfecting his discriminations about the world, broadening and sharpening his appetite, learning to bear the disappointments of life, becoming mature, seasoned—finally a unique creature in nature, standing with some dignity and nobility and transcending the animal condition, no longer driven, no longer a complete reflex, not stamped out of any mold. Then comes the real tragedy, as Andre Malraux wrote in **The Human Condition**; that it takes sixty years of incredible suffering and effort to make such an individual, and then he is good only for dying. This painful paradox is not lost on the person himself— least of all himself. He feels agonizingly unique, and yet he knows that this does not make any difference as far as ultimates are concerned. He has to go the way of the grasshopper, even though it takes longer.

Becker died of cancer shortly after this was published and before the book was awarded the Pulitzer prize in 1974. Sam Keen interviewed him in the hospital before he died or knew that the book had won the prize. Something he said deserves attention.

"I would say that beyond the absurdities of one's life, there are the tremendous energies of the cosmos using us for some purpose. We do not know. To be used for divine purposes, however we may be misused, this consoles. I think of Calvin's prayer, 'Thou bruiseth me, but since it is You, it is all right.' I think one does or should try to hand over one's life. The meaning of it, the value of it, the end of it."

The challenge of mortality is formidable and calls for a realistic and mature understanding of one's religious traditions in order to cope with it. The psalmist put his trust in God, his hope in the everlasting mercy of God, as the "home" of mortals. If Ruth's experience while at Mayo and Methodist Hospital was positive, it was not only because of the good quality of care she valued but because she had a rich background of resources garnered through a whole lifetime. Her experience of value was not just an immediate affair of the moment but an accumulation of earlier experiences that made that time richer. I can imagine what a dismal experience people without such a heritage must have when confronting their mortal limits.

The **time** factor, when would she die, had a significant bearing on Ruth's moral life. She wanted to extend life to the maximum length estimated by medical judgment; the radiation treatments would do that, she hoped. However, her age made a difference, too. If she had been 40 rather than 69, she may have been more angry and rebellious about having to die. Ruth, I surmise, realized that her time had come.

It seems to me that Ruth was able to make decisions based on her commitments, rather than compulsions, such as fear of death. She knew she was going to die, yet there is no evidence in my journal that she suffered compulsive anxiety about dying. At least she was not driven by fear of death to the point where her demands and actions were a problem for her care-givers.

214

She was able to talk to me about it, write as she did about her experience. Surely one must conclude that her religious outlook was a powerful influence on her attitudes and actions at this time.

Zoe, you asked about suffering, whether what we suffered had meaning. I read again what I wrote in my journal on December 13, 1989, to describe suffering as I was experiencing it at that time. The description is very brief but based on this view of the whole person as a physical, social, intellectual and spiritual being. That does not answer your question, however. Many people have thought and written, often in great anguish, about the meaning of suffering, especially because it seems so random, so unevenly spread, among us. Why was Ruth's suffering less intense than someone whose pain was more agonizing? Why was my time of caring for her so much shorter than it is for others? Are we dealing with chance, just random chance? With some kind of mysterious cause-effect relationship invisible to us? With the direct action of a powerful, mean, or partisan god who plays favorites? Which do you choose to believe? Which makes the most sense to you? Do any of them give you consolation as you endure or imagine enduring suffering?

Suffering is a fate to which we make a response. I choose to regard it as a challenge to meet as best I can, until I am no longer able. Ruth suffered. It is very consoling to me that in spite of her suffering she chose to live as well as possible until she died. Her example strengthens my resolve to do the same.

Ruth made a basic choice we each make when we awaken in the morning—to be or not to be, to live or to die. She wanted to live. Life was dear to her. Cancer was a threat to life, so she wanted the best medical care to diminish the threat, but the time had come to face reality, hard as it was, and she did. She accepted the medical opinions about treatment and prognosis. Radiation treatments had to be limited, and the dosage of decadron had to be reduced. There was no cure, none. That was hard to face, yet she did, with courage and commitment to make the most of her remaining days.

She also decided to write a "living will," which is dated November 17, 1989, before the diagnosis of terminal cancer came. I can't remember conversations about it with her, but I suspect she had an inkling that her death was coming. She was not feeling well at that time.

215

I can't help but speculate about why she accepted her fate. She could have sought a second opinion at another cancer treatment center, or tried some nontraditional treatments that claim to help when conventional treatments fail. We did not talk about such options. At one point I decided to pray unconditionally for Ruth's recovery, and in our prayers we expressed that hope. Ruth was hopeful, too, in January. Later, in March, reality hit her and she was more reticent to talk about dying, which she was more able to do at the beginning. Maybe it was too painful to discuss it openly, or maybe she was confused, or maybe she realized that it was irrelevant, that talk had become irrelevant. Maybe it was enough for us to be together and to share in this experience, too, as a part of our story, enough to continue living, talking as we were able, loving, praying as best we could.

As one at her side, observing and sharing to some extent what she was experiencing, I made several attempts to give her opportunities to talk, but she did not respond to them.

Kubler-Ross and others describe stages of feeling as one is dying, such as denial, anger, depression, peace. Ruth's reactions were not so clear-cut, but she obviously suffered more than physical pain. She was afraid, yes, and needed my presence; and she sometimes was irritated with me, such as about administering pain medication. I never felt that her dying cut her off entirely from me. The struggles we had during the last weekend of her life when I was alone with her were times of affection and even humor as we muddled our way through changing her garments and bed sheets.

I know that everyone's experience of terminal illness is unique, and some people have very painful ends, so painful they cannot bear to be touched. Then the illness is a cruel tyrant, much more destructive than Ruth's was. She had a relatively short final time, and low levels of pain. Her death came as a surprise to me, at an hour I did not expect, but maybe that is generally true. At least I was present, which has not been the case with some of my friends whose mates died away from home—or when they were absent. I do not want you to think I am generalizing from our experience to everyone's, Zoe. Martin Luther in one of his sermons at Wittenberg said that everyone goes to the ramparts alone. My experience of losing Ruth was sad but not grim. My grief is a mixture of sadness and gladness. I don't presume to understand the

216

experience of final time. There is, as I have said, a mystery about it that remains beyond language.

Whose Good? The Dilemma of Distribution

Dear Zoe,

You asked whether we had found an understanding organization to assist us. The answer is in the journal. Ruth and I received the best care the medical care system can offer at Mayo Clinic and Methodist Hospital, St. Peter Community Hospital and from the St. Peter Area Hospice Program, as well as the church community and the network of friends and family.

Mayo Clinic provided excellent knowledge and skill of specialists in diagnosis and treatment, and the technology they use. At St. Peter Community Hospital, Ruth received care appropriate for the terminally ill; the hospice program gave me the support I needed when I was in charge of Ruth's care at home. Our pastors were attentive and helpful. Family and friends surrounded us with loving attention and care.

Yes, excellent care, even elegant, but why am I hedging? Why do I have mixed feelings now as I review the story? I do not feel a need to complain, but to question and assess. Psychiatrist Willard Gaylin and ethicist Daniel Maguire have taught me to respect feelings as a warning signal that something significant is involved. Maybe the reasons for my ambivalence will be clear by an ethical assessment.

Social systems are complex organizations designed over time to provide services and supplies to people who need them. The medical care system provides its services to people who are ill or injured; and it also provides opportunities for many people to work for their own profit and satisfaction. The system should be organized to distribute these benefits fairly and frugally, and at the same time the services and supplies should be of excellent quality. Those criteria are moral matters, not just matters of technology and tactics that can be assessed by science, politics and economics. Persons receiving the care should receive what benefits them, or at least does not harm them. The persons providing services should receive fair compensation for their work.

Think about the basic ethical question, **whose** good ought to be served. Well, Zoe, a normal person's answer is, "Mine, I hope." Yours for sure, and mine as well. In other words, many people want and compete for the same services and supplies.

Ruth and I were among the privileged because of where we lived, and we had a friend who knew better than we did how to get into the system. We had access to that care, because the costs were covered under Medicare and our church's medical insurance program. We were spared the financial devastation that would have happened.

My reflections on access to medical care have made me see the dilemma of distribution.

Each of us wants to get the best care we can get, even though we know the price tag for health care is going up fast. As each specific doctor providing care for each specific patient acts to give the best care, the volume multiplies until it pushes the carrying capacity of the medical care system toward its finite limits. Then we, as a society, face the bleak choice of either limiting the quality of care and thus reducing its value, or limiting its distribution and thus reducing the fairness of the system we demand. Who of us wants to be among those with lower quality care or among those who are excluded? We surely did not.

In our conversations, Ruth and I did not ask about what care would cost, even though we were both familiar with how the costs have been escalating over the years. I could talk about the costs of medical care going up in my ethics seminars and philosophize about what to do, but when illness like this came to us, we didn't philosophize; we wanted the best medical care we could find.

At the time we went to Mayo, neither of us talked about the general problem of access to medical care. When our own welfare is at risk, each of us seems quite incapable of thinking about others' welfare. We want the best we can get to serve our needs. When we are hurting or someone we care about is hurting, we can't bear to think about cost or about denying them relief. Ruth and I had no compelling reason to do so, because we were protected from the burden of cost by medical insurance.

The public systems that organize the distribution of goods and services do not have unlimited resources. When policymakers act as if they do, the crunch eventually hits. Budgets impose limits on spending. Hard decisions about who gets what are inherent in moral life sooner or later.

We assume that others also can gain access to the medical care system, but that assumption is challenged by the fact that there are crowded emergency departments in large urban hospitals where people do not get immediate attention. There are too many in need and too few who have too little time to take care of everyone at once. There is unequal access to quality care; that is the reality. If we had lived in eastern Montana or in that pit of horrors today, Somalia, we would not have as ready access as we were privileged to have.

Over 35 million Americans do not have medical insurance. How vulnerable each of us would be without organized systems of distributing goods and services! I have to say, "Yes, but," because when the benefits of the system are not available to everyone who needs them, my sense of fairness is violated. A social system should distribute goods and services fairly and frugally. I have to say, "Yes, but," when I consider the high cost of medical care, which is going up so fast that it has put the entire American system of distribution of goods and services in a crisis.

I am getting into a sensitive matter when I raise the question of who should be served by the medical system. It is hard to face up to our own moral ambiguities. Maybe that is why many people shun ethics and sound analysis and resort to defense of and justification for what they do, rather than careful analysis. Self-interest is a strong force affecting decisions. Being able to identify with others whose needs are also important requires moral discipline that easily breaks down when our vital interests are at stake.

Self-Interest and Justice

Thinking about why some people have so much of the world's benefits and other people so little makes me feel uneasy. I want to turn away. Why? I am overwhelmed by the extent of pain and suffering. I want to walk around and away from the hurting and the homeless. I have enough burdens as

219

it is and can't see how I can bear their burdens as well as my own. It's too much.

I am upset by stories of human misery of people trapped in poverty, impoverished by the costs of illness or injury, some victims of the flawed system now operating and others suffering for poor judgment and misdeeds for which they have repented long ago. The consequences of destructive life-styles or abusive family systems last for years. Even the most ardent prayers of penitence and pleas for mercy cannot entirely erase those effects.

Sometimes I want to join those who say that people get what they deserve, but most of the time I side with those who say wait. There is not such a straight line between intention and act, and between act and consequence. We can cite experiences of our own in which good intentions did not produce appropriate action, and right action did not bring beneficial results. There is no simple diagram of moral experience; if one would do A, B, and C, the results would be Ar, Br, and Cr.

I want to blame myself and others for the style of life that is so costly to health and the economy, blame the medical profession for protecting its special privileges, blame the bureaucrats for the waste, blame the medical supply corporations for their greed, blame the politicians for being so timid and evasive, blame the randomness of nature, even God; there seems enough blame to hand out so that we can even include God! I know that the medical associations, the hospital associations, and the insurance business will crowd the halls of Congress and state capitols with lobbyists powerfully defending the interests of their clients; they will fight any changes that might affect their own interests. The American Association of Retired Persons lobbies long and hard to protect the system that benefits the elders; so on the scene comes the Children's Defense Fund lobby seeking the welfare of children.

There are people who defend this system in which the zealous promotion of self-interest seems the most feasible way to attain what is beneficial. They settle for an arrangement in which at least some benefit is attained by the clashes of powerful self-interest groups; and the lobbies of the groups I mentioned are among the most powerful. The claim others make on the same benefits and resources we want to enjoy challenges our natural inclination to act out of self-interest, most especially when our own cherished values are at stake. No one is exempt from the challenge, and all must make some decision as to how to deal with it.

Which is right—to be utterly devoted to our own self-interests or to be dedicated to fair distribution of goods and services? In principle, most of us would opt for fair distribution. Though self-interest is a powerful motivator, we also have a sense of injustice, and when that sense is violated, we feel outrage. We feel strongly about being treated unfairly, about being left out. We can imagine how we would feel if we did not have access to something as valuable as health care, so we should be able to imagine how others feel who do not have access.

It is that deep feeling that must be tapped to help us understand the plight of the deprived and oppressed. When we feel we have been wronged a cry comes bursting forth, "It's not fair!" When we ignore the cries of others in need, we violate the sense of injustice in us, and then we suffer a loss of something we value very much, our integrity. We want to be consistent, to think and act according to what we believe; and what we believe is a powerful energy in us. It seems that our own interests are at stake when we make decisions whether or not to care about others.

To ignore the cries of the oppressed and needy, however, is tactically shortsighted and dangerous as well. As each of us does so we come up against others who are doing the same, and then what? Conflict with the stronger winning the most, even at the expense of the weaker? Or some kind of wise cooperation, based on the realization that others have similar needs? Abused or neglected or exploited people can stand oppression or deprivation only so long, and they rebel. That has happened in countries where the people were deprived and oppressed. Even from a selfish point of view, it is wrong to neglect those in need because we will have angry people going at us in one way or another. If we are among the oppressors we are not safe. So we have our own interests at stake, too.

The Tradition of Justice

The rights and responsibilities of those who give medical care and those who receive it are not autonomous; they are regulated by a system of

221

rules, laws and professional traditions that shape decisions and action. Systems of regulation are not amoral or unnecessary inconveniences. Without them life would be chaotic. The way systems are set up is itself a moral significant factor in our experience; and so are their operations, which are only relatively efficient, effective and just. There are some things that individuals cannot do on their own, and we are all dependent on the system's working fairly and effectively.

The moral significance of the medical system becomes apparent in current discussions about changes needed in the way the system distributes and finances health care. Medicare rules had a distinct effect on decisions about moving Ruth to and from the hospital. What changes in the system should be made to support rather than undermine the rights and responsibilities of both those who receive and those who give care? That is a question so overwhelming that, at present, political and personal discussions seem to be unable to come to a comprehensive agreement.

Generally, rules give us guidance as to appropriate action. They are the distillation of experience and depositories of accumulated wisdom. We are governed by regulations much of the time; without them life would be chaotic. There is an imperative embedded in rules that we ignore at our peril—rules of good health, for example; habits of devotion that nurture faith, such as regular prayer routines, public worship, writing and reading.

The policies, guidelines and regulations of the medical system are necessary and generally they are helpful. Time must be allotted, talent and resources used in such a way that they are distributed fairly and without losing quality. The fact that the system is in crisis because of changes in knowledge and ability and population and expectations does not mean we can abolish the system.

Rules, however, are not synonymous with personal righteousness or with social justice. Systems can become so overloaded and burdened with obsolete procedures and attitudes that they become dysfunctional. They must be assessed and corrected. They are not utopias, and their managers are not gods.

To be a moral person is not synonymous with conformity; it is to have a perspective from beyond the law, so to speak, from outside the system, that enables us to assess ourselves and the system. We must have a point outside the system where we can take a stand.

I hear the roar of another waterfall, Zoe, coming from the poetry of the Hebrew prophet, Amos, which has stirred me for many years:

"Let justice flow down like waters,
And righteousness like an everlasting stream" (Amos 5:24).

Amos cried out against the injustices of his time in the eloquent poetry found in the book by that name. The story of the Hebrew prophet, Amos, is a major chapter in a long story. Amos was outraged, not because he was the one who was being mistreated, but because of injustice to the poor and powerless who lived in another country than his own, in the cities of Samaria. He decried the behavior and indifference of the powerful and wealthy in that society. How do we explain this strange capacity of Amos and other people to care about **other** people enough to come to their defense and their aid? He asserted that his message was not his own. It was the Word of the Lord that came to him in visions which he composed in poetic form. That tradition has been an everflowing stream that has shaped policies and action in our culture and has significant meaning in discussions about reforms of the medical care system to make it more fair and frugal.

"Do justice, love kindness, walk humbly with your God" (Micah 6:8).

This imperative, found in an ancient source, the book of Micah, provides a guide for decisions when we face the issue of whose good to attain and how to do so. What now is the force or energy that switches a person from pursuit of self-interest to the pursuit of justice, from overriding concern for one's own good to a commitment to the good of all?

Karen Lebacqz has provided a clue in her book, **Justice in an Unjust World: Foundations for a Christian Approach to Justice** (Minneapolis: Augsburg, 1987). "No theory of justice can be derived by reason alone. Reason, like theory, is secondary to experience. It is experience that gives shape to reason. If justice is grounded in remembrance, then the narratives that give shape to remembrance are crucial. If the story is not told, justice will die."

223

The foundation of justice is not the aggressive pursuit of our own self-interest and the sense of outrage when we are denied what we seek. Nor is the foundation of justice a social consensus between parties so that each believes he has fair compensation, whether price paid, product purchased, wages earned or services rendered. The foundation of justice was not in Amos, or his personal opinion based on being outraged by wrongs. The foundation of justice was the Word of the Lord that came to him, and that word involves his vivid experience of the presence of God as a spiritual force in the history of his people. The God Amos knew was a righteous God who cared about the oppressed, the poor, the alien, the hungry.

My tradition is Lutheran Christian; and that tradition, inspired by biblical views, has a resource that enables me, and others, to live under the law and yet beyond it. It sees the necessity of laws, and the limits of laws. The root of the Lutheran Reformation was not its reform of the church or of politics or any other system; it was the renewal of faith in a gracious God whose righteousness stands in judgment against all human achievement; yet a righteousness, revealed in Jesus Christ, that is a gracious attribution of righteousness to us sinners who fail more than we succeed—set free by forgiveness, not to be irresponsible but to respond by living boldly for each other, honestly.

I hear humorous comments about "Lutheran guilt," "Catholic guilt," or "Jewish guilt." The humor has a bite to it, in that its assumption is that it is somehow not good sense to be guilty. The humor is healthy in most respects, but it misses the point. If these constituencies acknowledge guilt, it is because they are freed by forgiveness to be honest about their failures and foibles, and to go on living and coping and muddling through the tests, trials and tribulations common to our fate.

Ruth and I, as members of a religious community that honors this tradition of justice, heard it over many years, read about it, and were influenced by it. We belonged to a community centered in the worship of that active God. That may have something to do with the decisions Ruth and I made about care during Ruth's final illness.

Is it consistent with "justice, loving—kindness and walking humbly with God" to expect and demand everything that medical care can give, no matter what the cost?

The "right to life" has been a guiding precept in medical care. That there may be a "duty to die," has very little status in the ethics of medical and health care. We prefer to ignore the very real fact of life, that there is a time to die as well as to live. Deciding to submit to that reality, not just stupidly but intelligently and responsibly and out of conviction, could be considered a way of "doing justice, loving-kindness and walking humbly." Who are we to demand everything possible when to do so results in injustice and harm to others?

It is common knowledge that a large portion of the nation's medical bill is spent on terminal care, especially care of the elderly and those who are critically ill or injured for whom modern technology can be brought into service to save their lives or postpone their deaths. Charles M. Johnston, MD, director of the Center for Creative Development in Seattle, asserts in **Necessary Wisdom: Meeting the Challenge of a New Cultural Maturity** (Seattle: ICD Press, 1991) that there is a need for medicine and culture as a whole to find a new relationship with death and that much of this need comes as a direct consequence of modern medicine's success in postponing death.

What a painful struggle we suffer to believe that even at the time of approaching death we have an obligation to do justice, love kindness and walk humbly with our God! Even Jesus struggled with that pain!

The issues of just distribution of benefits and costs in our society seem so overwhelming that one is tempted to think that it is beyond our power to do anything. However, there are ordinary ways of "doing justice."

Ruth and I made small contributions toward a more just and frugal distribution of medical care in several ways.

Ruth rejected options that were excessively expensive in relation to the probable benefits; for instance, choosing not to be placed on a life support system or to have an expensive surgery on her brain that would be of limited benefit. Each of us could limit the pressures on the medical system if we would recognize the limits of what medical science can and should do for us when we become terminal patients.

Ruth also accepted responsibility for her own health maintenance, as far as possible, by adopting a regimen of diet, exercise, rest and relaxation suitable for a diabetic. Abiding by current knowledge about healthy life-styles, she stayed healthier than she would have if she had bad eating habits. She may have reduced the need for expensive medical care associated with heart disease, cardiovascular disease and cancer. We had discussed these matters often and concluded that if less money is spent on critical medical care, more resources would be released for extending good care to others who are deprived of it.

Ruth and I accepted our duty of paying taxes, so that health care could be distributed through public programs designed to distribute it more fairly, such as the Medicare and Medicaid programs. Along with that obligation came another responsibility of influencing policymakers to see to it that the public funds were spent frugally and used wisely. Ruth wrote many letters to members of Congress on such matters. Mention the word taxes and the alarms begin to sound in citizens' minds. People think of taxes as a form of oppression by the government. I think we forget all the benefits we gain by being included in a system of distribution of benefits.

I belonged to and contributed to a private insurance system which spreads the burden of costs. I accepted the policy of the church to set aside part of my income for that purpose; the mutual benefits accrued to our advantage during Ruth's illness, because most of the cost was covered by Medicare and the ELCA medical insurance.

Doing volunteer work in the health care area is another way we all contribute to lowering the costs and distributing necessary care, such as being a volunteer in a hospice program, serving as a driver for elderly persons needing transportation, or delivering meals on wheels [which we did for a time].

When one's life story is shaped by such a larger story as the one in the Bible where mercy and justice are such common themes, then one's dealing with the end-of-life issues is shaped by that outlook.

Clinic and Hospital

Dear Zoe,

I feel this uneasiness about our experience, even though we had access to excellent care. Let me take you into Mayo and walk through the experience we had there.

Mayo is more than a particular clinic located in Rochester. It is a symbol of the whole modern medical system based on science, on objective knowledge gained from examinations, tests and treatments by a complicated team of workers, ranging from the specialists at the top to nurses' aides and orderlies and cleaning crews.

At the top, ruling all is the "mind," a vast brain called a computer that stores more information than any one or even a few specialists can handle on their own. One can almost imagine the doctors as servants reporting to and receiving orders from that Mind. Yes, a Mind to be respected, but a mind that cannot register feelings. If the system has strategies for dealing with specific illnesses, such as breast cancer, those are based on statistics from many cases. The treatment based on that vast knowledge is often effective and surely better than doing nothing.

Zoe, I want to describe how it feels to enter that system dominated by a vast mind. We chose to go to Mayo. The very sound of the word evokes submission to authority, the authority of medical science and practice.

Walk with us from the admission desk to the oncology department, wait with us and maybe try to fill the time by browsing through a magazine or doing a crossword puzzle; follow us to another floor where the radiation and X ray experts are, and wait again for Ruth's turn for a mammogram; then go with us to the specialist in diabetes; and then to the surgeon's consulting room where, a day after the tests, we hear the news from the resident surgeon and her supervisor, a famous surgeon, two courteous, competent, and candid professionals who know their work.

Notice their white coats, the diplomas and citations on the wall, the strange instruments lying about, the examination table, where one lies to be examined, poked, listened to and probed. Listen to the talk about what tests and exams have discovered. Hear the bad news, try to ask a sensible question when you feel so upset, and so vulnerable to the power and authority of that man and woman in white. They have science to back them up, and what do you have?

Ruth submitted to that authority, yielded her body's most intimate secrets to strangers with hardly a word of protest, and those strangers did tests that would yield information about her that even she did not know, information that ended up in the computer along with data from a thousand others, where it is compared and classified and studied. From that source the physician gets a printout about her and sees a profile of data that suggests what he can say in prognosis and suggest for treatment. In that vast Mind, Ruth is a number, a statistic. That is what she is in the system of scientific medicine.

Well, Zoe, Ruth and I asked for it, and I am not complaining. Much that is good can be gained from modern scientific medicine. Ruth gained something—27 months of freedom before she entered the dark valley and heard the distant roar of the falls, time to live and enjoy living, and temporary hope for a longer life. Without that expert knowledge gained by hard work and careful thought, many people would suffer much more and live less well and die sooner.

Yes, she got something beneficial, of course. So why the "yes, but"? First, that scientific medical establishment cannot do well what a person needs in the crisis of serious illness, and especially in a time of terminal illness. Its focus is on delaying final time, on repair work, on returning people to normal living as much as possible, on aiding them if they have chronic illnesses and need intervention to keep them going.

Its attention is on the body, even on specific body parts and their connections. But who knows the whole person in all of that business? Ruth was more than the sum of her body parts and the pulses that registered on the screens. Who cares for the whole person, for **Ruth**?

The clinic dismissed her. It gave her what it could—ten radiation treatments and decadron; kind, courteous attention while she was confined and during subsequent checkups. What the clinic does is not all that needs to be done. Modern scientific medical practice is not very skilled at helping people die; when the time comes and the roar of the falls gets louder, that whole system is at loss. She returned home for a few weeks, and we did our best to make life good.

After being dismissed from Methodist Hospital the middle of December, she was at home as long as she could take care of herself with my assistance. When her condition deteriorated, Gene Lund and I decided she needed to be in the hospital where she would have expert medical care, and Dr. Bauer admitted her to St. Peter Community Hospital. After a brief return home, when her care became impossible under conditions at home, she was taken to the community hospital hospice room. After 20 days she came home for her final days.

The best place to care for Ruth's needs was an important matter in the final days of her life. What are the moral factors in these decisions, which are not just medical matters but ones that involve values, duties and commitments? We need environments which sustain and nurture, not just the physical values we cherish but social, intellectual and spiritual life. We make judgments about which is the best place for medical care that will be most conducive to getting well, or for managing a chronic illness, or for living when we are in a terminal condition.

After the clinic's services, Ruth needed the kind of care a person should have during the terminal time when a patient is not going to recover and is approaching death. Where that can be best given and by whom were important **moral** issues. The shift was from therapeutic care to comfort care. It seems very important for patients and families to recognize and accept this change of care. It is difficult to do, because it must be based on accepting the reality of imminent death.

The care she needed could be given best in her own environment, by her family physician and others who knew her. When Ruth had to be put in the hospital, the local community hospital was most suited for that care for several reasons. The hospital had a hospice program designed for the care of the terminally ill, including a room designated and designed for hospice care. She was among people who knew her, in a familiar rather than a foreign environment. She was where family and friends had easy access to her. I was less than five minutes away from her when she was in the hospital, and immediately present to her when she was at home. The hospital staff and her family physician were dedicated to giving her the care she needed at this time.

Thus the decision to bring Ruth home for her final days was also related to this basic moral issue of what was best care for her during that time. It was a difficult decision for me, because I thought I was not as competent to give nursing care as were the skilled nurses; but Ruth's desire to go home was so evident that I decided to take the chance, with the understanding that I would have help from the hospice people.

Also, Medicare's so-called "swing-bed" rule which granted 20 days of coverage for hospital care in the hospice room was a factor. When that 20 days were up, she was dismissed to her home.

This raised the question of my motivation. There is no evidence in my journal that coercive pressure from others was a determining factor, although the pressure of hospital and Medicare procedures and Ruth's desire influenced me. I brought to this time of decision a realization that Ruth was more than a physical body that needed competent care; she was a person in need of companionship. She was lonely and frightened. She needed me to be with her, not just now and then or even frequently as visitor, but as one present to her at all times, as I could be if she were at home. Loneliness is essentially an experience of low quality, whereas my experience of companionship in her last days was an experience of high value, even though I was clumsy at giving her physical care. This is so evident during the difficult last weekend when I was alone with her. I considered my experience of being with her and serving her needs and being at her side when she died to be of high value, poignant though the experience must have been. It was a deep experience I would not want to have missed.

Hospice

Dear Zoe,

When you asked if we had an understanding organization to help us, you may have been asking if we had access to a hospice program. We did, and that was a blessing.

The St. Peter (Minnesota) Hospice Program is a well-organized and financed resource for terminal patients and their families. Ruth died the night before volunteers in the hospice program were scheduled to provide their services, but we had other benefits associated with the arrangement. The program was organized through the hospital and the public health program, so I had help when I needed it. Having available the services of Nancy, the nurse's aide assigned to us, was crucial such as when I called on her for help when Ruth was resisting medication. Her presence each day to give Ruth care gave me the breaks I needed.

However, even that fine program has limits, for I was alone in the middle of the night when Ruth needed much care, the man in the trenches, so to speak, who could not delegate the immediate task to anyone else. I am also aware of other people I know who have been the primary care-givers. Spouses whose mates had Alzheimer's disease have had longer periods when they were also the ones at the scene of action when others had left. Not all people have the care facilities and competent, responsible staff which we had. I know one person whose husband was in a nursing home where negligence by staff was so evident that she had to intervene and provide the care he needed whenever she could be with him, which was every day of his confinement.

In the story of the hospice team in Toronto, it was necessary for Margaret's friends to **organize** a team; that was less necessary in our town, for there was a natural network of friends and workers that was already there and served us well.

I wrote a letter to the nursing staff of St. Peter Community Hospital on April 2, the day before Ruth died. There is in it an important point about community hospitals that should be considered now:

> I am glad to live in St. Peter for many reasons, and now I
> have another. We have not just a hospital in the community, but
> we have a **community hospital** in the sense of having a family
> place where we are treated as people known, not as strangers and
> only a four-minute drive from home.

I commended the nurses, as well as physicians, who are present to those in pain with a quotation from **Suffering Presence: Theological Reflections on Medicine, the Mentally Handicapped & the Church** (University of Notre Dame Press, 1986), a book written by Stanley Hauerwas:

"Through their willingness to be present to us in our most vulnerable moments they are forever scarred with our pain. They have seen a world we do not want to see until it is forced on us. When we are driven into that world we want to be able to count on their skill and their presence."

In the letter to the hospital staff I acknowledged that "we all have much to learn about being present to one another in our illness, pain and dying; and that they are present to us, no matter who we are, or how foolish we have been about caring for our health or how fearful or angry or deluded; so you teach us the meaning of nonjudgmental and appropriate service to anyone in need."

I would say that to the extent that a local community hospital is that kind of a community, it offers what large clinics and medical centers find much more difficult to provide. Perhaps we must be wise enough to cherish what both kinds of medical centers can provide for us by way of care.

Whose Duty: The Physician-Patient Relationship
Dear Zoe,

The patient and the physician are the chief characters in the drama of medical care. Others play supporting roles of more or less significance. No matter how impressive and challenging are the technological advances that have made that relationship more complicated, that relationship is the focal point of the action. It is a **moral** affair, not just a professional relationship between an expert and a client. Ruth and her physicians had power and responsibilities that required collaboration.

It is the particular vocation of physicians and their colleagues to combine competence with compassion in their care of others. In **Suffering Presence**, ethicist Hauerwas has affirmed the **moral** commitment of the physician and others concerned with our care in illness to be present to us in our pain and illness, at a time when we are the most vulnerable; a commitment, he says is both a burden and a privilege for it is a time when our deepest fears and our profoundest hopes are exposed.

The observation can be made about all who are involved in the care of the sick, injured and dying, but since physicians have such key roles, I want to think about them in particular.

232

Why is the relationship a moral affair?

First, something happens that makes choices inescapable. Because of being hurt or feeling ill patients choose to come to a physician, who chooses to receive them. Those choices establish a collaborative relationship between physician and patient. Other decisions follow as the patient's condition is diagnosed. By seeking medical help at Mayo, Ruth and I made a choice that committed us to a responsible, collaborative relationship with the medical professionals, and they chose to enter that relationship by accepting Ruth as a patient.

Power is an inherent aspect of moral relationships, not a necessary evil, and in this relationship it is an important factor. The physicians' power resides in their knowledge, training and skill and their control of the medical resources to use in diagnosis and treatment. The ability to help or harm is enhanced by expert knowledge and skill. Patients have power as well, in that they know more about themselves, how they feel, and have the freedom to ignore or follow the advice of the physician. They can choose to be firm and assertive or weak and submissive.

The relationship between physician and patient is one of unequal power. Patients feel stripped of control, dependent and uncertain when they enter the medical domain, where the setting, the personnel, and even the language are foreign. One of my physician friends acknowledged to me that doctors often fail to recognize how scared patients are. They treat the physical condition more easily than the emotional needs. On the other hand, patients generally do not recognize the doctor's limits. The physician's power is limited by the lack of full knowledge of patients' feelings, capacity for knowing the truth about themselves, and level of moral rectitude necessary for carrying on a responsible regimen of treatment. Thus some kind of negotiation between patient and physician takes place, sometimes less effective than at other times. This unequal distribution of power obscures the power and responsibility of the care-receivers.

The physicians had the edge over Ruth and me in the power balance. They have the choice between using their position to dominate the patient, a tactic which in medical ethics is called "strong paternalism," or using that position to share information truthfully and to use diplomatic skills to

233

persuade the patient to give consent to what they believe is in the patient's best interests. They have a choice between listening to the patient's hopes and acknowledging fears or paying attention only to the results of scientific tests and lab reports and the patient's chart. They have a choice between humbly admitting their limits, or using their superior knowledge to control the relationship, in dealing with us who need their expert knowledge and skill.

Karen Lebacqz has called attention to the significance of humility, or a sense of one's limits, in the practice of medicine. She sees it as a virtue needed in medical practice, so that the relationship of professionals to their patients will be affected by recognizing their own limitations as professionals and needs as persons and also the worth of persons who come so vulnerable, poor, and oppressed. Humility also would dispose one to recognize the "peculiar wisdom" of patients and the limits of medical science and practice.

Humility is also appropriate as a virtue for patients, because it makes them more receptive to the knowledge physicians have. Furthermore, without it they could fall into a kind of pride that moves them to demand of care-givers more than is reasonable, particularly when they are unable to accept their mortality and their own responsibility for behavior that has brought on illness or injury, when such acknowledgment is clearly called for.

Conversations with physicians about Ruth's care revealed the difficulty of communication in this relationship. One physician told me that deciding when to tell patients that they have cancer or some other life-threatening ailment, what to tell them and how to put it is one of his most difficult moral judgments. The assumption that patients cannot handle information vital to their interests is based on a tradition of paternalism in medical history.

Second, how physicians use their power is a moral matter also, because decisions must be made about matters of significance to both care-givers and care-receivers. Success and failure of treatment, sickness and health, living and dying, are not trivial matters, and these are the stuff of medical care. Ruth's life was at stake; the physicians' reputations were also.

Care-givers have agendas, too, that may be harmonious or less than harmonious with the patients' benefit. There is a correspondence of interests. The patients want restoration of health and relief from suffering, whereas professional success in meeting those desires is a matter of high value for the care-givers.

The conflicts of interest come because of other purposes care-givers may have in mind. One of those purposes is medical research. Patients become statistical facts in the growing body of scientific knowledge. The question of potential conflict between the professional's interest in and obligations to advance the science of medicine and devotion to patient care must be faced. Large medical centers, such as Mayo, are places where significant research goes on. Although there are regulations to control this research, because many physicians have a strong interest in the science of medicine, they have a potential conflict of interest that could affect the patients they treat, if the science has higher priority than the practice.

Medical centers are also places where teaching future physicians and specialists takes place. Such places have a responsibility to that work as well as to patients' care. Among those who were involved in Ruth's care were resident physicians who were learning their craft under the supervision of instructors.

Another potential conflict of interest develops when, as described by a physician friend of mine, the entrepreneurial ethic intrudes into the medical realm. The fact that the practice of medicine is a matter of great cost and also great profit complicates the moral situation. For example, should doctors accept so many patients that they can't really get to know them well, because it satisfies their professional zeal or brings them a larger income?

On the other hand, doctors are not only professionals but persons who get tired and overworked, or who have personal concerns that are not related to the patient at all but may be intrusive. Should doctors refuse to see more patients who seek them because of their talent and knowledge because they have other interests or because they are tired? The tension between self-interest and justice is evident in this profession, too.

The moral drama becomes intense when the conflicts threaten to affect the care of patients. The patients' real needs, medical research and profit and loss are significant matters at stake.

A relationship of trust is inherent in moral experience and in the physician-patient relationship as well; but this trust is a tenuous, fragile

235

affair, because of the high stakes at risk and the unequal degree of power that physicians have. There is a serious decline of trust, evident in the number of malpractice suits by patients and their families and the practice of costly defensive medicine by doctors who want to avoid suits.

Another factor is the powerful influence of medical technology, which tends to separate the medical experts from their patients. The patient's chart, the tests, and the complex treatment techniques diminish the personal relationship. Making use of technology takes time and reduces the amount of time doctors spend listening to and talking with their patients. The scientific data does not give a doctor important clues about the patient's feelings. Feelings are sources of valuable information and also affect the results of medical care.

Ruth went along with medical experts' opinion about the outcome of her illness. They estimated that she would have two to four months to live, but they acknowledged that they could be wrong. Also, there is risk involved for both parties. They cannot predict with absolute certainty what the consequences will be. Mutual benefits or harms are going to result from the encounter. Medical science reduces risk as much as possible, but it cannot eliminate it entirely. Ruth chose the least risky of the alternative treatments they offered.

Ruth was grateful for the competent care she received at Mayo and Methodist, and I concur. Why do I say, "Yes, but" now? Ruth received the benefit of their precise knowledge of special medical problems and skill in coping with them. There was not just one but several specialists who had pieces of the action in her care. It is so obvious that there must be a complex design of interconnected services in the modern medical center.

Recently I talked to a friend whose husband died of cancer the day before. She was very disappointed in the way the oncologist who treated her husband withdrew from the scene and showed little sympathy for her. She considered him heartless. Her remarks prompted me to review Ruth's relationship with her oncologist and other specialists at Mayo.

Competence and courtesy come to mind as I remember the encounters with the surgeons, her oncologist, and other specialists, as well as the nurses. Her oncologist wrote detailed reports to our family physician after each examination, and wrote him to ask about how Ruth was doing just a couple of weeks before she died. He invited us to call him after Ruth was dismissed from Methodist Hospital if we had any problems or questions, and when I did so he treated them carefully.

There were three occasions that qualify my **yes** with a **but.**

In the consultation with the surgeons, when Ruth heard their diagnosis and recommended treatment, Ruth faced something she dreaded, a biopsy and surgery and the possibility of dying during surgery, and the news afterward that the tumor was malignant and might have metastasized. The treatment by the physicians was courteous and candid. There was no question about their judgment as to what Ruth should decide about having surgery. They made it clear that she might not live very long if nothing were done. She quickly submitted to such authority.

But what if what ails a patient is something larger and less understandable than the breast or colon or heart or cerebellum? Ruth was more than her body parts, more than a sociable person who needed to be acceptable, and more than an intelligent person who needed accurate information. She had feelings of fear in the face of probable death. She had a love of life, and a hope of survival. Who was listening to her fears and hopes, her longings and anxieties? She was Ruth, a whole, complicated human being with a history, a past, and an uncertain future. Who, in the medical system, pays attention to **Ruth**—not just who listens to her body language or her attempts to describe what is wrong with her body?

The second occasion came when Ruth was in Methodist Hospital waiting for the reports of the examinations and tests. Who came to tell her that she had from two to four months to live? That task was delegated to a resident, a stranger Ruth did not know, not the oncologist who had seen her for her regular checkups. I was not there either, but he would not or could not delay until I came to join Ruth in that moment of decision. I feel sad when I read the account of that moment and she told me the doctor hoped I would be there! I see that moment in the story of Ruth's relationship with the one in charge of her care as a time when his presence would have been very significant for her, when the physician could communicate to the patient his recognition of the patient's suffering, not just the medical options, which any skilled technician could do. The issue—central to the patient—is more than which of the medical options offered should she choose, but rather how shall she cope with this radical change in herself and her condition. Rational options are one matter medical specialists can present very well, but dealing with deep feelings about one's fate is beyond the scope of what scientific training can provide.

The expert's time and energy are rationed among many patients, so there is a delegation of tasks involved in patient care to others. Since the specialist in charge of Ruth delegated responsibilities to resident physicians working with him, I assume that he had to decide where to spend his time and with whom and on what aspect of Ruth's care. He apparently could not afford the time it takes to be present with each patient at that crucial time when the diagnosis and options for treatment are communicated. Maybe so. However, should the arrangement not give high priority to being with the patient at that time?

One specialist told me that he had about 30 patients to see in his office on appointment days. He frankly admitted he does not have time to engage them at more than a superficial level of friendship. His focus must be on the medical issues involved and on communicating them clearly. Ruth had to ask one of them to sit down long enough so he and she could talk about her situation; and he did with some reluctance, but then a fine conversation took place.

The commitment to be present to patients in their suffering, as Hauerwas put it, is less evident among many practitioners in high-tech settings such as specialty clinics, emergency rooms and intensive care units. In "A Medical Ethic of Suffering," an article found in the May 20-27, 1992, issue of **The Christian Century**, Arthur W. Frank notes that many specialists "make no pretense of knowing their patients." The communication at the bedside of their patients is rarely considered a topic of ethical relevance; whether or not a physician communicates his recognition of a patient's suffering is not seen as an ethical issue. The focus is on how universal principles and procedures are to be applied to a particular body of the patient.

These observations may partially explain the absence of the specialist in charge of Ruth's case when the moment came for giving her the diagnosis of her condition. He may not have seen it to be a primary responsibility to be present at that time, or he may choose not to be so involved when his efforts are not going to save the patient.

Should we who benefit from the expert care of specialists expect them to spend more time with patients to give them comfort care, as well as their expertise in diagnosis and treatment? There is an obvious and strong tendency of experts to become authoritarian when they deal with people who are not their equals; perhaps of necessity, given the limited knowledge of so many patients about medical care. We experienced this flow of power, especially from the medical specialists at Mayo. Even though Ruth had a strong sense of personal autonomy and resistance to that authority, it was impossible for her to resist it when her life was at stake. A family physician I know expressed strong criticism of specialists who fail to communicate with general practitioners like himself when to do so would help him give better care. Ruth's medical file shows that the Mayo oncologist in charge of Ruth's care wrote very informative letters to our doctor after her checkups, the sort of technical information in medical vocabulary that doctors use in communicating with each other. However, there was not all that much about Ruth the person there.

There is the matter of limits in the power and responsibilities of participants. Doctors are not divine and should not be expected to be all-powerful or even all-compassionate; yet people confer on them such high status that their judgments of what they can do are affected to the hurt of all concerned. When care-givers assume to have more power and responsibility than they can appropriately take on themselves, their judgment also is affected and can hurt themselves as well as others. In medical ethics this is a major issue. In stories, including those taking place in medical settings, there are interactions and interrelationships; seldom is any single person solely in charge, solely responsible, solely the one with the power to determine outcomes.

In the complex organization of the modern medical center something of value can be lost. The specialist loses something by distancing

himself from the bedside of his patients. And perhaps the patients do as well.
However, given the large number of people who come to a clinic such as Mayo,
would it be right for specialists to deny more people their expert knowledge
in order to give fewer people more attention and care?

The Family Physician

Our family physician, Dr. Thompson, was a general
physician/surgeon, not a specialist. He did not have the specialist's knowledge
and training about specific areas of medical practice, but he had the discerning
skill of knowing when to call on specialists for additional help in diagnosis
and treatment. Furthermore, he had the opportunity over a period of time
that stretched for years to get acquainted with Ruth and her family and their
circumstances, and also their moral perspectives and responses to illness and
suffering. Dr. Thompson had known us for many years. He not only knew
about, but also understood, the extent of our moral commitments to care for
each other and each for his or her own health; and he respected those
commitments. Thus he personified the virtue of humility in the manner
described by Lebacqz. He was at hand, available, when we needed his presence.
He came to our home when we had an emergency and sat after he had tended to
Ruth to talk to us, as if we were his friends, not just his clients. We had a
collaborative relationship, one in which he recognized and respected and
fostered our sense of personal responsibility for our own care.

Even so, there were moments in the story when communication was
strained. Facing the inevitability of death is difficult for physicians whose
work is aimed at cure. When the relationship lasts over many years, it is more
than professional. Because Dr. Thompson knew us so well, more intimately
than anyone outside the immediate family, and knew our bodies intimately, he
had a close relationship and one that must be based on trust and mutual
respect.

Should family physicians be expected to be present at crucial times of
need in the day-by-day story of a patient's illness? Their visits during hospital
rounds are necessarily brief, unless there is a special need.

Imagine what family physicians' burdens must be. They never know
what they will discover when each patient comes into the examining room,

when they will have to help a patient face the hard realities of a terminal condition. I have a poignant memory of that day in Dr. Thompson's office when he reported the tumors on Ruth's brain, how concerned and sad he looked, and with what affection his nurse hugged Ruth. If he needs to distance himself to some degree from patients who are dying, should we decry it as a failure of duty? I don't think so. Burdens, yes, but privilege, too, as Hauerwas has pointed out and my physician friend affirms; for the physician shares deep experiences of both joy and sorrow with patients, perhaps more than is possible in any other profession.

The third occasion that leaves a "yes, but" in my mind came during Ruth's confinement in the hospice room of the hospital. Who was paying attention to the way she was feeling? I was in and out. The physician's visits while on rounds were very brief. The pastor and I got into a professional discussion one day when came to visit her. The nurses were kind and attentive to her physical needs, but they had others to tend. Then one night the nurse called me because Ruth wanted to see me. She was in a panic of fear and loneliness, and visiting with her I realized how profound was her experience. The sound of that rushing stream and the waterfall was hardly noticeable to me, but it was a roar in her heart. She wanted to go home, and the conversations were awkward, truncated, back and forth, confusing at times. That experience now stands out as a major lesson about love that I have learned in this experience; it was a hard one that humbles me, and one I hope has given me more understanding of people who are facing death or other tearing separations.

What did Ruth need during her final time? Love, that I know, and we who cared for her gave it, maybe clumsily and with some uncertainty and much ignorance of that mystery of suffering that she endured. Our presence, so I am grateful that I had the opportunity to be present with her and to care for her in her last days, and I am sad about people I know who were denied that deep privilege, which was more than a compensation for the pain of loss.

Other Care-givers

The benefits of competent and compassionate care by nurses, nurses' aides and orderlies were very evident in our story. Should nurses have more responsibility than they are allowed to have? Given their intimate and frequent contacts with patients, their assessment should be and often is given much weight as to decisions about treatment at particular points. Some nurses criticize some doctors for being so authoritative that they do not listen well enough to nurses' assessments.

The hospice program provided us with help from a nurse's aide who came each day to take care of Ruth and relieve me. Nancy, the aide in our story, was assigned home care duties, under the general supervision of the nursing staff. Given the excellent care and assistance she gave, it seems unnecessary to question the delegation of such care to nurses' aides. However, friends of mine tell stories about nurses' aides in some nursing homes who do not give such good care as we received. All people are subject to the variables of such matters of fact as time, place and persons with varying motivations. Ruth and I were among the privileged who enjoyed excellent care.

Thus the moral questions come. What ought to be the motivations of people who are in medical care occupations? What ought to be their working conditions making excellent care possible?

What ought to be done by the patients themselves, and by family members who are at hand, as well as by friends? The options are to be passive victims, submissive to the authorities in the fields of care, or active, assertive and responsible. An ethics for patients places emphasis on patients' responsibilities as well as their rights. Some observers believe that medical care-givers and the system which regulates them should be more diligent in respecting the duty of us who receive care to be primarily responsible for our health and recovery.

There is a slippery slope here—a slide toward strong paternalism by care-givers and passivity by care-receivers. In our story, this happily was not the way matters were. My experience was positive in that the medical people gave me opportunity and responsibility and encouragement to take on Ruth's care in her final days. Should a clumsy novice be given such power? Should the system emphasize more than it has the individual's responsibility for her own health? I suppose we would answer yes, and no, depending on circumstances and persons involved. I was clumsy at basic physical care. I was not able to recognize the signs of dying when they started. Maybe others would be even more so, or emotionally unable to bear the burden.

I became the leading actor when Ruth came home, the one constantly at hand and especially during the night when we were alone. My role was ambiguous, for I was at times the stand-in for the physician and at other times Ruth's. This in-between position was sometimes a difficult place to be, as when Ruth told me I was not her best friend when I wanted to give her morphine and she did not want to take it. In the one role I was care-giver, and in the other the recipient of the professional care in that I needed help.

I had a difficult decision to make about sharing what was happening to Ruth with others. Should others be kept out of the story? Protected from this deep experience of loss? My decision to share the story was appreciated by many, and I discovered that others who love us wanted to be a part of our sorrow as well as our happiness. My children wanted to have a part in the care, too, and were troubled by the fact that they lived elsewhere and had other duties. Their presence and help were essential, in relation to Ruth's need for family. The presence and concern of friends, shown in visits, calls and letters, were a consolation that seemed to both Ruth and me an energy flowing into our lives.

Ruth was not completely passive in those final days; she resisted medication; she responded to other people who visited or were involved in her care; she did her best to do what she could about eating, for example. A most poignant memory I have is Ruth's efforts to wash her teeth even during the last day of her life and her insistence on feeding herself, even when she had difficulty placing food on a fork or spoon. Patients may not be as passive as we tend to see them.

Ruth passed beyond the time and condition where she needed effective medical therapy. What she needed doctors could not or did not provide; they had other prior claims on their skills. I also had needs—not of more skill but of consolation as I realized my helplessness and anticipated losing Ruth.

Our pastors' visits at Ruth's bedside at Methodist in Rochester and at home on the last Sunday of her life linked Ruth to the community of faith and that larger story of many generations when they served her communion. The rituals of the church provided that link in ways that transcend understanding.

At Mayo-Methodist in Rochester chaplains called on Ruth. They are not regarded as major actors, though, when important decisions about a patient's care must be made, according to one chaplain with whom I had coffee break one day. The focus was not set on an angle wide enough to include the spiritual aspect of a person's condition, so it seems that it is considered irrelevant.

Hauerwas challenges this inattention to the spiritual aspect in **Suffering Presence** by commenting on the relationship between prayer and medical care. Prayer, he says, is not a supplement to medical practice, something we resort to when it fails; nor is it a way of insuring medical success. Its purpose is to make God present "whether medical skill is successful or not." I would say, rather, it is the way we keep ourselves attentive to the presence of God, in whom we live and move and have our being. There is only a very poor reason available for thinking that prayer is a nonessential, the reason being a total disregard of the pervasive and widespread experience we call religious. Every profession needs a perspective outside of its own ideology, and outside of prevailing social views, lest it become an idol ultimately incapable of dealing with deepest human needs. The issue, Hauerwas says, is not whether medicine and prayer are antithetical, but "how medical care can ever be sustained without the necessity of continued prayer."

I sense I am touching on matters that go beyond ethical analysis. There is something mysterious and awesome about going through the experience of losing someone dear; it is a matter beyond assessment of good and bad. There is a mysterious depth in all moral experience. There is something we cannot entirely control or understand. It is something very powerful, although so subtle that we think we can evade dealing with it. There are times, however, when it surfaces and moves us deeply, sometimes to tears and sometimes to songs. The issues we face about medical matters are not just scientific questions about what we can know; and they are not just technological questions about what we can do. They are issues that come from the deepest and most mysterious regions of our humanity we often call our spiritual life. We struggle over questions of meaning. The region of the spirit lies beyond the safety zones of law and custom where we encounter awesome risks, where free choices are called forth. In that region we not only are born, thrive, hurt and die as biological and social beings. We experience deaths and rebirths, growth and change on a precarious journey through the perils of this world from birth to death. It is when we meet and acknowledge these experiences of mystery and death that religious traditions become important personal and communal concerns and not just conventional patterns to which we conform. Then we long for more than cures that will extend our life spans. We hope for healing of the various breaches of harmony that beset us. We long for meanings that will satisfy us as no bread or medicine can. Ethics does not fill this need, nor does medical practice. Both must be and can be transcended and fortified by what lies beyond them.

In his article "Religion, Theology, Church and Bioethics" (**Journal of Medicine and Philosophy**, Volume 17, June 1992), Martin Marty comments on situations in which families face crucial decisions that make me realize that judgments at such times have depths that call into question mere professional skills, even those of the professional ethicist. "One clinical ethicist in conversation put it this way: "When the patient's family is deciding whether to let the DNR sign appear, or in the crude language, to 'pull the plug on Grandpa,' they are not likely to invite in the academic philosopher to discourse on beneficence or nonmaleficence in Aristotle or Mill. They are more inclined to ask, 'What does my physician say? What does my minister think? What does my family want?' And these questions are rooted in the historical traditions, often in communities of faith, which have often been muffled, excluded or self-exiled.'"

I do not believe I am qualified to pass judgment on anyone in the system of care, nor do I want to condemn anyone, including myself. We are all limited, even the experts. No one can stop the stream that bears all of us away into the dark valley.

What makes me glad are the memories of such grace that makes our fate more tolerable—our doctor coming to our home to help with an emergency and then staying to talk awhile, a nurse named Smith at Methodist who glows in my memory as an example of competence and friendly affection for us, the courtesy and competence and honesty of Ruth's oncologist, the pastors' timely visits, the visits of friends and neighbors who just by coming gave us comfort, the anniversary party inspired by the Stroms' visit, Nancy's availability on her weekend off sharing herself as a person and her skills as a nurse, Marian's tribute to Ruth, the children's and grandchildren's presence and affection, and on and on until at last I think of Ruth, who by being Ruth, true to herself, remains alive in my life and gives me courage to live in the face of loss.

Your question was about whether we had found an **understanding** organization. How perceptive you were, Zoe. You did not ask about how competent or efficient or fair. Understanding has to do with seeing, really seeing, and responding, not just reacting on automatic pilot. Yes, we found understanding, of disease, of treatment, of care, of friendship; but there is a depth of the experience of dying and loss that remains opaque, distant, strange. That dark valley and that sound of the waterfall only can give us a premonition. We do not know, we cannot tell, what persons experience as they go into it. So what shall I, what can I, say about an understandable meaning?

About Meaning

Dear Zoe,

Finally I come to your question about meaning. What meaning does Ruth's death and my loss have?

Moral convictions and actions rest on the sorts of answers we give to the basic religious issues of identity, vocation, destiny and the relationship with what is the final reality we usually call God.

Vocation. The question of vocation is, "What on earth are you doing here?" I have to decide whether it is my calling to live as long as I can, work to lengthen my life span, as if longevity is the purpose of all that I do. If so, taking care of my health takes on the highest priority—so I had better go jogging, watch my diet, learn to manage stress, avoid conflict and be devoted primarily to my own well-being.

Is that all there is to it? Is it the calling of medical practitioners to increase life spans? There has been an increase, no doubt, as good health care becomes the norm. We have more people living longer. The earth's population is expanding rapidly; the proportion of older humans is increasing.

What if so many people live so long that the younger members of the human race will be deprived? If personal longevity is our vocation, then we have chosen our good rather than theirs.

There is an option—to see our vocation as making our lives count for the young, who are the future of the human race. This view of vocation would also impel us to take good care of our health, so that we would reduce the medical costs and keep ourselves fit for that work of service. There should not be a dualistic polarization of care for ourselves and for others, as if doing the one excluded the other. They are connected.

In the church community the vocation of members is defined by the stories and sayings in the biblical writings. Jesus said, "The Son of man came not to be served but to serve and to give his life as a ransom for many," (Matthew 20:28). Many similar statements inform our sense of vocation.

Destiny in the Story of God. The destiny question is, "What story do I believe shapes my life or, more to the point, **whose** story?" It is obvious that I do not live in an isolated story. Mine is but a small part of a larger story, one that began before I was born and continues after I die. How is my story connected with the larger story? Is that larger story my family story, or is it my nation's? Is it even more inclusive, all humanity's, or the story of developing life within the cosmic story?

We who at times need medical care in order to live and continue our stories have a very significant decision to make. We must decide that life is "full of sound and fury signifying nothing," or that it has purposes larger than our most colorful and hopeful visions.

I have to decide whether I believe Ruth's death was a meaningless, random event or the will of God, or a fate to which one must somehow respond, connected somehow to a larger story that I can believe to be meaningful.

What is the connection between advances in medical science and practice and the larger stories? Are the efforts to save lives and extend them as long as possible guided by a view of human destiny, that longevity **on this earth** is our proper destiny? Should the human story culminate in individual immortality? Or is there a destiny beyond history? Do I imagine my destiny to be acting on the leading edge of creation? Am I one of the latest experiments in creating life? Do I have a small but significant role in the long struggle to conserve and improve life? Is that an adequate hope about human destiny, or is it imperative that I believe that our earthly life is not the end of our personal stories? Is the hope of immortality a necessary, not optional, foundation for being a moral person?

During our life together Ruth and I had conversations and some differences of opinion about this basic question. Because she loved life and loved people, she had a strong conviction that death does not destroy her or those she loved. She was firmly rooted in this world, her body, the senses. In one of her articles she wrote:

"This is the moment for loving, for obeying and for delighting in God. If there is no thankfulness or joy or curiosity for what God has made, the soul—that flowering of the spirit—gets parched and shriveled like an apple left to rot in the cellar of boredom.

But who knows what happens to the soul that reaches, that stretches, that gravitates toward God? What happens to the soul that soars with curiosity beyond the limits of the body? Does that breath of life revive the same old body or does it take another form? Where will Jesus' gift of eternal life take us? What is the heaven Jesus talks about? What does God have in mind? It's exciting to think about, isn't it?"

Although Ruth was more skeptical than I, this hope about life after death was more essential to her than it was to me. For me it was enough to believe that my life was contributing in some way to a larger destiny, the shape of which was beyond belief. At best it could be imagined. Ernest Becker put it well to Sam Kean, "It is enough to know I am being used ... for purposes larger than my own."

Belonging to the Church. The membership question is, "Where do I belong?" When I am a stranger in a strange place, such as a large medical care center like Mayo Clinic, when I seem to be in a society of strangers, the question becomes especially urgent. Who is "family"? Where is my "home"?

Ruth wanted to come home from the hospital, to be with family. Friends were important in the exchange of support.

Ruth and I were of one mind about this question. The church was the community of faith we called "family." Her remark to Pastor Fahning ["Oh, you are family, too, John."] was not just an impulsive gesture of courtesy, but one that came naturally from her long association with the church. Ruth's love of the church was not an uncritical devotion, as our pastor, Don Ludemann, observed in his sermon at her funeral. Participation in the life of the Christian community was not optional for her, and she made no bones about her position on that matter. Family, nation, all humanity she saw as embraced in this inclusive body, the boundaries of which are known only to God. Far from seeing the church as an exclusive club, she regarded it as the center, the home, but not the circumference of her community. On that matter we were in agreement.

God of Steadfast Mercy. The god question is, "What or whom do I regard as the ultimate force with which, or whom, I must come to terms? A force so powerful and splendid that I am moved to give myself in unconditional trust and loyalty?"

The question becomes especially powerful and poignant when we face our mortality, or that of someone we love dearly. The God of tradition seems so remote when we are in pain and trouble, so silent, so absent. When we come down to the end, which is hardly easy or beautiful or rational, is death the **real** power that rules my life, or is there a Lord of death and life whom I can trust and for whom I dare risk my life?

God was, for Ruth, the central force in her life, and she cherished her experiences of transcendence of self, such as she had in Methodist Hospital during her confinement there. The most devastating time of her life was that period of her depression when she lost the sense of God's presence in her life. She rejoiced greatly when that period ended.

But the question persists. Given the bleak prospect of terminal illness, with its burdens of weakness and pain and decline of body and mind, is this reality we call God merciful and kind? Or is God essentially a violent, cruel God that remains impassive, relentless in his permission to let the forces of nature destroy us?

There is no incontrovertible proof that removes from us the risk of faith. To believe in a merciful God is a gamble, yet it seems a much more interesting position to take, and one having more energy in it for creative and compassionate work, particularly in the medical professions.

Christ is the clue for those who live in the Christian community, the clue to the meaning of our story, to the vocation we regard as most important, and to the kind of God. Christ is God's **yes** to humanity—Paul wrote in his letter to the Corinthian church—in which our value as persons is grounded and whose mercy inspires mercy in us and confidence that our lives ultimately have purpose, even if we cannot fully understand it.

There are optional answers. Yes, of course. That seems no reason to remain silent about the ones given within the Christian story and community. We have more to learn by listening to each other than by defensive silence.

Ruth gave a chapel meditation on the day after Nobel Conference XIX in October 1983, which dealt with issues of medical science. Her comments were based on a healing story in the gospels. She spoke with appreciation about the creative work of medical science.

> We can start with me. I have diabetes. That disease was diagnosed over 2000 years ago, and people who had it lived for a year or two at the most after diagnosis. It was not until this century that a way was discovered to use insulin. Twenty years of my life have been given to me by science that a simple faith in God would not have done.

She referred to a letter from a Mayo specialist, Richard DeRemee, about the theme of the conference in which he commented on the limits of medical science, about how the time comes when he can do no more for a person, and how grateful he is when a patient has a spiritual awareness that he can encourage when all else is futile. Then she said:

"We who worship here believe that God, that creative Spirit, whom we cannot see or hear or put under a microscope or view through a telescope, is with us in our lives and in our world; that there is an otherness, a beyondness that we celebrate with music, with prayer, with thanksgiving; that God is real, that this space is filled with the presence of God whom we cannot confine into any image, whose mind we cannot identify, a God so great, so infinite, we can never in one time or one generation understand or know him; that all eternity will never exhaust the creative action of this God. That is known as faith. Men and women from the beginning of time as we know it have worshiped this God and never has anyone made this God so real as the man Jesus who was able to say to the paralytic and to us, 'Your sins are forgiven' (Mark 2:5). For God, that Father of us all, is not only a creative but also a gracious God."

And What about Me?

Dear Zoe,

My understanding of God was also important in helping me deal with loss. Martin Marty's reflections on "wintry spirituality" helped me see that it is possible and plausible to include the negative side of experience within my spiritual life. My belief that God was at hand, even in the winters of my experience, was strengthened. Prayer and worship were not means to social or psychological ends but ways of keeping myself present to God and aware of God's presence. These developments enabled me to preach shortly before and soon after her death and to transcend my loss and to find new life.

The value of the disciplines of Christian spirituality, especially maintaining a consistent practice of daily prayer, physical exercise, and the like, points to the importance of such disciplines formed by that or other religious traditions.

Bringing to a difficult crisis knowledge and experience in reflecting about moral life, which I gained in my work as an ethicist, might be helpful to you, too, to understand what is happening. By interpreting medical care as a moral affair you might offset the tendency nowadays toward looking for technological fixes of human predicaments.

Drawing on the benefits of community, of reaching out to others, of accepting help but at the same time being willing to bear one's own burdens, seems something I hope others may learn from my experience. If I have any persuasive power left after all this, I want to use it to urge others to recognize and accept this communal aspect of experience.

Understanding the relationship of patient to physician as a moral matter, involving mutual responsibility and shared power has become a major feature of the way I interpret and experience that relationship; others who might enter those relationships with this perspective may gain more understanding.

I am not sure anything we learn can be taken over by others, but maybe we point to some possibilities that others have not seen. My experience may at least be a source of clues as to resources others can develop to enable them to live more fully and responsibly.

Am I better prepared to live in the face of my own oncoming death? I do not know. I haven't been there yet. I cannot foresee future consequences, so I can only say I hope that I will be able to do so with some degree of courage and wisdom. I honestly do not know how well I will respond to the discovery that I am going to die. I have learned something, though.

I had better be well prepared ahead of time because in that final time I may not be capable of clear thought, deep faith or any other human resourcefulness. I may have lost my mind, or be in intense pain that dominates me, or not have enough time to come to terms with my fate. Ruth was surely prepared by her strong Christian faith and experience to face death, but she lost much of her ability and strength to respond during her last days.

If I am aware of dying when my final days come, I hope that the habits of maintaining a prayer life will continue; even now I often discover myself reciting phrases from prayers, liturgies and psalms without thinking about them. They are like the pulse beat of my heart, almost as familiar and regular. As long as I am able I intend to maintain these disciplines, to live the praying life.

252

To the extent that I am able, I hope to enter that final time with some sense of my responsibility as a patient. I am convinced that patients have not only rights but duties, including the duty to communicate, even be assertive, about one's needs.

Finally, let go, let go, let go. I am trying to learn this ancient art of detachment by ways of meditating that help me to transcend my ties to time and place, to the things I have loved so much. Trust is essential, trust in God's eternal love, and so is faith that in that love I live and move and have my being. Hope is an essential virtue as well, for it is a perspective that enables me to transcend the limits of earthly experience, to imagine far more possibilities than the actualities I have experienced. And finally, love. Love endures. Love is virtually synonymous with life. If I love and when I love, I pass from death to life.

Beyond the Waterfall

I am caught, helpless, in a swift current,
tossed up and then submerged.
I see the valley shores and then they vanish.
I cry out, and my voice is not a sound.
The roar of water falling is in me and around me.
I am falling, doused in a blood-red stream,
All sound, all fury, all sight stop.
I fall into utter silence, total darkness
as in a deep cavern of the earth.
Out of the silence I hear a faint, distant sound,
a whisper as light as baby breath.
I see light as luminous as a dawn suffusing mist on a lake.
A figure appears, bathed in light,
from a ray of sun that has penetrated the mist.
I hear a voice, softly singing,
"There is a balm in Gilead
to heal the sin-sick soul."
The mist clears. I see trees,
budding with new, fresh, light green leaves.

I smell a fragrance as lovely as the smell of lilacs in May.

The figure comes to me.

She brushes a bouquet of lilacs, wet with dew, across my face.

The aroma comes in me, a healing balm.

Then I hear the sound of a distant throng,

that turns into a myriad choir singing a mighty song,

"Worthy is the Lamb who was slain...

To the one seated on the throne and to the Lamb

Blessing sing and honor and glory and might

forever and ever."

The vision ended, and I thought of Ruth and wondered if after the roar of the waterfall in the dark valley there was light and peace and no more pain and a glory beyond reason in a life beyond season.